The
CONSERVATIVE
SIXTIES

PETER LANG
New York • Washington, D.C./Baltimore • Bern
Frankfurt am Main • Berlin • Brussels • Vienna • Oxford

The
CONSERVATIVE
SIXTIES

Edited by
David Farber & Jeff Roche

PETER LANG
New York • Washington, D.C./Baltimore • Bern
Frankfurt am Main • Berlin • Brussels • Vienna • Oxford

Library of Congress Cataloging-in-Publication Data

The conservative sixties / ed. by David Farber, Jeff Roche.
p. cm.
Includes bibliographical references and index.
1. United States—Politics and government—1945–1989. 2. Conservatism—
United States—History—20th century. 3. Political culture—United States—History—
20th century. 4. Social change—United States—History—20th century.
5. Social movements—United States—History—20th century. 6. United States—
Social conditions—1960–1980. I. Roche, Jeff. II. Title.
E839.5 .F37   320.52'0973'09046—dc21   2002154225
ISBN 978-0-8204-5548-8

Bibliographic information published by **Die Deutsche Nationalbibliothek**.
Die Deutsche Nationalbibliothek lists this publication in the "Deutsche
Nationalbibliografie"; detailed bibliographic data is available
on the Internet at http://dnb.d-nb.de/.

Author photograph of Jeff Roche by Barry Rawson
Cover art, *God's Own Citizens,* courtesy of Lambert/Archive Photos
Cover design by Lisa Barfield

© 2003, 2010 Peter Lang Publishing, Inc., New York
29 Broadway, 18th floor, New York, NY 10006
www.peterlang.com

CONTENTS

David Farber and Jeff Roche

INTRODUCTION

The conservative sixties does, at first glance, have the look of an oxymoronic phrase. The "sixties," as conventionally portrayed, is the era of protests, social change movements, rebellion, and, even, revolution. It was the heyday of national liberalism; a time when the federal government massively extended its reach and power to fight racial discrimination, wage a war on poverty, clean up the environment, and regulate business practices. It was the era during which the rock-solid Cold War anticommunist consensus broke apart and the period when most every long-standing cultural tradition and moral verity was challenged by the "baby boomer" generation who dared to "question authority." All these descriptions are true enough. They are not, however, the whole truth.

Marilyn Quayle, who along with her husband, Vice President Dan Quayle, was the butt of many a joke during the last years of the twentieth century, bluntly and accurately reminded the nation during her speech at the 1992 Republican presidential nominating convention that even among the young during the 1960s "not everyone demonstrated, dropped out, took drugs, joined in the sexual revolution or dodged the draft." Contemporary pundit and former Newt Gingrich lieutenant Tony Blankley goes further, fondly remembering a conservative sixties radicalism: "I and my colleagues thought of ourselves as right-wing Trotskyites," he quipped in 1998. "We were as outraged by the government's domestic policies as the left was by its foreign policies."[1] What Quayle and Blankley describe has been, until very recently, largely ignored by historians, as it was ignored by the mass media in the 1960s.

During the 1960s and after, much was made—as it should have been—of antiwar rallies, civil rights protests, and counterculture "be-ins." Little, if anything, was reported about conservative women's grassroots movements against national educational reforms that included sex education, experimental pedagogy, and "progressive" school textbooks. Little, until very recently, has been written about the fight within the Republican Party between Goldwater conservatives—many of them young baby boomers—and traditional Republican moderates; a fight largely won by the conservatives. The power of conservative organizations like the fiercely anticommunist John Birch Society, the activist campus group the Young Americans for Freedom (who engaged in some fierce campus protests of their own), and the militant Minutemen, are usually ignored in most histories of the 1960s. Even less has been written about the impact both African-American urban riots and the huge upswing in violent crime (disproportionately committed by African Americans) had on the politics of the sixties era: when liberal politicians, by and large, offered only explanations and rationalizations, conservatives roared against "crime in the streets" and demanded "law and order." White voters, especially urban white voters who had traditionally supported the liberal wing of the Democratic Party, responded by voting for conservative politicians (Republican and Democratic) who promised to get tough on crime. As has been true of a great deal of American history written in the last twenty-five years, almost no attention has been paid to religious Americans' experiences. Both at the grassroots and at the organizational level, conservative religious Americans feared that American society in the 1960s was suffering catastrophically from a moral and spiritual breakdown. In response, they mobilized. In the 1960s, they laid the groundwork for their major political successes in the 1970s and 1980s. Self-proclaimed conservatives, with a few major exceptions like Barry Goldwater in 1964 and Ronald Reagan in 1966, did not, it is true, hold center stage in American society during the sixties era. However, institutionally, culturally, and politically, throughout the sixties, a new conservative coalition was coalescing and preparing to become a dominant force in American society.

Historians have been slow to catch up to the conservative ascendancy in American society that took place during the last decades of the twentieth century. If one read most of the professionally acclaimed histories of the last twenty or so years one would imagine that in the twentieth-century United States the most important political and cultural battles occurred within a powerful constellation of left-wing organizations, working-class neighborhoods and race-based communities. Few, if any, middle-class white people, let alone conservatives, play important roles in these historical accounts of American history. These histories have been critically important in expanding the scope of American history, but they don't always offer a coherent account of many critical turns in recent American history. Only in the last few years has a new generation of young historians begun to challenge what has become the traditional narrative history of the last half of the twentieth century in order to reckon with the primacy of conservatism, in its many facets, in American life. In this collection, several of these new historians of conservatism, joined by a few "Old Turks," provide short takes on key aspects of the conservative sixties. Without an understanding of sixties conservatives, our own recent history remains incomplete.

* * *

Scholars of contemporary conservatism in the United States, who almost all recognize the 1960s as *the* crucial era in the resurgence of a vibrant right-wing political movement, have begun to refocus the narrative of the 1960s. To do so, they have had to challenge the traditional interpretation of the decade and forty years' worth of popular imagery. Unlike antiwar demonstrations, civil rights marches, and the antics of the counterculture, which gained so much popular attention, most conservative organizing took place outside the purview of the mainstream media. Americans formulated a conservative political ideology in countless coffee-table discussions with neighbors, whispered conversations in the college library, heated debates around the break-room snack machine, over fifty-pound bags of seed at the rural feed store, and, most important, at the precinct meetings of the Republican Party. While Abbie Hoffman manipulated the media with his absurd behavior and Eldridge Cleaver devised ways to scare suburban white America, countless local business owners, self-made professionals, and traditional housewives met regularly with other committed men and women and mapped out a plan to take over the local school board, the county commission, the state Republican Party, and the national political agenda. Operating under the national media's radar, they went largely unnoticed. Indeed, when conservatives did show up in popular magazines or on television news broadcasts, they were often the subject of derision or ridicule. Excavating the history of conservatism has only recently begun in earnest.

Several fine biographies of national conservative politicians have led the way. Robert Goldberg's excellent biography of Barry Goldwater has done much to elevate "Mr. Conservative's" historical status. Mary Brennan's examination of the 1964 Republican Party, *Turning Right in the Sixties,* has clearly demonstrated how Goldwater's nomination represented the beginning of a new and powerful movement. In *Before the Storm,* Rick Perlstein locates the epicenter of modern politics within that 1964 campaign. (Until recently, in both popular and academic accounts, Goldwater was too often portrayed as the last gasp of the old anti–New Deal Right.) Matt Dallek's superb examination of Ronald Reagan's successful 1966 campaign for governor of California not only aptly demonstrates how Reagan came to replace Goldwater as the leader of the conservative movement, but also helps to explain Reagan's enduring appeal. Dan T. Carter's award-winning biography of Alabama governor and perennial presidential candidate George Wallace makes a forceful argument that the "guvnah" introduced southern-style racial politics into conservatism. It was race, Carter contends, that represented the final piece of the political puzzle for conservatives. Other scholars have agreed that Wallace tapped into a vein of racial resentment among whites, especially urban ethnics in the North and Midwest, over issues of housing, affirmative action, crime, and Great Society welfare programs. Indeed, the proponents of this "backlash" school, who also stress Americans' anger over hippies, feminists, antiwar protesters, and drug users, argue that the moral, political, and economic excesses of the 1960s broke the back of the New Deal coalition and destroyed the liberal ideal.[2]

Several recent overviews of modern conservatism, however, have stressed continuity between the old anticommunist Right of the 1950s (and the old anti–New Deal Right) and the New Right of the 1960s. Jonathan Schoenwald, Jerome Himmelstein, and Godfrey Hodgson each present the emergence of the conservative movement in the 1960s as a logical result of postwar anticommunism and its intellectual underpinnings.[3] Several organizational studies of groups like the Young Americans for Freedom or the Republican Party demonstrate how conservatives moved from intellectual critiques of the modern state to building a coherent and cohesive political movement within the GOP. Kurt Schuparra's examination of the evolution of the California GOP and David Reinhard's study of the national party are particularly enlightening and useful.[4] What has only just begun to emerge are studies of the conservative movement at the grass roots. Historian Lisa McGirr's outstanding *Suburban Warriors* shows how everyday conservatives articulated a political ideology, organized around their principles, and came to dominate the politics of southern California.[5] Several recent dissertations, including work by Jeff Roche and Michelle Nickerson, have also focused on grassroots conservatism. These new studies reveal much about not only the organizational tactics of conservatives, but also the ways that they articulated a preexisting, if not fully coherent, set of political ideas.[6]

The essays collected in this volume attempt to both summarize the new history of the conservative sixties and point out directions for further inquiry. Although each author considers a different aspect of modern conservatism, the essays share thematic and interpretive coherence. First and foremost, these are primarily studies of conservative politics at the grass roots, whether the organizing of the Minutemen in Missouri, the opening of a conservative bookstore in southern California, or fighting over textbook selection in Texas. The women and men whose voices appear in this book fought for their beliefs on their neighbors' front porches or in school board meetings, not on the pages of the *National Review* or in the halls of Congress. Second, the authors, by carefully considering the ways that everyday Americans come to understand conservatism, narrow the gap between the Old and New Right. Focusing on the 1960s reveals a clear continuity in conservative philosophy among these Americans. Lastly, and perhaps most interestingly, what these essays reveal are the ways that Americans came to articulate their politics over time. Anticommunism, extremism, Goldwaterism, Reagan Democracy, religious fundamentalism, and "law and order" become ways to communicate a deep-rooted set of beliefs. This interpretation shifts the way we think about conservative politics.

In our first essay, David Farber argues that many Americans rejected liberal elites' attempts to devise and implement national standards of racial justice and cultural practice. Conservatives, he states, best articulated and acted on Americans' fear or rejection of centralized authority and their complex, contradictory demands for local power or group identity.

Jonathan Schoenwald's examination of the John Birch Society (JBS) moves beyond simple critiques of the national organization and its leadership to explain the role of this "extremist" organization in grassroots activism. Through national campaigns, like the movement to impeach Supreme Court Chief Justice Earl Warren, and local efforts to control school boards and city commissions, the JBS members changed the nature of American politics. For many conservatives, the JBS represented a necessary step, a "trunk line" in the formulation of their political philosophy, from fretting over communism to establishing ideological dominance over the Republican Party. These conservatives were not dejected by Goldwater's 1964 defeat; they were energized by the Goldwater candidacy and came to comprehend (and exercise) their immense power in the post-Goldwater Party.

Evelyn A. Schlatter, in her essay on the militant Minutemen, "Extremism in the Defense of Liberty," demonstrates continuity in the conservative philosophy of groups across the spectrum of the political right. She argues that although the gun-toting Minutemen differed in degree from groups like the JBS or Young Americans for Freedom, they drew from the same ideological well: intense anticommunism and a fearful outlook for the American future. While other conservatives might work to elect a local county commissioner or judge, the Minutemen stockpiled weapons and trained for a war against the communist-dominated U.S. government.

Historians have long recognized the importance of women to the conservative movement, but few have examined the impact of gender on conservatism. More-over, the contemporary dismissive description of the "little old lady in tennis shoes" further obscured the creative impact of women conservatives. In Michelle Nickerson's essay on southern California's "Moral Mothers and Goldwater Gals," she describes the crucial role of women in grassroots organizing and political par-ticipation. Building on a body of literature that describes how women have ex-tended their control of the domestic sphere into public policy debates, Nickerson not only connects conservative women to 1960s politics but makes critical links to the larger women's movement. Using a wealth of oral histories, Nickerson allows these women to tell their stories and fill an important gap in our understanding about women's role within the conservative movement.

Mary Brennan's essay on the 1964 Goldwater campaign challenges the funda-mental assumption of a "New Right." She argues that Goldwater provides the cen-tral link between classic Cold War conservatism and the emerging social conserva-tism of the late 1960s. Rather than portraying Goldwater as the progenitor of a new movement (a John the Baptist to Reagan's conservative messiah) or the last gasp of old-school anticommunism doomed to oblivion by the wacky antics of the far right, Brennan shows that Goldwater was the embodiment of a progression of conservative ideology. His message blended the 1950s Right (a hatred of commu-nism and a distrust of labor unions) with dire warnings about the political and cul-tural issues of the 1960s (a misguided U.S. foreign policy, a misplaced emphasis on personal rights, and a mistaken policy on welfare).

In many ways, Goldwater was the national symbol of what Jeff Roche describes as "cowboy conservatism." In his study of the conservative Texas Panhandle in the 1960s, Roche explains how local people came to formulate a political ideology as national issues came to have local resonance. In the early 1960s, many Panhandle Texans used anticommunist rhetoric to describe their intense dissatisfaction with modern life. They joined or supported anticommunist groups, like the JBS, in an attempt to convert that dissatisfaction into political action. As local versions of na-tional issues—student protest, Black Power, the counterculture, and busing—ap-peared on the plains, Panhandle Texans' anticommunism evolved into what Roche calls cowboy conservatism. Local conservatives defined and defended a political ideology created from their vision of whiteness, a faith in traditional family roles, a respect for free-market principles, and a demand for unswerving patriotism. They then looked to political candidates who most closely reflected their ideals.

In 1968 (and again in 1976, 1980, and 1984), cowboy conservatives strongly favored Ronald Reagan. Kurt Schuparra, in his essay on the creation of Reagan the politician, demonstrates how conservatives across the nation saw the former actor as a beacon—a "great white light." Reagan's political journey mirrored that of millions of other Americans who had supported the New Deal, feared the expansion of communism abroad and growth of liberalism at home, and wondered aloud about the direction of their political home—the Democratic Party. As Schuparra explains, Ronald Reagan was himself perhaps the first Reagan Democrat. Through a careful examination of the way that Reagan expressed himself on the issues that dominated the 1960s, Schuparra retraces the journey of many Americans who came to describe themselves as conservatives.

Another icon of the conservative movement, Phyllis Schlafly, further exemplifies the evolution of conservative ideology between the 1950s and 1970s. Donald Critchlow, in his consideration of conservative activist Phyllis Schlafly's long career, shows how grassroots activists like Schlafly come to articulate their vision of conservatism in response to contemporary politics. Rather than the more common portrayal of Schlafly as a radical opportunist grasping for issues, Critchlow explains how a generation of conservatives adapted their message to address a shifting American political culture. In this essay, he not only shows a great continuity in thought and action among conservative activists, but reveals the ways that local conflicts played out on the national stage. Critchlow argues that Schlafly, who operates both locally and within the upper echelons of conservative institutions, represents a crucial link between grassroots activism and national policymaking.

Scott Flipse explores a similar nexus in his examination of evangelical Christians. As he describes the importance of "below-the-belt" politics, he explodes many of the myths surrounding the creation of the religious right. Basing his study on national leaders of the evangelical Christian movement, Flipse explains how their attempts to offer moderate stances on sexual issues—sexuality, contraception, equal rights for women, and, of course, abortion—left them vulnerable to grassroots attacks from their own congregations and to the rapidly shifting cultural landscape of the late 1960s. To maintain control of their movement, evangelical leaders moved right from their original positions and into alliances with other conservatives, including, for the first time, Catholics. Flipse's essay goes a long way toward explaining the political and ideological journey of the religious right and greatly expands our understanding of the conservative sixties.

Lastly, Michael Flamm's essay, "The Politics of Law and Order," analyzes the emergence of "law and order" as both a campaign tool for conservatives and an issue for urban voters. Basing his study in 1960s and 1970s New York City, Flamm demonstrates how local citizens came to politicize crime and law enforcement. People in the 1960s who demanded "law and order," Flamm says, were not simply racists (though some may have been). Flamm explains how citizens' concerns over exploding crime rates led them to organize at the grass roots, which, in turn, created a fundamental shift in the political culture of New York. Emblematic of urban politics across the country, the law and order issue enabled conservative politicians to roll back much of the urban liberal agenda of the previous two decades.

In the 1960s, a multifaceted, multiconstituent conservative movement grew in strength and numbers. National leaders like Barry Goldwater, Ronald Reagan, and Phyllis Schlafly articulated a broad vision of conservatism that provided popular answers to the domestic and international challenges of the Vietnam War era. The civil rights movement, a failed war effort, antiwar protesters, massive domestic federal programs and regulations, cultural revolts, and a widespread breakdown in civility and lawfulness all fed a growing disgust on the part of many Americans with liberal leaders and liberalism in general. Conservatism, often developed at the grass roots without much fanfare and certainly outside the mass media spotlight, had become by the end of the 1960s a powerful political and cultural force that would soon gain ascendancy in the United States.

David Farber

DEMOCRATIC SUBJECTS IN THE AMERICAN SIXTIES: NATIONAL POLITICS, CULTURAL AUTHENTICITY, AND COMMUNITY INTEREST

Many of the most interesting and popular recent historical treatments of the American Sixties begin, I think, with a premise: that the left-wing social change or social justice movements of the 1960s era significantly figure the meaning and practice of democracy in the last third of the twentieth century.[1] And so they do.

I would like, however, to *re*-figure that political process by placing those movements in a larger framework. This framework, I hope, will still give political potency to radical activists and non-electorally oriented political actors while explaining the reasons their actions might have been historically timely and capable of shifting critical boundaries in American democratic practice. This framework will also help to explain the fragmenting of many of these social change movements and, at least as important, the power of conservatives to limit the victories of the left-liberal activists in the late 1960s and to become politically dominant by the late 1970s. Rather than regard left-wing and right-wing political movements of the 1960s and 1970s as opposing forces, I believe that a great many Americans across the political spectrum shared a political common ground: the desire for community political control and local cultural self-determination. A great many Americans came to see the national policymaking of liberal politicians, the national legal standards created by liberal jurists, and the national cultural values championed by a liberal (or, at least, cosmopolitan) mass media and intellectual establishment as impediments to their rights to local, democratic self-determination. While few of these Americans would convert to the traditional social conservatism of a William Buckley or the free-market conservative libertarianism of a Milton

Friedman—indeed, a small minority would become left-wing radicals—they would in large numbers by the late 1960s become politically not liberal. A populist conservative political realignment would result from that antiliberalism.

At the heart of the crisis politics of the 1960s was that most traditional of American democratic dilemmas: where should sovereignty lie in regard to the public affairs of the citizenry? From the New Left and the nascent New Right, from Black Power activists, Chicano militants, white southerners, and white urban ethnic blocs came impassioned calls for a more direct democracy built on local control and community right to self-determination. Besieged Great Society liberals and their allies defended the necessity of national policy conceived and administered by trained experts. The central debate was as old as the struggles over the Constitution. And that aspect of the debate that created the greatest heat—the one centered around the intertwined categories of national politics, cultural authenticity, and community interest—was, as it had been at least episodically for so long, focused first of all on issues of race law or racial justice. Could and should there be a *national* legal standard governing race relations in the United States? This question of racial justice organized much of the formal domestic political fireworks of the 1960s, incorporating radical activists from the left and the right, as well as a great many local, state, and national officeholders.[2]

In part this struggle over national racial justice had such explosive ramifications because it helped to produce a rancorous public debate about the political vitality and political saliency of local and community ways of self-governing. People asked to what extent and in what specific areas of public life (and thus private life as well) did the federal government have the right to enforce one standard for everyone? What of local traditions and local self-determination; that is, culturally "authentic" practices?

Race played out most spectacularly in regard to political jurisdiction with white southerners. However, by the late 1960s, outspoken whites in communities in all regions of the nation had become bitterly opposed to the idea that the federal government had the right both to set the standard of racial justice and to intervene in Americans' neighborhood schools, union locals, places of business, and housing choices. As early as 1966, the virulently racist Mississippi Senator James Eastland gleefully told his followers: "The sentiment of the entire country now stands with the Southern people."[3] National laws mandating racial integration and outlawing racist practices, backed up by powerful new federal bureaucracies, such as the Office of Federal Contract Compliance and the Equal Employment Opportunity Commission, had made "states-rights," local-rule "Confederates" out of many whites around the nation.

During the 1968 presidential race, Alabama Governor George Wallace (whose national reputation had been made in 1963 when he personally refused to allow a black student to register at the University of Alabama) most successfully blended traditional southern state's rights rhetoric with a principled-sounding conservative defense of local political self-determination. On "Meet the Press," where he coyly first announced his bid for the presidency, he denied being a racist and even insisted—against all prior evidence—that he held no brief for racial segregation. What he believed, he said was "that the states . . . [must] continue to determine the policies of their domestic institutions themselves, and that the bureaucrats and the theoreticians in Washington [must] let people in Ohio and New York and California decide themselves . . . what type of school system they are going to have." He continued, "there's not any backlash among the mass of American people against anybody because of color. . . . [T]here's a backlash against big government in this country."[4] Some three years earlier, when Wallace first hit the national stage, he told a bemused *Playboy* magazine interviewer: "Originally, a liberal was a believer in freedom. But the name has been taken over by those who believe in economic and social planning by the federal government to interfere in everybody's private business. The liberalism of today shows a loss of faith in the individual. Conservatives still believe in the individual, in private enterprise. . . . [t]hat the state should protect the people's welfare does not mean I believe the government has the right to tell a businessman whom he can hire and whom he cannot hire, a café or restaurant or motel owner whom he can serve and whom he cannot, a homeowner whom he must and must not sell his house to. A conservative tries to preserve freedom for business and labor."[5] Wallace never said the obvious, that many whites' anger at big government was not driven by abstract political philosophy but by their government's decision—via the 1964 Civil Rights Act and subsequent legislation—to make racial discrimination in employment, public accommodations, and housing a federal crime.

The major conservative political leader of the early 1960s, Barry Goldwater, recognized the electoral efficacy of this equation of conservatism with the individual right to be a racist employer, a racist businessman, or a racist property owner, even as Goldwater was, personally, not a racist. In his 1960 best-selling autobiography, *The Conscience of a Conservative*, Goldwater had been more outspoken in his praise of the ideal of school integration than then presidential hopeful, Senator John Kennedy. Goldwater wrote: "It so happens that I am in agreement with the objectives of the Supreme Court as stated in the *Brown* decision. I believe that it is both wise and just for negro children to attend the same schools as whites, and that to deny them this opportunity carries with it strong implications of inferiority." But Goldwater was not at all willing, as he put it, "to impose that judgement of mine on the people of Mississippi or South Carolina. . . . That is their business and not mine. I believe that the problem of race relations, like all social and cultural problems, is best handled by the people directly concerned."[6] Goldwater voted against the 1964 Civil Rights Act because he believed it dangerously expanded federal power and would result in a "police state" and "the destruction of a free society."[7] But he also opposed the legislation because he believed it was good politics. In an oft-quoted remark, he told Republican Party activists that their party was "not going to get the Negro vote . . . so we ought to go hunting where the ducks are."[8] A large majority of southern whites, Goldwater knew, were more than ready to leave the Democratic Party because its national leaders supported federally enforced civil rights laws that would end southern white communities' right to maintain their racist way of life. Goldwater was happy to make common cause with these fierce defenders of local rights, promising to "support all efforts by the States, excluding violence, of course, to preserve their rightful powers [to maintain legally prescribed segregation]."[9]

Other issues, which I will not discuss in detail here, also fed this claim about the right of democratic self-determination in different places or among different "communities": the banning of prayers in public schools (such prayers having been a century-old practice in many small towns and rural America) was a piece of this quandary.[10] So was the question of criminal suspects' rights, which had varied immensely in practice across the nation but for which the Supreme Court would set a national standard in the sixties.[11] By the mid to late 1960s, the issue of national standards versus local or for the late and post-sixties, equally important "community" ways would bleed across the political spectrum and energize groups as diverse as the Black Panthers, the National Welfare Rights Organization, and the 1968 supporters of the presidential aspirations of both Alabama Governor George Wallace and California Governor Ronald Reagan.

In America, in the 1960s, nationalizing a standard of justice—most of all, racial justice—created a crisis in democratic practice that mobilized disparate voters, interest groups, and self-described communities. That the nationalization of racial justice in the 1960s created such political turmoil should be a reminder of how resistant at the local level many whites had long been about accepting racial integration of neighborhoods, schools, and the workplace. As soon as black southerners began moving North in large numbers, first during the World War I era, and then in larger numbers during and after World War II, multitudes of northern urban whites had enlisted in a grassroots fight against what they perceived as African-American incursions into their communities.

Historian Thomas Sugrue points out that in Detroit between 1943 and 1965 whites organized some 192 neighborhood organizations aimed at keeping black people out of their neighborhoods and their schools. Sugrue quotes Allen B. Crow, president of the Economic Club of Detroit, who watched with interest as white working-class, labor-union families began to rethink their political identities in response to the city's changing racial demographics: "Men and women who own homes, which they have purchased to raise their children in congenial neighborhoods, have invested their stake in Detroit. . . . It has been well said, 'A Liberal is one who is liberal with the other fellow's money, and a Conservative is a man who has saved a little money and has a home of his own.'"[12] Long before the so-called white backlash in the 1960s, urban northern whites had made it clear to local politicians and to black urban migrants that they meant to preserve their neighborhoods as whites-only communities. Such long-standing insistence on local control of their own communities' race policies is a critical indicator of how uneasy so many Americans have long been about centralizing political authority, particularly regarding racial justice, in the federal government and of how recent that process of political nationalization has been in the United States.[13]

This national debate took modern root in obvious ways in the New Deal years of the 1930s when the federal government began to nationalize social provision (unemployment compensation for the out-of-work and pensions or welfare subsidies for the elderly, the disabled, and other targeted needy populations). Critically, racial justice during the New Deal years was consciously omitted by national reformers (going so far as to exclude most African-American and Mexican-American workers from key provisions of the Social Security act).[14] Racial exclusions then were engineered by southern, racially reactionary congressmen. Franklin Roosevelt defended his actions to Walter White, head of the NAACP, in regard to his seemingly egregious failure to support federal antilynching legislation: "I do not choose the tools with which I must work. Had I been permitted to choose them I would have selected quite different ones. . . . The Southerners by reason of the seniority rule in Congress are chairman or occupy strategic places on most of the Senate and House committees. If I come out for the anti-lynching bill now, they will block every bill I ask Congress to pass to keep America from collapsing. I just can't take that risk."[15] Racial justice — perceived for so long by the political elite, and, in fact, by most whites, as a regional southern problem — was bracketed by liberal forces in the 1930s in order to achieve some national, class-based relief for the economically hard-pressed.

By the World War II years, New Deal liberals' internal debates and complex negotiations with locally minded elected officerholders produced a new mainstream in liberal elites' approach to national governance. The relatively weak economic redistributive faction of the New Deal lost. So did the more orthodox national planning wing, which called for government development of American economic resources. The winners were those who believed that liberals could instead best legitimate, develop, and deploy national state power through expert, technocratic management.[16]

Two linked forms of this technocratic, expert state management developed rapidly. Growth liberalism focused on managing domestic macroeconomics to facilitate national prosperity. Cold War liberalism focused on managing international global security to provide peace and international trade. The creation of the Council of Economic Advisors through the 1946 Employment Bill (a centerpiece of Truman's Fair Deal) and the National Security Council and CIA via the National Security Act of 1947 were a few of the many institutional building blocks in national liberals' new technocratic, expert state management.[17]

In this new national politics, centralized decision-makers and decision making were supposed to create public policy that had national and even international level impacts (i.e., not a district-by-district game of congressional pork barrel politics but a standard system of rationally constructed policy impacts would change the nation's approach to basic institution building). These systemic policies and the kind of rationally trained policy actors they depend on were not altogether new. However, their electorally legitimated, congressionally approved, and, thus, normalization, multiplication, and powerful role in governance in the post–World War II years was a new development in American democratic practice and a fundamental structural and instrumental basis of post–World War II liberal policymaking.[18]

The legitimation of large-scale federal administrative power is only one part of the complex story of the nationalization of both politics and public policy and the simultaneous weakening and delegitimating of locally oriented and community-based governance. Network television and the potency of other forms of national mass media played a critical role in creating a national political audience. The regularization of a mass, national consumer marketplace—which had been so disrupted by the Great Depression and then World War II—helped, too, to craft a connective tissue among the American people. The Cold War, immediately following the sacrifices of World War II, molded a national patriotism, in which "our way of life" needed to be defended and demonstrated as superior. All these factors intensified the national—as against local—nature of the American people's democratic vision of self-governance.[19]

Specifically in regard to racial justice, this nationalization process was a godsend for civil rights activists. The national scope of domestic politics (with its clear implications for the international project of winning the Cold War in Africa, Asia, and other places inhabited by "people of color") transformed the race issue.[20] As a result, the political location of race relations, which white southerners had for so long successfully claimed as their special regional issue, which they alone had the moral right, political jurisdiction, and appropriate knowledge/experience to handle, was ready to be moved to the national arena.

Even prior to any semblance of a mass movement by African Americans or their allies, this political opening had become obvious. President Truman, speaking about Americans' Cold War international reputation, had desegregated the armed forces. The northern movement of millions of African Americans had caused some northern politicians, seeking black votes, to speak out about the disgrace of southern racism. In the *Brown v. Board of Education* decision (1954), the Supreme Court, recognizing the nature of the modern national economy and the place of all God's children within it, began its unanimous repudiation of segregated southern schools by acknowledging historical change: "In approaching the problem we cannot turn back the clock to 1868 when the [14th] amendment was adopted or even to 1896 when *Plessy v. Ferguson* was written, we must consider public education in the light of its full development and its present place in *American life throughout the Nation* [emphasis added], only in this way can it be determined if segregation in public schools deprives them [African Americans] of the equal protection of the laws."[21] In the post–World War II years, race and racial justice was being successfully nationalized as a public concern by an array of elite operators both inside the African-American movement (and, to a lesser extent, within the Mexican-American activist community, too) and by powerful liberal elites whose motives varied but whose national—and even international—orientation (cosmopolitan and not parochial) was a unifying principle.[22]

Enter the activists.

In the early 1960s, activists as diverse as Roy Wilkins of the NAACP and Martin Luther King—the first deliberately and the second ever more consciously—sought to make racial injustice in the American South an issue of injustice in the United

States that therefore necessitated federal intervention. For the older African-American activist community this project reached its climax in 1963, first with the Birmingham protests—Project C for Confrontation—and then in the March on Washington for Jobs and Freedom. The first act, Birmingham, was aimed at creating a national sense of crisis. This crisis would be conveyed by mass media representation that would increase the political saliency of racial justice for northern white liberals and the Kennedy White House, which, in turn, would increase the likelihood of national civil rights legislation and federal intervention in the South. The idea was not, fundamentally, aimed at getting folks in Birmingham to work out their differences. The opposite, in fact, was true: the idea was to show a national constituency that the white folks in Birmingham could not be reasoned with. The March on Washington culminated this nationalization of civil rights protest. The target was no longer any specific, tangible, situated racist practice or practitioners. The goal was a national demonstration aimed at effectuating civil rights legislation.

It is at this point that the civil rights movement famously, if not yet publicly, divided. Most of the younger activists associated with the Student Nonviolent Coordinating Committee (SNCC), the group of youthful organizers developed out of the 1960–61 sit-in movement, saw the march as a waste of time. In accord with Malcolm X's witticism, "The Farce on Washington," SNCC organizers had come to believe their activism was not aimed at focusing a national response to southern racism. Instead, they sought the empowerment of black people. SNCC organizers had started to create a new race politics based not on an abstract notion of equal opportunity guaranteed by national law, in which, to use Martin Luther King's hallowed words, "my four little children will one day live in a nation where they will not be judged by the color of their skin but by the content of their character." Increasing numbers of SNCC activists meant, somehow, to enable black people to gain tangible control over the *communities* in which they resided.

SNCC's Stokely Carmichael, a few months after the march, explained his basic political premise: "the national conscience was generally unreliable. . . . specifically, black people in Mississippi and throughout this country [can]not rely on their so-called allies."[23] And then, two years later (1966), in a more codified fashion, Carmichael spoke for the vast majority of SNCC activists and supporters before a crowd of cheering black Mississippians: "The only way we gonna stop them white men from whuppin' us is to take over. We been saying freedom for six years—and we ain't got nothin'. What we gonna start saying now is Black Power!"[24]

Stripped of their violent rhetoric and deliberately intimidating stance, many Black Power activists were, fundamentally, moving in the political direction many white urban ethnics (going back to the Catholic and Jewish urban immigrant experience in the 1870–1920 period) had taken at the local political level and much of the nation had practiced at the congressional level through geographically bounded political communities (in plain speech: delivering the pork to the home district). To gain status, security, and opportunity, Black Power activists turned to this model of political community. Instead of championing abstract national models of fairness and individual opportunity, they insisted on the need for communities to stick together and control what territories and resources they could in order to deliver the goods to fellow community members. Urban political machines had long used this ethnic system of community reward and community representation.[25] And throughout the nation's history, legislative governance at the state and national level, as exercised by white Americans, had long depended on a practical politics of geographical solidarity in which resources and legislation were supposed to benefit given spatially derived communities.

Black Power was a return to an older model of American democracy in which prescriptive community ruled. That model of community politics, in which congressmen parceled out pork on a district-by-district level by log rolling, or in which (at the intra-urban level) ethnic communities shared in the spoils through machine politics, was a rejection of late New Deal and post–World War II national liberal policymaking.[26] It dismissed abstract political ideals, systemic national planning, or provisioning of the New Deal/Fair Deal sort, and the national, bipartisan solidarity preached by Cold War presidents. In the Black Power model, the national liberals, with their rationalistic, technocratic orientation, were poor partners— "undependable," Carmichael said—for ensuring a kind of racial justice in which equality was not just an ideal but an outcome.

Less well publicized, at the First National Chicano Youth Liberation Conference in March 1969, Mexican-American activists codified an analogous discontent with liberals' promises of a nationally secured equal opportunity, nondiscriminatory society. They scorned national integration of any kind: "we can only conclude that social, economic, cultural, and political independence is the only road to total liberation from oppression, exploitation, and racism. Our struggle then must be for the control of our barrios, campos, pueblos, lands, our economy, our culture, and our political life."[27] Local community control by like-minded (racial) majorities, ironically enough, had become the demand not just of white racists in urban enclaves across the industrial Midwest or the rural backwaters of the Southeast, but of Black Power advocates in the ghettos of New York, Chicago, and Oakland and of Mexican-American militants in the barrios of Los Angeles, Denver, and San Antonio.

White liberals' active support for civil rights legislation had been gained, in part, by black activists' ability to show white supremacists as atavistic, irrational barbarians who could at their very best defend themselves by declaring that white supremacy had to be maintained because it was their . . . tradition. Nationally oriented white Americans recoiled at Mississippi Governor Ross Barnett's pro-segregation rally (1962) held at halftime during a University of Mississippi football game, in which he defended racism to rapturous approval by echoing Hitler's call on Blood and Fatherland: "I love our people, I love our ways, I love our traditions."[28] Civil rights, Martin Luther King and white liberals argued, was a national issue because it was not about local communities working out their local problems. The civil rights struggle, they argued, was about ensuring a national standard of justice as guaranteed by our fundamental national beliefs. Local communities could not use local history, local understandings, or even local political majorities to override those national beliefs. Ross Barnett and white supremacists, Confederate flags a-waving, disagreed. Black Power adherents, while abhorring the particular values and traditions of Barnett, though locked in combat with racists in the South and the rest of the nation, did agree with Barnett's analysis of how political communities actually operate. By the mid-1960s, a vocal number of African-American political activists, whether they were open housing advocates in Chicago or voting rights protesters in Alabama, as they faced off brickthrowing and firebombing white mobs, had begun to lose faith in the possibility of national solutions. Their experiences with a racially minded multitude made racial integration and the nationalization of racial justice seem both unlikely and, increasingly, undesirable. "How long? Not long," King had preached. What if he was wrong?

In New York City such doubts erupted in 1966 when African-American parents and community activists became fed up, they said, with the unmet promises of liberal political leaders to create good schools for black children. Rather than demand integrated schools ("We must no longer pursue the myth that integrated education is equated with quality education," decried one activist), they fought, instead, for community control of their all-black schools. A Harlem community leader, Preston Wilcox, speaking for the Ad Hoc Parent Council, told New York Mayor John Lindsay and School Superintendent Bernard Donovan that black New Yorkers demanded the right to select the principals and to control the direction of their neighborhood schools so that "one can expect the school in the ghetto to become what schools in more privileged areas already are, a reflection of local interests and resources, instead of a subtle rejection of them. For the operating philosophy of the existing system is too often manifested in a conscious or unconscious belittling of the values and life styles of much of its clientele."[29] In such concrete institutional battles the rhetoric of Black Power was given substantive meaning.

National liberals, politicians such as John Kennedy and Nelson Rockefeller, federal administrators such as Wilbur Cohen and Joseph Califano, and public intellectuals such as Arthur Schlesinger and John Galbraith, dreamed of an electorate capable of voting for men who had the training, intellect, and discipline to craft a compassionate society, unified against global threats, which transcended historic divides of race and region, religion and ethnicity in large part through government-managed free-market-based, globally secured, national prosperity.[30] The fact that elite liberals had been so slow to embrace the civil rights struggle was in large part because they realized that race or racial justice was the issue most likely to reveal the fragility of their enterprise. The election of 1968 fully revealed this fragility. A large majority of Americans across the political spectrum, and on all sides of the quest for racial justice, rejected national liberals' faith that federal officials—the liberal, national government—had the moral wisdom and practical knowledge to orchestrate nationally applicable solutions in many critical areas of public life.

Richard Nixon, politician extraordinaire, took full advantage of the electorate's growing antiliberalism and distrust of the national government. In his 1968 acceptance speech at the Republican National Convention, he stated the matter plainly:

"America is a great nation today, not because of what government did for people, but because of what people did for themselves." He ended that speech with a pitch-perfect call on the humble icons of local community, thanking, first and foremost, his hardworking father and loving mother for his good fortune, and then "a great teacher, a remarkable football coach, an inspirational minister."[31] In an era during which television flashed innumerable, violent images of faraway places (whether urban ghettos or Southeast Asian villages) into so many (white) Americans' homes, Nixon's conservative call on the supportive environs of the individual hearth, the community church, the neighborhood school, and the local playing field resonated across partisan political lines.

During the 1968 presidential campaign, Nixon made explicit the political implications of his cultural iconography, promising Americans that we would return to "the states, cities and communities . . . decision-making powers rightfully theirs."[32] (And he later made partially good on his promise by replacing nationally managed federal social programs with "block grants" to local governments who would then devise and run their own programs.) Nixon stated that if elected president he would oppose all federal efforts to force communities into busing their children from one racially homogenous neighborhood into another in order to achieve integrated schools. While Nixon was not completely adverse to new uses of federal power—in particular, in order to bring "law and order" to American cities' crime-ridden streets—and while he was not a racist reactionary like Governor Wallace, he understood that a great many Americans yearned for the small-town aura and community-centered ethos of the conservative Eisenhower years—even if such a time was more fable than lived experience for most Americans and even if such conservative leadership had largely dismissed the rights and dignity of America's minority populations.

Nixon's careful domestic conservatism repudiated the national social experimentation of much of the Great Society. Again and again, he proclaimed: "I say it is time to quit pouring billions of dollars into programs that have failed in the United States of America."[33] Yet Nixon was careful in how he couched his rejection of the racial policies of the Great Society. In his speeches and even in his back-room politicking with southern reactionaries like Strom Thurmond, he made it clear that as a pragmatic matter he supported open-housing legislation and he told prospective southern supporters that he would not support federal government funding of segregated schools or racially discriminatory programs, of any kind.[34] Nixon believed, at least from a political perspective, that while a hard-core racist white vote existed, it was not a majority. Many whites, Nixon believed, were not so much committed racists as they were unlikely to support racial justice measures that affected their own rights to community self-determination or their obligations to family members. He was right.

And as has been emphasized, not just whites felt this way. In the late 1960s, as Black Power advocates (and African-American urban rioters, the *lumpen* version of the revolt), in part in response to the obdurate racism of specific white "communities" (whether in Cicero, Illinois, or the Mississippi Delta), the limited nature of federal protection against racist law enforcement, the limits of federal redistributive efforts, and entrenched structural forms of oppression (such as "redlining"), began themselves to reinvent a new sort of local community politics. The liberal, Great Society dream of a new national politics—inclusive of racial justice—began to crumble. Over the last thirty years, even as equal protection before the law became normative as American practice, the saliency of race as a marker of social division and as a site for political wedge issues—issues that divide Americans into separate political communities—has remained extremely potent. That division is driven by both blacks and whites who have accepted in different ways for different purposes, based often on different understandings, the idea that race figures critical aspects of self-identity, cultural practice, and, thus, group politics.[35] Race politics, forever America's most daunting democratic challenge, at first despite and then because of 1960s activism, not surprisingly served to damage the liberal political dream of a nationally oriented electorate interested less in interest group parochialism and more in technical problem solving aimed at the realization of nationally agreed-on abstract ideals.

The racial politics of the 1960s on which I have dwelt here tell only a part of the story of the defeat of national liberals and their dreams of technical problem solving and the return of a localist politics that puts little faith in the power of the federal government to solve big problems and emphasizes instead the likelihood that local communities should most often look after their own affairs. The failures of Big Picture technocratic liberals like Robert McNamara to manage Vietnam and, thus, to fulfill Cold War liberal/economic growth liberal John Kennedy's boast that "we shall pay any price, bear any burden, meet any hardship, support any friend, oppose any foe to assure the survival and the success of liberty," mortally wounded Americans' sense that democracy could be entrusted to a caste of non-elected national whiz kids who could solve problems in a nonpolitical, bipartisan way. The failure of the more grand aspects of the War on Poverty, which was colored black by many government officials and American voters, intensified the sense that the alternative to community, local politics—a technically astute class of national officials—was not only an exercise in distant (and thus hard to reach) governance but a public policy disaster. They didn't know how to fix things any better than local actors. All they did, said many traditional and neo-local and community-oriented citizens and politicians, was take away the pride of local self-rule, dismiss the value of local ways, and weaken the ties that enabled communities to solve problems effectively in accord with community needs and desires.

Many conservative politicians, who had never cared enough to do anything to solve racial-based injustices or entrenched poverty, castigated liberals during the late 1960s, and for the next several decades, for making a hard situation worse. In 1994, after the Republican Party regained control of the House of Representatives, conservative Texas congressman Dick Armey provided a revisionist history of Martin Luther King's national campaign for racial justice and federal legislation, such as the 1964 Civil Rights Act and the 1965 Voting Rights Act, when he declared: "To me all the problems began in the Sixties."[36] In large part, Armey and his conservative allies meant that when local communities lost the right to govern themselves according to their traditional cultural values (even if those values included racist practices) the nation's social fabric tore and its moral fiber was dangerously weakened.

The irony of race politics in the 1960s went like this: white liberals enabled a successful mass African-American civil rights movement by forging a national government—and other national institutions—capable of challenging and defeating the traditional, regional politics of American apartheid and localized forms of racial discrimination. To do so, such liberals accelerated the late (or final form of) New Deal to turn to a faith in nationally applicable, technocratic, rational, often extra-legislative state management of society. As this form of state management began to carry out the project of racial justice, often through expansive court decisions and powerful administrative agencies, many Americans of all persuasions found the federal orchestration unacceptable. Some argued that local ways were being callously—and undemocratically—destroyed. Some believed that the ability of local actors or specific communities to maintain their own authentic cultures and to determine their own collective fates was being destroyed by elites who promised (in bad faith, critics argued) inclusion in some abstract "Great Society" that would never exist. Big government, necessary to create a national standard of justice, was beloved by too few, as its alienated, distant sort of governance satisfied few communities' desire for democratic control over their own fates.

In final irony, the American white "sixties" radicals who got so much press then and now, had tried to forge a new politics—a "New Left"—amid the contradictory desire for a national standard of racial justice (and other idealistic hopes) and the democratic practice of local self determination. The driving force of the New Left was "participatory democracy," that hard-to-define notion that people in direct, unmediated fashion could and should determine their own political fates.[37] What they meant, in practice, was that people who had already accepted certain beliefs—that is, not members of the Klan or the John Birch Society—should work together at the grassroots community level to establish consensual plans that benefited everyone. By the late 1960s, such New Leftist hopes had mainly dried up. First, they had watched the American people vote overwhelmingly in the 1968 presidential election either for a racist conservative populist, George Wallace, or a Cold War conservative artfully deploying conservative populism, Richard Nixon. Second, many realized that their political faith in local organizing and community building had little to say about big problem solving: how do local citizens, even if they are united in democratic communities, successfully regulate or control the decisions made by globally based business corporations? And third, the political coalition of young students brought together in the early 1960s by the horrors of southern racism had itself fragmented over questions of racial identity, gender politics, and ideology; as a result they could no longer hold together their own political community to work together to face an increasingly hostile majority of the American citizenry. Many in the New Left leadership realized that "participatory democracy" had not worked and turned, usually only for a short time, to politically suicidal and morally corrupt Stalinist or Maoist forms of "democratic centralism."[38]

Many white radicals, with far greater success, escaped this political dead end by creating group "liberation" movement struggles—national communities of people tied togther by identity politics—somewhat modeled on the Black Power struggle (Gay Liberation and Women's Liberation). In such social change movements new forms of political community based on personal identity, not geography, were successfully created for tens of millions of Americans.

As vital as these liberationist struggles were for a more inclusive and equitable American society, more successful at the electoral level from the 1968 election to nearly the end of the twentieth century would be a growing network of community-based islands of resistance to the Great Society dream of a nationalized system of social provision, equality, justice, and resource management. Driven by the older dream of local control and local standards based on culturally authentic, traditional values, by the late 1960s the New Right was being born.[39] Following in the footsteps of that John the Baptist figure, Barry Goldwater, and animated by thousands of grassroots community groups, many of which predated the mid-1960s "Movement" culture of leftist social change movements, this New Right called for a return to community control over the basic forms of cultural and social reproduction (schools and abortion), public provisioning (welfare, in particular), and resource management (public lands included). In the dual attack on liberalism by both the Left and Right, racists and new racialists, made possible through the gross domestic and foreign policy failures of Great Society liberals and a widespread rejection of national management of public life, it would be the Right, not the Left, that would best succeed in reinventing local, grassroots democracy in the post-sixties era.

Jonathan M. Schoenwald

WE ARE AN ACTION GROUP:
THE JOHN BIRCH SOCIETY
AND THE CONSERVATIVE MOVEMENT
IN THE 1960S

As late as 1958 there was no "conservative movement" to speak of. Conservatives, or those Americans who opposed statism or centralized power embodied in communism or socialism, and who supported a limited central government, a strong national defense, the nuclear family and its concomitant values, the primacy of the individual, and an ordered society were, in many ways, politically isolated.[1] Though such periodicals as *Human Events, National Review,* or *The American Mercury* provided intellectual forums, most interested people still only read about conservative ideologues or perhaps listened to pitchmen. National conservative organizations were rare; conservatives were essentially alone. If this was the case in 1958, how did conservatism, a political ideology barely more than a decade old in its modern iteration, grow from a scattered intellectual network to a coherent political movement, which, by the mid-1960s, experienced surprising success? Though no single answer satisfies this question, one might begin with the John Birch Society (JBS).

Founded in 1958 by candy manufacturer Robert H. W. Welch, Jr., the JBS became a trunk line for a number of conservative Americans, many of whom believed that traditional politics were no longer sufficient to solve the country's problems. Appearing at a time when most Republicans seemed comfortable with Dwight D. Eisenhower's "me-tooism," the JBS represented an opportunity for isolated and frustrated conservatives to join a national organization that not only bound them together ideologically, but also distinguished them from their fellow citizens who were unwilling to act boldly to achieve their goals.[2]

The JBS is typically identified by scholars with extremist conservatives who suspected internal subversion at the highest levels of government, who hoped to end or circumvent the "Eastern Establishment's" dominance of the American political process, and who sought to widen participation in the electoral process through active citizens' groups. Though at first a term of derision used by their enemies, some conservatives co-opted the word "extremist" and wore it as a badge of courage that distinguished them from complacent moderates or liberals. Within the Republican Party, a majority of mainstream or electoral conservatives relied on the GOP as the sole vehicle to assess, develop, and win political power. Throughout the 1960s, the two general divisions, extremist and mainstream, never officially demarcated, developed a symbiotic relationship, borrowing policies, strategies, and infrastructure in the hopes of reshaping the political, social, and cultural contours of the country.[3]

For tens of thousands of conservatives, the JBS represented a transformation from thinking about what it meant to be conservative to acting conservative. For years dismissed by most political pundits as a group of conspiracy theorists composed of "wealthy businessmen, retired military officers and little old ladies in tennis shoes," the society demonstrated that tens of thousands of Americans wanted to help chart America's course, and for those on the Right it presented one of the first opportunities to join a grassroots movement.[4] Though it rarely acted as a political kingmaker, its impact was wide-reaching: it organized citizens; publicized issues; and promoted legislation, all in an effort to awaken America to the dangers of communism, changing cultural mores, and duplicitous and ineffectual political institutions. In other words, conservative ideology needed a conduit to reach local activists, and the JBS served that purpose peerlessly. Within a few years, for example, the society's home office in Belmont, Massachusetts, could put out the word to members to flood Congress with thousands of telegrams and letters; or local chapters, on their own, might run a member for the school board, aiming to create a majority that would determine policies on everything from textbook choice to teacher hiring. Conservative Americans had been waiting for such an organization. As one conservative put it in a 1959 letter to Robert Welch, "The John Birch Society is a God-send. Your plan is Divinely inspired. And you, Robert Welch—you have become the key to one of mankind's greatest opportunities. The need was for inspired leadership; and we didn't have it."[5] For these Americans, a new day had dawned.

Since its founding, most scholars and other critics have typically classified the JBS as another faction of a radical Right composed of everyone from fascistic groups to fundamentalist Christians. Contemporary studies of the society usually fall into one of five general categories. In 1960, after its existence became public knowledge, a flurry of mass-market paperbacks appeared in response to the media attention showered on the JBS. Most of these accounts tried to expose the evils of the society, positing it as a right-wing equivalent of communism, or associating it with racist or anti-Semitic groups like the Ku Klux Klan or the American Nazi Party.[6] About a year later, studies conducted by organizations—frequently religious—that felt threatened by the JBS began to appear.[7] The press investigated Welch and the society from its earliest days, its klieg lights burning most brightly in 1961.[8] Beginning in 1963, academic studies analyzed the society by employing social science methodology and member surveys.[9] Finally, conservative and liberal journals and organizations examined Welch and the society, the former to decide whether to encourage their readers to join, the latter to illustrate the group's inherent dangers.[10] While each of these studies was aimed at different audiences, they all sought to answer similar questions: who would join such a group? Did Birchers represent a threat to American democracy? Is America shifting rightward?

In recent years a handful of scholars have begun reexamining the JBS. Rather than categorizing Welch and his followers as somehow abnormal, these researchers have tried to understand why the society became so popular and what impact it had on the conservative movement and politics in general. This latest wave of historical examinations takes the society—and Welch—seriously, acknowledging their impact, trying to understand their attraction, and considering how they played a part in the conservative movement.[11] In essence, each of these scholars argues that the JBS was a crucial strand in a conservative web, which connected isolated individuals to a national network and enabled a particular brand of conservative ideology to be applied to political and social situations at a community level.

Among conservative organizations the JBS was unique. Welch's ideas emerged out of his life experiences: a precocious childhood, a successful business career, and growing respect from his peers as a political prognosticator. Welch built the JBS like a business, selling ideology to members just as he had sold candy to customers. His timing was crucial; the society tapped into contemporary suspicions born out of a series of Cold War events (such as an increasing number of liberal Supreme Court decisions, the creation of the Warsaw Pact in 1955, and Nikita Khrushchev's 1959 visit to the United States) that seemed to indicate that the federal government could be aiding and abetting the communist cause. Lastly, given the absence of national activist groups, the JBS gave citizens a forum in which to commiserate, plan, and act locally and nationally. In essence, the society was an amalgamation of Welch's business and political worlds, its internal logic nearly indecipherable to those who did not feel similarly. And yet, to members, it made sense. For example, mimicking its enemies, the society's infrastructure was based on local chapters, an organizational decision borrowed from communist cells. Though not totally clandestine, the JBS never made membership lists public or disclosed its annual income. Though the society professed nonpartisanship, it backed candidates in spirit if not with its checkbook, and frequently tried to recruit politicians to its membership roster. To fully understand the society, however, one must begin with its founder, Robert Welch.

Welch was born to a fundamentalist Baptist family in rural North Carolina in 1899. He entered the University of North Carolina at age twelve, graduated at sixteen, briefly attended the Naval Academy, and for two years was enrolled at Harvard Law School. In the mid-1920s, Welch followed his brother into the candy business and became an expert salesman who later penned such works as *The Road to Salesmanship*. Welch began to make his name in conservative circles in the early 1950s when, after running in and losing the Massachusetts primary for the lieutenant governorship, he turned to writing political tracts, giving speeches, and publishing his own journal, *One Man's Opinion*.[12] An unapologetic alarmist, Welch's writings focused on the internal subversion wrought by communist agents, dupes, fellow travelers, and "comsymps," or communist sympathizers, who intended to soften up American psychological and moral defenses. In 1958, Welch outlined the basic strategy for the communist conquest of the world: seize Eastern Europe, take over Asia, and finally capture the rest of the world, including the United States. According to Welch, the first step had been completed in 1950, and the second step was about three-fourths accomplished.[13] America's only defense, he argued, was its people.

The timing of Welch's tocsin was perfect. The Cold War was a constant source of tension for Americans, and most politicians, Welch claimed, offered only platitudes. In fact, he insisted, politicians—whether Democrats or Republicans—promised only more of the same. Only the staunchest conservatism that was relatively free of the debilitating compromises inherent in politics could provide an alternative. Postwar conservatism, though containing divisions, was fluid, with a variety of individuals and ideas influencing its course. By the late 1950s and early 1960s, conservatives could be generally categorized as traditionalists, libertarians, or anticommunists.[14] These divisions were permeable; individuals and groups borrowed ideas and political strategies from each other. Out of this broad ideological heritage Welch created an inclusive society, inviting conservatives of all stripes into the fold, which, in many ways, mimicked the enemy's efforts at creating a "popular front." Though he emphasized anticommunism first, Welch was also an anti-statist libertarian and a solid traditionalist, values the society would personify in its projects and pronouncements.

Throughout the 1950s, Welch delivered speeches, wrote pamphlets, and sharpened his message. Welch realized that not only did anticommunists need a symbol, but also that anticommunism was only one small part of a larger conservative undertaking. Small government, free enterprise, and agrarian, small-town values, he believed, should rule the day. During the depths of the 1950s Cold War, Welch concluded that communist victories around the world could have only been accomplished with American help. The question of why America failed to act when even a paltry gesture might have prevented another domino from toppling brought only one answer. Foreign and domestic policy betrayals were aided by "insiders" in the State Department; the Supreme Court; the United Nations; the mass media; various "fronts" like the civil rights movement and liberal church groups; and, most important, the president.[15] In 1954, Welch published *The Life of John Birch,* which eulogized a hardheaded Baptist missionary killed by the Chinese communists ten days after the end of World War II as the first victim of World War III. That same year, as Welch's conspiracy theories hardened, he began writing a long "letter" describing America's decay in world stature since World War II. Sitting at his desk in Belmont, Massachusetts, Welch revised multiple drafts of the letter, and eventually concluded that President Dwight D. Eisenhower "has been sympathetic to ultimate Communist aims, realistically and even mercilessly willing to help them achieve their goals, knowingly receiving and abiding by Communist orders, and consciously serving the Communist conspiracy, for all of his adult life."[16] By 1958, the letter was more than 300 pages long. Welch bound hundreds of copies in black, first calling it *The Black Book,* and later simply *The Politician.*

Introduced to like-minded doctors, lawyers, and businessmen, Welch's ideas found a receptive audience. Welch first duplicated *The Politician* by mimeograph machine; later he set up his own publishing house, Western Islands, which became an integral part of the society's vigorous propaganda machine. By 1970, Welch claimed to have sold 200,000 copies of the tome, almost all of which were distributed by the JBS and through word of mouth.[17] *The Politician*'s conclusions, for many, required but a small leap of faith. They had already suspected that Eisenhower was colluding with the enemy and that Dean Acheson had helped to give away Eastern Europe. But Welch made it clear. As one reader said, "I have read the introduction and first chapter and agree completely. The facts and conclusions are not new to me, but I am extremely grateful to have them actually written where they don't get lost and blurred."[18] *The Politician* fused hundreds of disparate facts and ideas into a coherent whole, giving readers the chance to experience a eureka moment.

But Welch understood from his business experience that it was not enough to mail newsletters or write books to create a critical mass of believers. If he were to recruit the million or so Americans he thought necessary to oppose the communist subversion, he had to organize face-to-face meetings among eager patriots. Therefore, on December 8, 1958, Welch met with eleven men in a brick Tudor house in bitterly cold Indianapolis to unveil the John Birch Society. Welch lectured the men for two days, taking breaks only for coffee, lunch, and dinner. His notes became *The Blue Book,* the society's seminal text and a guide to fighting the growing conspiracy.[19] At the meeting Welch assumed the title "Founder" and told the men that the society would be monolithic, since "democracy is merely a deceptive phrase, a weapon of demagoguery, and a perennial fraud."[20] Drawing on his experience as a salesman, Welch believed that above all else the JBS needed a strict hierarchy, which convinced him to create an advisory council that rubber-stamped his decisions, a network of paid organizers, and, eventually, hundreds of local chapters.

Eager to see the light, new members of the JBS lapped up copies of *The Politician.* The published version, however, did not contain the original incriminating statements by Welch about Eisenhower. Most famously, Welch originally claimed that Eisenhower was "a dedicated, conscious agent of the Communist conspiracy," and not simply a communist "stooge."[21] Welch had been trying to explain how various fellow travelers, communist sympathizers, stooges, and full-time agents constituted an enemy matrix, which planned to overthrow the United States. Eisenhower, he said, was the linchpin of that assembly, the most important of all of the Kremlin's recruits. Since *The Politician* was written before the creation of the JBS, however, members did not necessarily have to agree with its conclusions, unlike

The Blue Book, which was the society's official doctrine. Nevertheless, when reporters began tracing Welch's background and found unpublished versions of *The Politician,* which contained the inflammatory quote about Eisenhower, the society paid the price for Welch's claim. Though the society and Welch himself tried hard to differentiate between the founder's writings prior to 1958 and those that came later, journalists, politicians, and most of the public made a permanent association between his rants about Eisenhower and the JBS.[22]

Not all conservatives agreed with Welch's conspiratorial outlook. For example, William F. Buckley, Jr., who had relied on Welch among many conservatives to fund *National Review* (which Buckley founded in 1955), told Welch "I for one disavow your hypotheses. I do not even find them plausible."[23] General Albert C. Wedemeyer, himself a prominent conservative speaker and under whose command Birch had served in China, told Welch that although he did not "question your sincerity of purpose or motives . . . I do question your judgment."[24] This was the beginning of a growing divide between "responsible" conservatives—as they labeled themselves—and the Far Right. Buckley, Wedemeyer, Richard Nixon, theorist Russell Kirk, *National Review* publisher William Rusher, and many others quickly began searching for ways to distinguish their own brand of conservatism from Welch's. Welch thought politics were a sham; they did not. Welch believed internal communism was a worse threat than the external. Though acknowledging an internal threat, responsible conservatives thought it was secondary to the realities of Soviet and Chinese expansionism. Welch wanted to create a coalition with the JBS at its center. The others also wanted unity, but were loath to accept someone so radical in his beliefs. And on and on. But Buckley and the others were also in a bind; they knew that although tens of thousands of Americans would follow Welch, the vast majority of the electorate would not. The question was: how could they depose Welch without turning away his followers? This quandary would plague conservatives throughout the 1960s.

Welch opened an office in Belmont and by late 1959 the society was mailing information to thousands and scheduling dozens of Welch-led weekend seminars, which recreated the founding meeting in Indianapolis. The society engaged in massive fundraising and membership drives. The day-to-day operation of the JBS clearly reflected Welch's business acumen and background. Welch stood atop the organizational pyramid; below him was the council, the support services and staff in Belmont, regional coordinators, individual chapter leaders, local chapters, and individual members. The number of members, its potential for growth, and its geographic area (a regional coordinator had to cover his territory by car) determined the size of a region. Chapters consisted of no more than twenty members; if they grew too large, a new chapter would split off. This way, reasoned Welch, the chances of communist infiltration and subsequent damage were kept to a minimum. If any region had too few members, individuals were invited to affiliate with the home chapter. Home chapter members could correspond with Belmont simply by ripping out a page from the JBS *Bulletin* and sending it to the Member's Monthly Messages (MMM) Department. They contributed their suggestions, questions, and, of course, monthly dues and donations. Dues for men were $24 per year, while women paid half of that figure. In 1962, the society's income reportedly exceeded $1 million.[25] One year later the figure had almost doubled.

The MMM Department provides a good example of how Welch understood that he had to satisfy Birchers as if they were customers. The JBS appeared at a time when some Americans were eager to make a difference. Just as liberals heeded John F. Kennedy's advice to "ask not what your country can do for you—ask what you can do for your country," activist conservatives were energized by liberalism and the Cold War threat, and the JBS helped channel their enthusiasm through Welch's ideology. He gave members reason to believe that they made a difference in the struggle against communism. Thus, MMMs and services like it developed regular exchanges between members, Belmont, and regional organizers. Members wrote in to suggest how to maximize the efficiency of national projects, offered slogans for bumper stickers ("Let's Give Red China Our Seat [in the UN]"), proposed compiling lists of communist fronts in their communities, and thought of ways to recruit new members ("Why not have Junior Birch Society Members starting at the age of ten?").[26] Sometimes chapters reported local projects that they thought might work well nationally. Welch and his advisers knew that being a Bircher was different from being a member of, say, Americans for Democratic Action or other liberal groups, which asked for dues and at times encouraged members to write a letter to a representative or senator. Though some Birchers simply paid their monthly dues, the majority were active on the local level and many perhaps on the national level, which made them more likely to remain within the fold.[27]

Welch's business model worked wonders. He knew that he needed to reach a national market, and that the key was through local retail efforts—the chapters. Therefore, even though the chapters were at the grass roots and did not ultimately have a voice equal to Welch's or the council's in making decisions, the society was structured to support the chapters, not the other way around. Though members could have been content purchasing books by mail, Welch insisted on opening American Opinion bookstores. By focusing on action—monthly projects, society news, and providing updates on various campaigns—the *John Birch Society Bulletin* supplemented the more theoretical monthly *American Opinion*. By 1963, the society had a hundred bookstores across the country, a paid circulation of about 27,000 for *American Opinion,* weekly expenses nearing $35,000, and the home office in Belmont had dozens of staffers, not including about forty paid organizers scattered around the country.[28] These regional coordinators were essentially traveling salesmen whose purpose was to promote local chapters. They spent long hours on the phone and behind the wheel, shuttling from meeting to meeting, giving speeches to city councils during the day and in members' living rooms at night. Coordinators observed meetings, made suggestions to chapter leaders, and evaluated the performance of recruits and veterans. Sales of the ideological product were measured quantitatively: the number of new members a coordinator recruited, the number of letters a chapter sent to the editor of the local newspaper, or the number of signatures a chapter collected to impeach Earl Warren from the Supreme Court.

The society grew rapidly in the early 1960s, and even though membership rolls were secret, most contemporary observers put the figure at between 40,000 and 100,000.[29]

Being a Bircher meant implicitly or explicitly supporting Robert Welch, whose conspiracy theories often earned the ridicule of the press, liberals, centrists, and many conservatives. And associating with the group could even jeopardize one's standing in a community, workplace, or family. For example, after Welch appeared on "Meet the Press" on May 21, 1961, one viewer wrote that the society "should be disbanded immediately! They are out to confuse the public, so utterly, so completely, so thoroughly, that we will be ready to follow them blindly, because according to them we won't know what to think, what to believe, or what to do about our leaders our politicians, or our civic groups."[30] Knowing that neighbors, friends, or business associates supported Welch's ideas and tactics could raise doubts about their judgment. It would be hard to look at a friend the same way knowing that he or she had apparently sworn allegiance to Robert Welch.

Birchers were overwhelmingly white, middle and upper class, and Republican. One 1965 academic survey found the typical member to be a forty-one year-old white male who lived in a less densely populated state and in a smaller community than most Americans. Almost half were Protestant and went to church regularly. One-third of those surveyed had attended college, with most majoring in engineering or business. Few had gone to elite institutions.[31] The normality of members was not lost on contemporary observers, many of who seemed to think that Birchers would somehow set themselves apart from everyone else:

> When Welch travels on speaking tours, he draws large audiences, most of them middle-aged and from the upper middle class. They are not unemployed malcontents or crackpots; they are patient and enthusiastic men and women, willing to wait on a line, four abreast, for an hour, to buy tickets to hear him. Reporters who have talked to them say many speak like educated people. From their dress and social poise most of them seem economically well off.[32]

Birchers saw themselves as patriotic, respectable Americans, a fact that not only helped them recruit more members, but also weather storms of negative publicity.

Although most researchers agree that the majority of JBS members were men, women played critical roles in chapters across the country. Across the Sun Belt women constituted a preponderance of chapter leaders and members. Since many of these women were homemakers, they felt they could devote their time to the fight to roll back communism and liberalism. Knowing that women had not only the time, but also the energy and acumen to take on such responsibilities, coordinators often targeted them specifically. Consequently, women's confidence grew as their rosters filled, and their projects gained momentum. For these women, the society acted as a liberating agent, clarifying their political priorities, illustrating their potential as contributors to a cause, and helping women to enter the realm of political organizing in the early 1960s.[33]

Ironically, the independence some women gained in the JBS ran counter to the society's position on women's rights. According to Welch, women's liberation was simply a ploy designed to overthrow a social order based on the nuclear family and specific gender roles. Women might have thought that they were releasing themselves from their traditional bonds, he posited, but they were actually playing into the designs of the communists. Day care centers, for example, were nothing less than a direct assault on the nuclear family. Connecting these threats against traditional gender roles to the communist and liberal menace, the society reported that at a protest against the 1969 Miss America Pageant, leaflets announced "We are tired of having sole responsibility for caring for our children. [We want] state-supported, community-controlled day care centers and nursery schools, and compensation for mothers who choose to care for their children at home, as this is work vital to the whole society."[34] Members did not need more evidence to understand that a communist conspiracy was behind yet another so-called revolution. Though working in the society gave women an excuse to "let a sink full of dirty dishes wait," relinquishing one's responsibilities for the children was not an option.[35]

Men and women in the society focused their efforts on both national and local projects. Welch, with some help from the council and other staff at Belmont, dreamed up most of the national projects. One of the longest-lived, the campaign to impeach Earl Warren, flooded the offices of senators and representatives in state legislatures and on Capitol Hill with thousands of postcards and telegrams, urging action against the Supreme Court Chief Justice. Locally, anti-Warren billboards dotted the landscape. In Pampa, Texas, a banner urging Warren's removal hung over Main Street.[36] Bumper stickers adorned cars in Georgia, California, and Pennsylvania, and thousands signed petitions demanding his ouster. Welch knew that cases like 1954's *Brown v. Board of Education,* which ended segregation, and 1962's *Engel v. Vitale,* which took the first step in outlawing prayer in school, struck a chord with Americans who believed in states' rights.

Projects like the Warren impeachment drive tested the limits of the JBS. Though it was virtually impossible to impeach a Supreme Court justice, JBS members took on the task with relish. Even Welch knew that the project would not work. As he wrote to a member of the council, "I am not deceiving myself that we have very much chance of really bringing about the impeachment of Earl Warren. Although we might. But I don't think that is really as important as dramatizing to the whole country where he stands, where the Supreme Court as now constituted under him stands, and how important it is to face the facts about the road we are now traveling so fast."[37]

The JBS was neither immune to nor unaware of what was perhaps the most penetrating issue in 1960s America: race. Some conservatives used states' rights as a cloak to hide racist beliefs, while others openly declared their opposition to desegregation in the South and elsewhere. Like many other conservatives, Welch attacked the civil rights movement as a communist Trojan horse. The society, however, was not racist; all internal and external communications point to the position that it saw civil rights as part of a communist effort to undo America using internal strife.

In 1956, Welch argued that the communists had no "interest in the welfare of either the colored people or the white people of the South. It is not desegregation as an end in which they are interested, but the bitterness, strife, and terrors of mob action which can be instigated while that end is supposedly being sought."[38] By fomenting hate between the races, communist organizers could achieve their real goal: overthrowing the United States. Of course, argued many liberals, such an analysis could also be used to camouflage a racist position. Nevertheless, the solution to racial unrest, said Welch, was not to follow Martin Luther King or his disciples, but instead to handle problems locally. Welch often repeated the tale of Americus, Georgia, where, after a black teenager killed a white teenager, tensions in the town ran high. A Birch chapter helped reduce mistrust by first educating county citizens, and then organizing meetings that preached "not hate, but love." As one Bircher pleaded at the town meeting, "We must not retaliate against Communist dupes, and give them the bodies that they desire."[39] Knowing the value of civil unrest, reasoned Welch, the Kremlin encouraged Americans to upset the status quo.[40]

The society's position on American foreign policy, specifically that of the country's involvement in Vietnam, illustrates how Welch and many members perceived a holistic effort by the communists to defeat America. Beginning in the early 1960s, for example, Welch and his staff opposed American involvement in Vietnam. The caveat, though, was that as long as America was involved it should win quickly, set up an anticommunist government in Saigon, and get out. The greatest peril, reasoned the society, was that Vietnam served as a smokescreen for more insidious leftist actions at home. The federal government's actions both at home and abroad, argued Welch, encouraged subversive activity as part of an elaborate con game, in which the American people would throw their support behind the federal government, allowing communist and communist-sympathizer politicians to secretly grab more power with the public's approval. Moreover, antiwar protests justified an increased use of military and police forces, all while ignoring the true danger, that of a growing communist state in America. Welch, in fact, famously proclaimed the defense department's buildup in the early 1960s as "wasteful . . . a phony defense against an external enemy."[41]

The society worked hard to marshal evidence to support its position. One Birch analyst pointed out the ties between the North Vietnamese and the protesters on the homefront: "Our enemy is not only aware of the decay within America, but he takes it into account in all his calculations—and depends upon the supporting role to be played by his openly active fifth column."[42] According to the JBS, soldiers "agreed that the war had to be won in the United States before it could be won in Vietnam."[43] A North Vietnamese think tank had "endless files on every partisan they can count on in America—from fatuous housewives lulling away the dull days of their suburban lives by playing at revolution, to officials at sensitive posts in our Foreign Service, professors, physicians, lawyers, sociologists, and student leaders."[44] Such explanations reduced a multiplicity of problems to a comprehensible few. Thus, in the same way that Moscow directed the communist insurgency, the unrest in America, the JBS explained, was co-managed by North Vietnam, encouraging both the naive and the malevolent to engage in insurrection.[45]

Although Welch believed that giving local chapters some control over which projects they pursued independently of the national agenda could jeopardize the society's defenses against communist infiltration, he realized that members needed to know they were making an impact in their own communities. Rather than writing letters to legislators demanding that Earl Warren be impeached, for example, a chapter might attempt to boycott a local media outlet it thought was too liberal or book an unsanctioned guest speaker to address the community. Local projects could benefit chapters and the entire organization since they "provide our members with an opportunity to see the tangible results of their efforts which can be a powerful factor in keeping the morale and esprit de corps of the chapters at a high pitch."[46]

Many chapters managed to pursue projects independent of Belmont's directives, and it was often the enthusiasm with which they took on these tasks that earned the JBS its reputation for ruthlessness. In California, chapters ran slates of candidates for local school boards. They hoped to gain control and regulate the curriculum, textbooks, and teacher hirings.[47] On one August day in 1964, New York chapters in Manhattan, Brooklyn, the Bronx, and Long Island passed out 80,000 reprints of a JBS article that opposed citizen review boards for local police departments.[48] Other chapters besieged union locals, church leaders who belonged to the National Council of Churches (thought to be a pipeline for communist ministers), and local merchants suspected of being communists. Welch, though, worried about chapters gaining too much independence and losing interest in national projects, so the home office issued directives on running meetings, giving presentations ("The battle for saving our Republic could well be won or lost in our living rooms."), and starting discussions ("Should Communist teachers be allowed to hide behind the doctrine of academic freedom?").[49] Welch even took to sending out monthly taped messages to chapters so his voice could fill living rooms across the country. As Belmont reminded constituents, "We are neither a study group nor a discussion group. We are an action group and our meetings should reflect this fact at all times."[50] "Action," however, could mean anything from reading society publications to running for the local school board. This flexibility helped convince the rank and file that they were helping to chart the society's course, which gave them reason to struggle on another day. In some ways the members pushed the society further than Welch, attracting the attention of not only potential recruits but the Leviathan itself: the federal government.

By 1962, the Federal Bureau of Investigation and the Democratic Party were paying close attention to the JBS. The FBI received thousands of requests for information about the society from citizens who wanted to know if it was a proper outlet through which to channel their anticommunist sentiments. J. Edgar Hoover, who ran the FBI for nearly half a century, was America's most trusted authority on communism. Surely he would know whether to support the society. Typical of such inquiries came from one writer contemplating joining who told the director:

> I am a member of the City Council, the local school board, the official board of my church, and I attempt to be a good citizen. I do not want to be involved with any organization that is not 100% American and above board. I have a very great respect for you and the organization which you have built; your opinion will be greatly appreciated.[51]

The Bureau's responses ranged from condemnation to a limited endorsement; after all, the JBS was attempting to educate the public about the dangers of communism. This, however, did not prevent the FBI from scrutinizing the society. Anyone who wrote to the agency and declared his or her allegiance to the JBS was noted in bureau files. If the society opened a bookstore, sponsored a rally, or somehow attracted attention, local agents documented the activities.[52] Although officials assured citizens that they were not investigating the JBS, the fact that they devoted time and energy to collecting information belied their disinterested tone.

The FBI, however, was only part of a larger investigation into the JBS. The Democratic Party under Kennedy and then Johnson saw the JBS as both a threat and a potential political windfall. Both presidents refrained from commenting publicly on the Far Right except in news conferences. As the controversy over *The Politician* hit the front pages in April 1961, for example, Kennedy offered only a mild rebuke to the society: "I'm not sure that the John Birch Society is wrestling with the real problems which are created by the Communist advance around the world."[53] Nevertheless, Democratic advisers—especially Kennedy's—churned out reports that suggested ways to counter and perhaps exploit the Right. A typical analysis by Kennedy aide Myer Feldman noted that while candidates for public office who aligned themselves with the Far Right were relatively rare, those who did exist garnered a fair amount of support: "While none of the 4 candidates for Congress who were avowed Birchites were elected in 1962, each ran a surprisingly strong race and polled about 45 percent of the vote cast. . . . They raised and spent almost a quarter of a million dollars."[54] Birchers who ran for office typically came from conservative strongholds in southern California or the South. While not all benefited from their affiliation, the devotion their supporters displayed to seeing their fellow members attain office shocked many liberals. The numbers did not look good to the Democrats.

At the same time, the Republican Party was powerfully affected by the JBS. For years conservatives had criticized the party as being a middle-of-the-road institution ruled by the Eastern Establishment. The advent of a conservative coalition, which included Birchers willing to work for candidates, contribute money, and forge a new agenda, meant that the GOP had to pay attention. The influx of Birchers into the party machinery created a real dilemma for the GOP. Should party leaders ignore conspiracy theories, Welch, and occasional despicable tactics in order to gain tens of thousands of voters who would canvass neighborhoods, call and write representatives, and work to elect local candidates? Or should the party repel extremists who not only threatened to tarnish the Republican name, but also might drive out moderates and liberals? Though no single decision ever determined the GOP's path, the party tried to pursue a pragmatic course, tacitly accepting help from individual members while never publicly embracing the society. Consequently, Birchers often took over local party machinery. As Birchers worked to make themselves indispensable, the national party, for the most part, accepted them into the fold.

In 1964, the "popular front" strategy—the idea that conservatives of all hues should band together to fight liberalism—helped Barry Goldwater receive the Republican nomination over moderates like Nelson Rockefeller and William Scranton. Birchers worked tirelessly for Goldwater, and he and his advisers decided not to disavow their support (as demanded by many moderate Republicans). The danger of coddling these "extremists," of course, was that moderate and liberal Republicans would be so repelled by their presence in the party that they would flee to the Democrats or stay away from the polls. Birchers and other Far-Rightists were fueled not only by getting their man nominated (and maybe elected), but also wresting control of the GOP from the Rockefeller/Scranton faction.

With no faith in the federal government, Welch claimed the society was nonpartisan and apolitical, arguing that education was the key to awakening the public. However, as early as 1960 or 1961, some Birchers had, on their own initiative, begun organizing to make Barry Goldwater the GOP standard-bearer. It was dangerous, therefore, for Welch to condemn the Arizona senator simply for being a politician. As Welch noted in 1963, "I personally think that Barry Goldwater is a very patriotic American and a very able politician, who is determined to use his political skills to do all he can towards saving our country from the dangers now closing in on every side."[55] But a politician could never really be trusted, and Welch thought the apparent candidate would be "far smarter if he were less of a politician." Reinforcing his position, Welch noted that Goldwater thought that "direct political action" was the best method by which to fight communism, and concluded simply, "We disagree."[56]

The upshot of including extremists—tacitly or explicitly—was to indelibly link Goldwater with the John Birch Society. Goldwater and his advisers did little to dissuade voters of the connection, even though many electoral conservatives, like William F. Buckley, Jr., tried to convince him to publicly disavow any relationship with the JBS.[57] Goldwater, the consummate westerner and outsider, relished the chance to snub those easterners who had dismissed him, and refused to turn away the support. The ultimate rejoinder from the Goldwaterites to their liberal and moderate comrades came at the 1964 Republican National Convention, when, instead of uniting the party, Barry, in his acceptance speech, thundered, "I would remind you that extremism in the defense of liberty is no vice! And let me remind you also that moderation in the pursuit of justice is no virtue!"[58] Goldwater later admitted that he and his advisers were not "in a conciliatory mood."[59]

Goldwater lost the election for a number of reasons, one of the most important being the association voters developed between the Republican Party and the Far Right. Post-election analyses by electoral conservatives openly blamed extremists. George H. W. Bush, who had run unsuccessfully for the Senate in Texas, noted that a "negative image remained . . . partly because of the so-called 'nut' fringe." Undecided voters, Bush argued, "would be pounced upon by some hyper-tensioned type armed with an anti-LBJ book or inflammatory pamphlet. . . . They pushed their philosophy in Goldwater's name, and scared the hell out of the plain average non-issue-conscious man on the street."[60] Thus, in 1964, the GOP encountered and learned the consequences of dealing with radicals within their own ranks. Taking the discouraging lessons to heart, in 1965, conservatives began to strip the JBS of its political power.

Still, the party and conservatives reaped some benefits in 1964. Conservatives captured the party from the moderates. The presence of extremists made the positions of responsible conservatives seem more acceptable to moderates and liberals. As they began to untangle themselves from the Far Right, Republicans secured an emerging conservative middle ground. In January 1965, the Executive Committee of the Republican National Committee met to plan the expulsion of extremists from the party apparatus. In the first of many moves, the executive committee ousted RNC chairman Dean Burch, a symbol of the Goldwaterites who had welcomed Birchers with open arms. Following polls in which 29% of Republicans called Goldwater a "radical," the leadership began refocusing its efforts on softer-edged yet still conservative candidates like William F. Buckley and Ronald Reagan. Buckley, who ran for mayor of New York City in 1965 and had long been a critic of Robert Welch, rejected Far-Rightist help, ran on a platform of staunch conservative values, and drew 13% of the vote in liberal New York as he demonstrated that Americans would support viable conservative candidates. Reagan, the GOP leadership's ultimate champion, used his personality and advisers to deftly deflect the Radical Right problem during his successful 1966 California gubernatorial campaign, and proved that the GOP could be conservative and succeed without appearing to kowtow to the JBS.[61] In other words, the GOP began to seek out candidates who, while ideologically driven, had personalities that made them acceptable to a wider range of party members. This choice allowed the leadership to rely more on the rank-and-file Republicans and less on fanatical Birchers who jeopardized the party's internal cohesion.

After the 1964 race, the society's power began spiraling downward. The GOP's decision to disavow their efforts was traumatic for some Birchers; they saw the party opting for political expediency over ideological purity. Others, however, understood that winning political power first and then molding the party in the image of Taft, Goldwater, Reagan, and perhaps Welch made more sense. By 1968, the Far Right's influence in the GOP had declined dramatically, while ironically the party—and the country as a whole—had moved Right.

Few groups on either the Left or Right in the 1960s translated ideology into action as effectively as the John Birch Society. Students for a Democratic Society (SDS), for example, became known by the mid- to late-1960s as the leading liberal and then radical student group. But SDS's official roster only numbered around 10,000 in 1965 and its ideological opposition to organizational hierarchy prevented it from being as effective as it might have been.[62] The Left's internecine battles furthered the impression that many liberals were left-wing radicals, and all radicals were somehow associated with the Democratic Party.

Like a third party, the JBS encouraged politicians to address such issues as a growing cultural licentiousness and a continuing communist threat and, in turn, the Republican Party adjusted its agenda to incorporate these issues into its platform. By 1968, the Republican leadership had assimilated the most useful elements of Birch strategy and limited its contact with the Far Right. The Democrats, on the other hand, failed to quell their radical wing, and lost both in 1968 and 1972. The JBS continued to act as a buffer for electoral conservatives, deflecting criticism that might have otherwise focused on the electoral conservative wing of the party. In effect, the presence of the JBS on the Far Right helped shift the GOP toward the center of the political spectrum. In the end, one might argue, Robert Welch and his legions helped the GOP as much as they had hurt it in 1964.

Although postwar conservative ideology was robust in the 1950s, it lacked channels to reach American voters who, frustrated with years of liberalism, were ready to challenge the status quo. The John Birch Society played a critical role in opening lines of communication among conservative leaders, the Republican Party, and activists-in-waiting. Welch and the organization's members developed a dialectical relationship. The founder built the society's structure, dictated policies, and created and oversaw projects. Birchers, however, often came to view the organization as an outlet for grassroots activism, manifested primarily through local projects over which the home office exercised minimal control. Some members saw the projects and their roles in the society as a means to an end, a prelude to the real confrontation with the enemy, while others were satisfied attending meetings, watching films, writing letters, and educating themselves about the conspiracy. Although most Americans looked on the JBS with disdain and more than a little fear of what it indicated about the direction in which the country was headed, for tens of thousands of members the society represented hope, a chance to challenge the status quo, and a place to have one's innermost thoughts affirmed by a group of neighbors, friends, and acquaintances.

The JBS, indelibly identified with 1960s conservatism, has been much less celebrated than leftist radicals, but was perhaps more powerful in changing American political culture. Electoral conservatives co-opted its strategies, candidates borrowed its messages, and grassroots activists professionalized its operations. Was the society successful? If judged by its ability to complete projects, the answer must be no. Earl Warren was not impeached, the United States did not leave the UN, and communism survived the 1960s. But if the society is viewed as both an outlet for frustration and a training ground for budding conservative activists, the answer must be yes. Even if members abandoned the society as it spiraled downward in the late 1960s and into the 1970s, scores continued organizing for conservative causes, focusing on single-issue politics like abortion, prayer in school, immigration, and busing. The emergence of Christian fundamentalism as a political force in the 1970s provided a new vehicle for numerous former Birchers, helping them organize against pornography, sex education in schools, and the dramatic rise in the number of legal abortions performed each year. Other former Birchers railed against increased taxes, gay rights, and expanded welfare rights. In 1980, they campaigned vigorously for Ronald Reagan, his triumph vindicating years of effort. Many of these activists first cut their political teeth in the JBS; their experiences ensured continuously evolving grassroots activism that aided causes and candidates for years to come. Intellectuals might have begun the conservative movement, but these activists turned it into a viable political force by challenging the complacency of the American people and government, and reconfiguring the GOP. If its ideology was not enviable by detractors on both sides of the aisle, its ability to politicize the average Americans was. The John Birch Society permanently altered the American political landscape in the 1960s.

Evelyn A. Schlatter

"EXTREMISM IN THE DEFENSE OF LIBERTY": THE MINUTEMEN AND THE RADICAL RIGHT

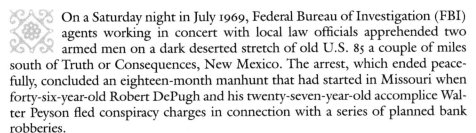 On a Saturday night in July 1969, Federal Bureau of Investigation (FBI) agents working in concert with local law officials apprehended two armed men on a dark deserted stretch of old U.S. 85 a couple of miles south of Truth or Consequences, New Mexico. The arrest, which ended peacefully, concluded an eighteen-month manhunt that had started in Missouri when forty-six-year-old Robert DePugh and his twenty-seven-year-old accomplice Walter Peyson fled conspiracy charges in connection with a series of planned bank robberies.

Peyson and DePugh eventually ended up in this small New Mexico desert town, where they rented an isolated house on a bluff overlooking a mostly deserted U.S. 85 and the Rio Grande. DePugh was an avid outdoorsman and spent as much time as he could working on his survival skills in wilderness areas. He was attracted to New Mexico because it struck him as "off the beaten path"—a place where he could disappear or pass unnoticed while furthering his rightist goals.

They'd been in town about six weeks and the locals had only good things to say about them, so it was with a great deal of surprise and trepidation when they learned that "Ralph Cooper" and his "nephew, Jim," were charged in Albuquerque with conspiracy to rob at least four banks in the Pacific Northwest. Some may even have shaken their heads in disbelief when FBI agent Thomas Jordan told the *Albuquerque Journal* that the money the men hoped to accumulate during their heists would go toward funding a violent revolution to combat a Communist[1] takeover of the United States.[2]

DePugh and Peyson had been working underground for five years with a network of sympathizers to accumulate weapons and money in their battle against Communist subversion.

DePugh was the founder of the Minutemen, an organization dedicated to armed resistance against a Communist takeover of the United States. The Minutemen predicted that this takeover would occur at some point in the early 1970s. Consequently, they trained in paramilitary techniques and weaponry; they operated in small, secret cells of five to fifteen men; and they printed and disseminated anticommunist and anti-U.S. government literature. By the late 1960s, a few Minutemen cells, in their struggles against a perceived Communist threat, had committed bombings and other violent acts.

The Minutemen were, from almost any contemporary perspective, extremists. And they were, inarguably, rightist extremists. Like the John Birch Society (JBS), which was also derided by many as a part of the conservative movement's "lunatic fringe," the Minutemen helped to define conservatism in the 1960s.

Many conservatives, especially long-standing Republican Party activists, struggled to exclude the radical elements that operated within their camp. But as their liberal counterparts would discover in the late 1960s and early 1970s, so-called mainstream conservatives had a great deal of difficulty distancing themselves from their radical wing. A major reason was the fact that mainstream and more radical conservatives shared many of the same core beliefs. Both the mainstream and the "fringe" in the early to mid-1960s greatly feared the threat of Communist subversion and the inherent dangers of a tyrannical federal government. While mainstream conservatives and right-wing extremists differed about the degree of such threats and about the means by which these threats should be fought, much united them.

In the first years of the decade, people across the political spectrum struggled to make a distinction between mainstream conservatives and the extreme right. Dire warnings about the dangers inherent in the rightist "fringe," as it was called, graced the pages of the *New York Times* and other establishment media venues from a variety of sources—mostly written by church and political leaders.[3] Bishop Donegan of the Protestant Episcopalian Diocese of New York stated darkly that the JBS and groups like it were endeavoring to reverse American traditions of democracy, oppose civil rights, and paralyze federal government. They were, he continued, trying to turn back the clock of American history. Donegan did distinguish between mainstream conservatives and radical elements that were finding expression under the larger conservative umbrella. To call the hard right "conservative," he exhorted, is a "misnomer."[4] Reverend Virgil Lowder, executive director of the Protestant Council of Churches in Washington, D.C., buttressed Donegan's remarks in 1961 when he called on Protestants, Jews, and Roman Catholics to resist the "'self-styled patriots of the far right.'"[5]

Earlier that year, North Dakota Republican Senator Milton R. Young blasted the JBS for calling Eisenhower a "Red." Montana Senator Mike Mansfield, then-majority leader, backed his colleague's comments.[6] A month after Young made those statements, Wyoming Democratic Senator Gale W. Welch verbally reproached Robert Welch, national leader of the JBS, for his views and his perceived attempts to undermine democracy.[7] Jacob K. Javits, moderate Republican senator from New York, spent most of the first half of the 1960s excoriating the radical right and accusing members of extreme right groups of trying to infiltrate his party, an occurrence, he warned, that would cause its collapse.[8]

Former New York Democratic Governor and Senator Herbert Lehman called the radical right "a force for evil in our country which in its potential harm is certainly equivalent to McCarthyism." He went on to cite a recent report that some 2,000 rightist groups existed in the country and 8,000,000 people claimed membership in them; the JBS could count on 60,000 supporters. Lehman compared the extremist right to Communist subversion from within, and called it just as threatening.[9] Even President Kennedy weighed in on the extremist right, at a speech in Los Angeles: "There have always been those fringes of our society who have sought to escape their own responsibility by finding a simple solution, an appealing slogan or a convenient scapegoat . . . men who are unwilling to face up to the danger from without are convinced that the real danger comes from within."[10]

As the elections of 1962 drew closer, many Republicans disavowed their party's right-wing "fringe." Democratic politicians seemed to revel in the disagreement the hard right had introduced in Republican quarters and enjoyed suggesting that extremists were taking over the Republican Party. Democratic National Chairman John Bailey called the upcoming 1962 elections a test of strength between Democrats and right-wing Republican extremists. Republicans, he warned, were in thrall to "reckless radicals of the far Right and echoing the efforts of these extremist agitators to breed fear and suspicion in our society."[11] Later that year, Bailey told happy Democrats that the Republican Party was polarized between moderates and a "radical Right-wing faction."[12]

In southern California, a hotbed of conservative and extreme right activity in the 1960s, the Republican Party was deeply divided and a powerful hard-right faction vied for party control. Many of the most conservative groups were evangelical in organization and practice; a few called themselves "survivalists." Among the latter were an estimated 2,400 Minutemen.[13] California congressmen John H. Rousselot and Edgar W. Hiestand were active members of the JBS. They were, however, unseated in the 1962 congressional elections—a fate of many rightists in those elections.[14] Nonetheless, even after the right suffered those losses in California and elsewhere, disagreement about the role of the "hard right" in the Republican Party at the state and national level didn't subside.

The issue of the extremist right nearly split the Republican Party at the 1964 convention in San Francisco's Cow Palace. New York Governor Nelson Rockefeller blasted his fellow Republicans for not taking a definitive stance against the radical right. Moderates pushed for an anti-extremism plank in the Republican Party's platform, but they lost the bid by a vote of nearly 2 to 1. Arizona Senator Barry Goldwater—the party's presidential nominee—deliberately alienated the moderate wing of his party by declaring in his convention acceptance speech: "extremism in the defense of liberty is no vice!" The senator was directly responding to the moderates' anti-extremism call.

Goldwater, to say the obvious, saw nothing wrong with the extremist wing of the conservative movement, which included groups like the JBS and Minutemen, the racist and traditionalist National States' Rights Party, and several major religious right organizations.[15] He respected, in particular, their belief in a limited federal government and their firm—even fierce—anticommunism. He also recognized their growing role in the conservative movement. By 1964, the JBS, for example, was pulling in around $7 million annually.[16] Public opinion polls indicated that at least 5% of Americans could be counted on as supporters of the JBS and other groups whose members and affiliates insisted, among other things, that Communists directly controlled the U.S. government, public schools, and the National Council of Churches.[17]

Whether or not Communists were in fact infiltrating the United States during the 1960s isn't as important here as the fact that a range of conservatives—from mainstream to hard right—believed that such a threat existed. Anticommunism proved itself a point on which many Americans in conservative camps could agree, and it would prove a strong ideological bridge between mainstream and fringe.[18]

Minutemen founder Robert DePugh, for his part, supported many mainstream conservative positions, including unfettered capitalism, unbending nationalism, and proud patriotism. He believed in a strong national defense and in strictly limiting the power of government. DePugh also believed in strengthening America's "Christian heritage," though he also believed in the constitutional separation of church and state.[19]

He held these stances throughout the 1960s, even while engaged in paramilitary activities with the Minutemen such as gun caching, survival training, and preparation for an eventual war with invading Communist forces. Where he differed from mainstream conservatives and other radical conservatives (like the JBS) had more to do with ultimate goals and methods than basic ideology. DePugh's primary goal was to save the United States from Communist forces, some of whom he believed had already entered the country and were operating incognito in high government positions. The way to defeat Communist threats, he thought, involved not only educational seminars, meetings, and readings along JBS and Young Americans for Freedom (YAF) lines, but also military preparation for armed conflict.

DePugh's focus on weapons training and survivalism was at the core of Minutemen extremism. DePugh encouraged his Minutemen to break into bands of five to fifteen members working independently of each other and guided by one coordinator.[20] This may have been the first true use of so-called "leaderless resistance" among modern extreme right groups in this country. The concept has remained and been encouraged among rightist extremists since then.[21] DePugh, like most mainstream conservatives, was not anti-Semitic or racist; he hated Communists and feared for the future of the free market and individual freedoms at the hands of big government.[22]

DePugh laid out the Minutemen's goals and beliefs in a 1961 manifesto. Like Robert Welch, founder of the John Birch Society, he emphasized that Communism was not some distant threat but had already arrived. Its insidious hold on the country had already begun. [23] Such language was, in many ways, reminiscent of the not-so-distant speeches of Senator Joseph McCarthy. Unlike McCarthy, who had been discredited in the minds of many, but still respected by numerous conservatives, DePugh believed that Communists could not simply be rooted out of American society through public exposure and legal trial. It was too late for such gentle measures. He explained: "[T]he objectives of the Minutemen are to abandon wasteful, useless efforts and begin immediately to prepare for the day when Americans will once again fight in the streets for their lives and their liberty. We feel there is overwhelming evidence to prove that this day will come." [24]

DePugh's apocalyptic rhetoric came amid a wave of similar sentiments. The John Birch Society had engaged in a massive letter-writing campaign in 1961 aimed at stirring up a congressional impeachment of Supreme Court Chief Justice Earl Warren. The Birchers believes Warren to be a "knowing instrument" of the Communist Party. Since the JBS believed that both major parties were controlled by Communists, Warren's impeachment seemed unlikely. [25] Also in 1961, General Edwin A. Walker and a number of other high-ranking army and navy officers had sponsored or participated in a series of anticommunist seminars around the country, aimed primarily at active duty servicemen. [26] Speakers warned that the Communist attack on the United States had already begun. DePugh was not alone in fearing that the Communist menace was already entrenched in the United States and on its way to victory.

Robert Bolivar DePugh's rise to leadership in the radical wing of the conservative movement came in stages. He was born in Independence, Missouri, in April 1923. His father gave him the "Bolivar" as a tribute to Simón Bólivar, whom the elder DePugh considered a valiant revolutionary. Ralph DePugh was a deputy sheriff in Jackson County for years; the job itself was part of a political patronage system that DePugh worked with aplomb. His son Robert was exposed to politics at an early age and later claimed that he had developed a sense of cynicism about the political process watching his father work the Democratic machine. [27]

DePugh himself provided conflicting information to the media (and, I suspect, to his only biographer, J. Harry Jones, Jr.) after he had formed the Minutemen and was attracting media attention. He claimed, for example and at various times, military service alternately with the Signal Corps, the Coast Artillery, and the Air Force. The only military record he actually had, though, was in 1943–44 with the Coast Artillery in Fort Monroe, Virginia. [28] He also claimed to have spent a year in Signal Corps training in 1942 during World War II at the University of Colorado, which has no record of his ever having attended the school. [29] He has also claimed to have attended Kansas State University for about a year and a half in 1946, but again, there seem to be no records of his having done so. [30]

He married sometime around 1943. Between 1947 and 1954, he held several jobs, mostly in sales. He and his wife had gone back to Missouri and, in 1953, De-Pugh started the Biolab Corporation, which specialized in supplements and foods for animals. Within two years of opening, the company went bankrupt after the IRS forced him to pay his back taxes—an event that influenced his views about overbearing government interference in private enterprise. DePugh would resurrect the company later, but on a smaller scale. Also in 1955, DePugh had his first brush with the law in Kansas when he was caught passing bad checks, probably to cover his losses in Biolab. He was arrested and released on bond. He did eventually pay the money back and, a year later, the charges were dropped.[31]

During the 1950s, DePugh became more interested in what he perceived as restrictive gun laws, another example in his eyes of the intrusiveness of the federal government. He himself didn't own a gun until 1960, but his avid pursuit of outdoor activities had perhaps made him sympathetic to hunters and sport-marksmen. His burgeoning suspicions of the government in the 1950s weren't uncommon among conservatives and certainly would not have marked him as part of a "lunatic fringe."

By the late 1950s, he also began to espouse a fierce anticommunism and discussed with his friends and business associates the necessity for military preparation to stop a Communist takeover of the United States. Locally, he was well known for his outspoken opinions. A neighbor in Norborne later told a reporter: "He's a very peculiar sort of fellow . . . I can't make out whether he's a genius or a screwball."[32]

At some point prior to the founding of the Minutemen in 1961, DePugh joined the John Birch Society, which didn't suit him because he felt that Birchers were mostly talk and not enough action. Nonetheless, during his association with the JBS, he learned grassroots organizing methods and he borrowed JBS rhetoric.

Sometime in late 1959, DePugh and nine hunting buddies began their own JBS-like reading group. In June 1960, according to DePugh's account, the friends were building a duck blind at a small lake in Missouri. Talk turned to the Communist threat and one of the men joked, " 'Well, if the Russians invade us, we can come up here and fight on as a guerrilla band.' "[33] Another man in the group who allegedly had special forces training remarked that it wouldn't hurt Americans to know a little more about defending themselves if things degenerated into a last-ditch stand. The following week, he brought some of his training manuals to the lake and shared them with the other members of the group and slowly, "the joke turned into a serious project."[34]

DePugh and his cohorts chose the name for the little group. It stuck and De-Pugh was well aware of its historical origins and implications. Like their eighteenth-century predecessors, he and his growing organization meant to prepare themselves to confront and face down a tyrannical government. As DePugh himself explained: "The Minutemen were first formed in the American colonies in 1774 as volunteer military companies. Their members were patriots who banded together for the purpose of defending their traditional liberties. They were called Minutemen because they pledged themselves to take the field at a minute's notice in defense of their freedom."[35]

DePugh further explicated that "any male United States citizen, loyal to the principles of liberty for which the Minutemen fought, may join providing that he is at least fourteen years of age." He told the *New York Times* (which ran a series of stories on the right wing) that the organization was open to "anyone," but, in practice, that may not have been the case. All official members whom I've come across were white men.[36]

The Minutemen set about recruiting to develop a network, though DePugh had been encouraging leaderless resistance since the beginning. They took out benign classified ads in local papers and they distributed typed information sheets through church groups, hunting and gun clubs, and word of mouth.[37] DePugh also ran information seminars in a number of cities. He claimed that he had conducted sessions in Newark, Philadelphia, San Antonio, Omaha, Columbus (Ohio), and Kansas City (Missouri).[38]

DePugh's ideas caught on quickly with sympathizers. A couple of weeks after a Denver seminar, held 8 October 1961, seventeen men, one woman, and a boy were arrested in Shiloh, Illinois. They had been planning to perform military-style maneuvers using information they had acquired at a seminar on guerrilla warfare. Law enforcement agents seized this Minutemen group's arsenal, which included recoilless rifles, mortars, and machine guns.[39] DePugh's message was finding an audience and in remarkably short order, though it's still difficult to determine the actual extent of the organization's popularity. An article in a 1978 issue of the *Kansas City Star,* based on interviews and research, claimed that at its zenith in the mid-1960s, the Minutemen had between 10,000 to 15,000 dues-paying members, an impressive number for a group organized on the principle of individual cells and leaderless resistance.[40] DePugh himself claimed that the Minutemen numbered at least 50,000, but that number has never been verified.

The 1962 election year, as we have seen, brought increased media scrutiny of the extreme right and hallmarks of its activities like weapons stockpiling and paramilitary maneuvers. A few well-publicized incidents increased the public's perception that extremist right-wing groups could be violent. In February, the California homes of two vocal critics of the radical right were pipe-bombed (no one was injured). Authorities linked the incidents to an attempted bombing at the American Association of United Nations in Los Angeles. The week prior to the house bombings, a cruder device exploded at the Los Angeles Communist Party headquarters. Blame immediately centered on the extreme right, but the John Birch Society was quick to deny any involvement and to assure the public that the society's members did not advocate violence.[41] Whether the perpetrators were affiliated with the JBS or the Minutemen remains unknown, but the bombings were likely the work of rightists.

In 1963, DePugh began publishing a monthly news-type magazine called *On Target.* The "O" was made to look like the crosshairs of a rifle scope. Within its pages, he reported on presumed Communist activities and described alleged government activities against American citizens. As in the 1 April 1964 issue, he printed a "Warning to Patriots!" in which he claimed that American Patriots (people involved in the struggle for "liberty" like him) were being arrested. Government-mandated disarmament of American citizens loomed, he stated, and he further claimed that "90%" of the 1964 Civil Rights bill was designed to give the federal government police state control over free enterprise. He advised his readers to buy a gun "NOW" and to avoid talk that would label them as fearmongers or racists. He encouraged readers to stay low and "blend into the background."[42]

By 1964, DePugh's rhetoric was becoming more violent and apocalyptic. He claimed that Communists were promoting racial violence and that the United Nations supported world Communism and he warned of economic collapse and ensuing chaos.[43] The apocalyptic streak in DePugh's literature and later stockpiling behavior most likely was inspired by a warning that had been circulating in extreme rightist circles since 1961. Fred Schwarz, executive director of the rightist and fundamentalist Christian Anti-Communism Crusade, had predicted that the Communist flag would fly over Washington, D.C., in 1973. He made the remarks at a forum held in Briarcliff Manor, New York. He stated that Communist propaganda and subversion would enable a bloodless coup.[44]

By 1964, the Minutemen were involved in national politics; members enthusiastically supported Barry Goldwater's presidential bid. In an August interview with *New York Times* reporter Donald Janson, DePugh claimed that on Johnson's nomination in the 1964 presidential campaign, members of the Minutemen would infiltrate Democratic campaign headquarters all over the country and sabotage communications. He claimed that the group had already successfully utilized such techniques in several local 1962 election campaigns and had placed twenty-four Minutemen on state delegations to the 1964 Republican convention (though he provided no specifics). When Janson questioned him about Minutemen membership, DePugh claimed that the number was greater than law enforcement estimates of 25,000 nationally.[45]

During the interview, DePugh also exhibited a rare racism. When queried about his thoughts on events in Mississippi and Civil Rights protests, DePugh stated flatly that "Negroes" are not capable of voting intelligently and he dismissed African-American participation in government as part of a larger Communist subversion.[46]

A few other incidents in 1964, prior to the election, brought more attention to the Minutemen and the extreme right in American politics. That summer, tax agents seized an arsenal in Clinton, Illinois, at the home of Richard Lauchli, purported Midwest regional director of the group. Lauchli had already been in trouble regarding illicit firearms in 1961; in this instance, he and his associates had accumulated over 100 submachine guns, five .50-caliber machine guns, a flame thrower, a 15-mm recoilless cannon, mortars and shells, automatic pistols and rifles, and several 25-pound aerial bombs. Lauchli had purchased the armaments as scrap, but his skills as a machinist had enabled him to put everything in good working order.[47] As a result of the Lauchli arrest, law enforcement agencies planned to have a closer look at members of rifle clubs in the United States and, by extension, at DePugh's activities. Though the latter would claim throughout the 1960s that he knew nothing about individual cells and their operations, law enforcement and government agencies dogged him whenever a Minuteman was arrested or sought for questioning.

In the mid-1960s, DePugh was infusing the movement with a new sense of urgency and greater militancy. In his biography, DePugh indicated that he had started envisioning Communism almost solely as an internal threat. That is, rather than worrying about Communist troops arriving on American shores ready to do battle, DePugh had come to believe that Communists had in fact been infiltrating the country for years, may be Americans, and had secretly taken over government agencies. The showdown between the Minutemen and Communists, therefore, was going to entail battling forces affiliated with the American government and it was going to require greater paramilitary preparation. National and world events made the transition in DePugh's ideology easy. Frustrations over Vietnam, the actions of the Left, civil rights, and the growing influence of liberal politicians like Robert Kennedy indicated to DePugh that the problems of the United States originated and spread from within, making threats to individual liberties all the more insidious.[48]

DePugh's troubles with the law began in earnest in 1965, when he was arrested on kidnapping and bomb possession charges. Two young Kansas City women claimed that DePugh had held them captive for two weeks in June, urging them to use sex as a weapon to blackmail Communists. The kidnapping charges were later downgraded to contributing to the delinquency of a minor (Linda Judd, one of his accusers, was sixteen when the incident occurred), but DePugh faced years of legal battles.[49]

Despite his run-ins with the law, the Minutemen's leader still managed to found a third political party in 1966. The so-called Patriotic Party was born, fittingly, on the 4th of July at a two-day gathering held at the U-Smile Motel in Kansas City, Missouri. DePugh declared himself the party's chair and indicated that members would be encouraged to work secretly for both major parties in order to gain political experience and sabotage Republican and Democratic campaign efforts. The party's goals included severely limiting government and maximizing individual freedom. According to the press, 400 people attended the founding, including a few JBS members. DePugh's relationship with Birchers by then was prickly at best, however; he felt that the society thought the Minutemen were somehow in competition with them.[50]

At the retreat, DePugh appointed all in attendance "executives and leaders" and encouraged them to bring the 27 million people who had voted for Goldwater into the fold. Attendees planned regional conferences in August in New York City, Birmingham, Alabama, and Phoenix. State meetings were scheduled for September and state chairmen were appointed for 43 states.[51]

DePugh ran into more trouble after the July conference. He was indicted in Kansas City, Missouri, in August 1966 for conspiracy to violate the U.S. Firearms Act—possessing firearms without paying required taxes or registering them. He would spend the next few months dealing with trials and appeals to overturn the charges. Like left-wing radicals of the late 1960s, he accused law enforcement agents of "Gestapo" tactics, including drugging a witness to obtain a conspiracy charge against him. In 1966, he ironically turned to the very powers he mistrusted and called for a congressional investigation of federal agents and their alleged use of illegal coercion and searches.[52]

While DePugh had his hands full with his own indictments, a group of Minutemen on the East Coast would bring further heat to the group and its erstwhile leader. In October, New York state officials uncovered a Minutemen plot in Queens that involved attacking and burning three separate compounds designated as Communist or Communist sympathizer. The compounds were leftist retreats and communal living experiments located in Connecticut, New York, and New Jersey. Nineteen Minutemen were arrested after a ten-month investigation. The group's twenty members were planning to attack and destroy the compounds with heavy weaponry. The uncovered arsenals included bazookas, mortars, machine guns, semiautomatic rifles, machetes, crossbows, garroting nooses, and over a million rounds of ammunition.[53]

In the wake of these arrests and the subsequent investigations, state and local officials discovered that Minutemen membership included policemen, armed forces members, doctors, teachers, employees in "sensitive industries," and public employees. The investigations occurred in New York and spilled over into fourteen other states. Interviews revealed details about field maneuvers, arms, explosives, bombing plots, and propaganda. These findings prompted New York State Attorney General Louis Lefkowitz to call for a law making association with or membership in illicit paramilitary groups a class C felony.[54] An assistant district attorney in upstate New York also resigned his position in the fallout from the October 1966 raids. He admitted that he had once sought membership in the Minutemen and though he wasn't currently a member, political pressure forced him from his post.[55]

Nineteen of the New York Minutemen were linked to DePugh a week after their arrests. The Minutemen leader got word that he would be "invited to testify" before a Queens grand jury.[56] While he waited for further instructions, he and two associates were convicted in November of violating the Federal Firearms Act. After six days of testimony—including that of two former members of the group—a jury returned guilty verdicts in just over an hour.[57] DePugh claimed that his trial was the result of a massive effort of government officials politically inspired to convict him by any means necessary. Furthermore, he continued, the U.S. government was under the control of a "liberal-Communist-Socialist" conspiracy.[58] DePugh faced four years imprisonment, but he was allowed to remain free on bond while clearing up the earlier indictment on bomb possession. The year 1967 had not started well for either DePugh or his Minutemen.

Shortly after his sentencing in January, DePugh resigned as national leader of the Minutemen, stating that the organization would continue to operate secretly. Members would develop codes that only other members would recognize, and, in this fashion, they would spread propaganda and work to undo Communist subversion. DePugh announced that though his work with the Minutemen was probably at an end, he would nevertheless remain with the Patriot Party and help with further organization.[59]

Most likely, in the face of negative publicity generated by the New York raids and his own conviction, he decided to lower his public profile. The terms of his probation probably stipulated also that he was not to associate with paramilitary organizations so he publicly announced his resignation to dissuade further investigation. Regardless, he secretly resumed his national coordinator post by May 1967. In July, the Patriotic Party nominated George Wallace as its presidential candidate at its convention in Kansas City, Kansas. One media estimate put attendance at 380.[60]

Though DePugh was publicly trying to maintain a certain image, his biographer, J. Harry Jones, Jr., notes the increasing radicalism of the group's founder in a 1967 conversation:

> "Your purpose seems to be to frighten people, to frighten the government, from going too far to the left," I suggested, somewhat naïvely. "No," DePugh said, "the purpose is to provoke the government into taking harsh and repressive measures against the general population so people will be turned against the government. . . . [A]ccording to our theory, the Communist-Socialist clique is taking over the country according to a very skillfully programmed timetable. They do this in such a slow and insidious manner that the conditions become gradually more restrictive. . . ." [Jones] "The goal, then, is a revolution?" [DePugh] "The goal is counterrevolution. There's already been a revolution, a non-violent revolution in which the original constitutional republic of the United States has been superseded by an alien, socialist ideology."[61]

And so though DePugh busied himself with the workings of the Patriotic Party and the 1968 elections and waited for a decision on his appeals regarding his conviction on violating the National Firearms Act, he was perhaps planning radical activities and printing literature that echoed his beliefs. Nevertheless, the remainder of the year passed relatively peaceably. He continued his life in Independence and Norborne, Missouri, busy with the Party and Biolab. His closest aide, Walter Peyson, had been living with the DePughs in Norborne for at least a year. I suspect that the two men continued working on disseminating Minutemen literature beneath the eyes of the law. Regardless, they kept their noses reasonably clean. That all changed in February 1968.

On 20 February, a federal grand jury indicted DePugh for conspiracy in a Minutemen plot to rob four suburban Seattle banks and blow up a police station and power plant as diversionary tactics. Seven men were arrested in the 26 January sweep. Upon his indictment, DePugh denied the men's connection to the Minutemen and denied knowledge of the plot. Shortly after he received notification of the new indictment, DePugh and aide Peyson went missing from Norborne. Bail for each man was set at $30,000 and the FBI initiated a massive manhunt.[62]

Throughout 1968 and half of 1969, the two men remained at large. Upon his arrest, DePugh would claim that he and Peyson had been helped by an underground network of Minutemen and sympathizers. He also stated that he had prepared for just such a contingency and had ensured that he and Peyson had access to false identification, supplies, and survival gear. They traveled in a variety of disguises, including what DePugh called "hippie" outfits. He noted that they probably could have eluded authorities "indefinitely" had they concentrated on hiding rather than producing and disseminating Minutemen literature—a million pieces, DePugh boasted, including books on guerrilla warfare training.[63]

During the period that DePugh and Peyson were on the lam, Minutemen incidents occurred sporadically in various parts of the country. In June 1968, the director of the Friends Center Workshop in New York City received threatening literature signed "Minutemen." In November, a homemade rocket launched across from the Houston, Texas, federal building scattered thousands of tiny leaflets also signed "Minutemen." A week later, a mortar exploded near the White House, apparently intended to shower the back yard with Minutemen leaflets. The bomb went off early, blowing a hole in the side of a National Park Service tool shed. Two other leaflet bomb incidents occurred in Kansas City, Missouri, and Wichita, Kansas.[64]

At the University of Chicago in February 1969, ten college-aged men burst into the administration building brandishing Minutemen leaflets that warned traitors "to beware." They initiated a fistfight with leftist student protestors who were there staging a sit-in. Later that month, bombs exploded in Dallas and Carthage, Texas, and in Little Rock, Arkansas, scattering more Minutemen leaflets and causing nearly $2,000 in damage. In Dallas, a bomb exploded in a parking lot near a First Baptist Church and Internal Revenue Service offices. The Little Rock blast occurred in the parking lot of television station KTHV and the Carthage bomb was actually dropped from a plane, damaging several cars. Leaflets stated "Fight the Parasites," "Stop the Bureaucratic Tyrants," and "Death to Socialism."[65]

Eventually, De Pugh and Peyson arrived in Truth or Consequences, New Mexico, where they rented a house from an absentee landlord. The house sat a couple of miles south of town and was known for its string of odd tenants, so two more elicited no response from local residents. Distant neighbors did notice a number of people coming and going but no one who raised eyebrows in the community.[66]

A local sheriff tipped off the FBI when he recognized the truck parked outside their house as wanted in conjunction with the two men. After the arrests were made, authorities entered the house and discovered an arsenal that would have rivaled a military base. Every corner, an officer reported, was filled with weaponry, survival gear, and ammunition. The inventory included forty-eight rifles, carbines, shotguns, pistols, revolvers, thousands of rounds of ammunition, drums of explosives, homemade antipersonnel mines, large quantities of dynamite, homemade hand grenades, pipe bombs, blasting caps, cases of fuses, cans of tear gas, homemade silencers, high-powered rifle scopes, stacks of bandoliers, and magazines loaded with cartridges. They found flare pistols, equipment for remote detonations, bows and arrows equipped with impact grenades, handcuffs, hunting knives, survival kits, and camouflage clothing.[67]

Law enforcement authorities in the country were aware that "militants" in the United States were stockpiling illegal weaponry that often included machine guns and submachine guns. Many also managed to acquire dynamite and hand grenades and though the extent of the caching was unknown at the time of DePugh's and

Peyson's arrests, authorities noted that in the year 1968–69, individuals taken into custody for weapons violations included members of the Minutemen, the Klan, the Black Panthers, and the Mafia. Caches of illegal weapons had been discovered "in every section of the nation in 1969." Many of the machine guns were foreign-made and were at one time military-issue, some circulating since World War I and modified. Literature included with the caches indicated that many of the groups were adopting tactics of the U.S. Special Forces. Assistant Chief of Law Enforcement for the Treasury Department William Behen noted dryly in one instance that " 'the right wing seems to have a propensity for automatic weapons.' "[68]

After DePugh's 1969 arrest, the Minutemen largely dropped off from establishment media radar and, in fact, the group all but disappeared after DePugh and Peyson were apprehended on that lonely New Mexico highway. Whether this was because the very visible DePugh was no longer able to work at furthering his goals through the group or because of increased government and law enforcement crackdown on extremist activities is open to debate; probably both factors played a role. Consequently, the Minutemen did not have the longevity that the JBS did into the 1970s and beyond.

The paramilitary bent of the Minutemen in the 1960s increasingly ensured their isolation, even from other rightist groups like the JBS that did not emphasize weapons and survivalism. It also ensured the organization's alienation from the larger conservative movement, even as Minutemen shared many key political beliefs with mainstream conservatists.

Friction between radical rightists and mainstream conservatives had rapidly intensified in the mid-1960s. By 1965, noted conservatives, including William F. Buckley, attacked the radical right, with specific emphasis on the John Birch Society, in the pages of the *National Review*.[69] Still, the attempts of some mainstream conservatives to isolate the extremist right during the 1960s did not obscure commonalities and ties. Mainstream conservatives and extremists often supported the same causes, sponsored the same committees, appropriated money from the same sources, and shared leaders and ideas. For example, the conservative journal *Human Events* offered a joint subscription during the mid-1960s with *American Opinion,* the journal of the JBS. Scott Stanley, a Young Americans for Freedom official in the early 1960s, later edited *American Opinion* for a number of years. And the active participation of Republican Congressman Larry McDonald in the John Birch Society did not seem to hinder his popularity among conservative voters.[70]

However, membership in paramilitary groups like the Minutemen remained taboo among mainstream conservative politicians. Though the JBS was often lumped with the Minutemen in vitriol directed toward the extreme right from both liberal and conservative corners, the latter was considered more dangerous on the whole than the former because of the paramilitary aspects and the violent actions that some members of the Minutemen undertook during the 1960s. Though the JBS may have been condemned by noteworthy conservatives like Buckley, membership in that organization was not necessarily a hindrance to a conservative's political career. Membership in the Minutemen, however, seems to have been tantamount to political suicide among conservatives — at least on the national level. While the Minutemen would play essentially no role in the mainstream conservative movement after the failed presidential bid of Barry Goldwater in 1964, it would continue to influence the tactics, strategies, and beliefs of the rightist militia and survivalist movements that continue to capture the imagination of numerous Americans across the United States.

As for the Mintemen's founder and leader, Robert DePugh, after being paroled he returned to Norborne in the early 1970s. He steered clear of the law throughout the 1970s and 1980s, but he never disavowed his beliefs.[71] Though a Communist flag did not fly over Washington in 1973 as he had expected, DePugh nevertheless worked on developing vitamin tablets and foodstuffs that would sustain armed survivalists in their inevitable freedom fight.

Michelle Nickerson

MORAL MOTHERS AND
GOLDWATER GIRLS

In November 1961, a group of parents in Los Angeles' San Fernando Valley gathered at Gledhill Elementary School for their regular PTA meeting. School board member J. C. Chambers was their speaker that evening and his topic was "How the Communist Menace Influences the Minds and Thinking of Our Youth." Chambers warned his audience that communists at Harvard and Columbia were using textbooks to brainwash American schoolchildren. Some women stood up to point out that communists were closer to home than that: they taught at U.C.L.A., U.C. Berkeley, and other California colleges. The discussion then turned to a recent development at Gledhill. The patriotic hymn "Columbia, Gem of the Ocean" no longer appeared in the second-grade songbook. Instead, folk tunes like the Ukraine's "Cut the Grain" took its place. When one woman spoke up to defend the decision, noting that "Columbia" was too difficult for second graders, the others booed her. They believed that "Cut the Grain's" peasant themes and place of origin should be taken seriously—that this was precisely the way communists slowly and insidiously opened vulnerable minds to radical thinking.[1]

The tension and suspicion that underlay this gathering at Gledhill was characteristic of the high-pitched political battles happening around Los Angeles and all over America during the Cold War. Dominating the discussion was a formidable group of political agitators—homemakers and mothers. From Orange County to Pasadena, from Hollywood to the San Fernando Valley, women increasingly made it their business to stop communism from infiltrating their communities. After World War II, when California reached new heights of electoral importance as the most populous state in the nation, Los Angeles and its burgeoning suburbs became a hotbed of grassroots right-wing activism. The region's economic boom, fueled by the growing military-industrial complex, kindled a pro-defense, free-enterprise, limited-government program of conservatism. In the 1960s, the movement picked

up energy and supporters in response to civil rights activism and Vietnam War protests; and in 1966 it propelled Ronald Reagan to the governorship. Just as the Free
Speech Movement in Berkeley and Gay Liberation in San Francisco have made
northern California a focal point of the standard 1960s narrative, southern California deserves equal recognition as a nucleus of conservative activism.

The conservative movement spread quickly and pervasively throughout Los Angeles because its organizers mobilized effectively at the grass roots. Women,
mostly homemakers and mothers, executed much of the work behind these homegrown efforts. Women conservatives built important organizing networks from
their living rooms and kitchens, balancing these tasks with child-rearing and
housekeeping, embracing political work as an extension of their household duties.
Few of these women participants in the conservative movement actually sought
high political office for themselves or made any efforts to secure gains for women
as a group.[2] Sometimes they invoked their roles as housewives and mothers to get
attention, but most often they spoke up on the basis of their own political expertise, cultivated through intense study and research with other women. They entered politics as informed, self-educated super citizens. Mostly white, middle and
upper class, few of these women worked at paid full-time jobs. Instead, they took
advantage of their time and flexible schedules to do political work. These activists
shaped the conservative movement in ways that reflected their concerns for children, family, and community. They politicized their PTAs and school boards,
opened patriotic bookstores, formed anticommunist study groups and letter-
writing networks, wrote politically conservative literature, and composed anticommunist music. With these activities, women drew the battle lines of the Cold War
at the most fundamental levels of civic and cultural life and built a grassroots movement in the process. As one South Pasadena housewife active in the Republican
Women's Club and John Birch Society remembered, women were "the core of the
conservative movement."[3]

Women's involvement in right-wing politics increased alongside an emerging
conservative era in the California Republican Party. When conservative Senator
William Knowland became the Republican front-runner for governor in 1958, his
more militant anticommunist, anti-labor faction began to dominate the party.[4] Although Knowland ultimately lost to Democrat Pat Brown, his candidacy signaled
the decline of President Eisenhower's moderate "Modern Republicanism" in the
California GOP.[5] By the early 1960s, a vibrant, energetic conservative movement
swept Los Angeles and its environs, helped Barry Goldwater win the 1964 Republican presidential nomination, and contributed to Ronald Reagan's victory in the
1966 gubernatorial race.

This conservative movement was jump-started by charismatic figures like Barry
Goldwater, Robert Welch, and Fred Schwarz, who put forth a fresh, exciting, and
intelligent vision of conservatism. Goldwater's *Conscience of a Conservative* (1960),
for example, outlined a compelling "Conservative position," declared war on the
nation's moral and spiritual decay, and summoned patriotic Americans to mount
"Conservative demonstration."[6] Robert Welch, who founded the John Birch Society

(JBS), named after a Baptist missionary slain for his anticommunist efforts in China, offered a "total program" for fighting communism in 1958.[7] Men and women all over the country formed JBS chapters in their homes. Although the communist conspiracy theories propagated by the society struck most Americans as extremist, Welch's patriotic, antistatist message resonated even with conservatives who chose not to join. The society also educated and cultivated many of the most important leaders, both men and women, of the burgeoning movement in L.A. At roughly the same time, Australian Dr. Fred Schwarz, who based his operation in Long Beach, opened immensely popular "schools of Anti-Communism" and held youth rallies in several U.S. cities.[8] Schwarz's Christian Anti-Communist Crusade introduced a highly appealing evangelical conservatism that electrified audiences from the Disneyland Hotel to Patriotic Hall, the Hollywood Palladium, and the L.A. Sports Arena.[9] The breadth and popularity of this invigorated conservatism became apparent with the right-wing takeover of the Republican Party. The three major Republican volunteer organizations, the California Republican Assembly (CRA), the Young Republicans (LAYR), and the newly formed United Republicans of California (UROC), became a powerful conservative bulwark within the party. The members of these groups proved instrumental in the election of Birchers John Rousselot and Edgar Heistand, in Barry Goldwater's 1964 presidential nomination, and in Ronald Reagan's 1966 gubernatorial victory.[10]

While white men played the most visible roles in this conservative movement, women dominated the activist grass roots. As historical subjects, conservative women of the 1950s and 1960s do not fit the mainstream women's history written about their era, which focuses on Cold War domesticity and feminism. By not calling attention to themselves as women and not working toward a set of goals specifically for women, these activists fit awkwardly in the history of the women's liberation movement.[11] Politically aware and active, they defy Betty Friedan's *Feminine Mystique* model of the depressed, unfulfilled housebound American homemaker.[12] As housewives and mothers, they mobilized behind conservatism while accepting and even leveraging their traditional feminine roles. Although the lives of activist wives and mothers mirror the revived domesticity often associated with the 1950s, they challenge the assertion that this ideology, as historian Elaine Tyler May argues, effected an "apolitical tone."[13] On the contrary, southern California's women conservatives shored up traditional gender roles and laid the groundwork for the conservative movement. Within the John Birch Society, the CRA, the Young Republicans, and UROC, men and women worked together—but women worked during the daytime, weekday hours as well. Women generally expressed the reasons for their conservatism in the same terms as men. They thought government was getting too big, that domestic communism posed a serious threat, and that social disruptions like loosening sexual standards, student activism, and civil rights demonstrations made America vulnerable to communism.[14] Gender might not have colored their core beliefs, but women experienced politics differently from men and chose to confront the threat of communism in their own ways. Believing that the educational system was the nation's Achilles heel—where children would become either patriotic Americans or disillusioned radicals—many women felt compelled to become political. They often viewed their work as a crusade. As the president of California's Federation of Republican Women challenged her 50,000 members in 1958, "No longer is it possible for [women] to stay home keeping aloof from all outside. . . . Are we through apathy and ignorance going to allow this great dynamic idea we call the U.S.A. to go down the drain of governmental controls and dominance under Socialism?"[15]

Education battles presented women with the opportunity to extend the domestic realm into the larger world of politics. Though the not-so-cold war over education started well before the 1960s, the grassroots movement turned a corner with the election of Max Rafferty as state superintendent in 1962. His shocking victory represented a new show of strength for conservatives. Rafferty was a firebrand educator, writer, speaker, and school superintendent in the wealthy LaCañada school district. He championed a "back to basics" program for education: local control of schools, the use of wholesome *McGuffey* Readers, the emphasis on patriotic "heroes" in American history, and the "three R's."[16] Dr. Rafferty excoriated the "red psychological warfare" being waged on school children and denounced the "unwashed, leather-jacketed slobs" and "greasers" who disrupted classrooms and terrorized other students.[17] Though roundly criticized for the racial undertones of his rhetoric, Rafferty resonated with Angelenos who were anxious about rebellious youths and afraid of communism. He came to personify the educational agenda of the conservative movement in Los Angeles.

In 1961, a "Draft Rafferty" office opened in Orange County. A group of wealthy businessmen from the California Club—oil company executives, bankers, and real estate giants—made hefty contributions to Rafferty's campaign that played a major role in his election.[18] Women, however, played the key role as the grassroots activists in his campaign. When draft Rafferty efforts got underway in Orange County, Newport Beach homemaker Patricia Gilbert, the wife of a traveling salesman, invited ten women to her house to strategize. "We sat around the table," she remembers, "just like we were planning a senior prom or something."[19] The women merged their Christmas card lists into a mailing roster and organized a letter-writing campaign to draft Rafferty. When Rafferty finally decided to run, Gilbert formed Parents for Rafferty. Adopting the little red schoolhouse as their symbol, Parents for Rafferty set out to reach as many Californians as possible; theirs was a genuinely "homespun effort."[20] The group distributed over three million pieces of literature, most of which were printed on a mimeograph machine in the Gilberts' garage.[21] Parents for Rafferty built an 8,000-person mailing list and opened 260 chapters around the state.[22] Telephone calls, canvassing, mass mailings—all activities that mixed well with their daily routines as mothers—became their modus operandi.

Patricia Gilbert's own political awakening originated from her interests as a mother. Busy at home with small children, she had paid little attention to politics before the Rafferty campaign. She had, however, grown concerned about communism enough earlier that year to attend Fred Schwarz's School of Anti-Communism.[23]

Schwarz left a strong impression on her political thinking, but it was her focus on children and education that catalyzed her activism:

> I always loved children and I always worked with them . . . teaching them numbers and colors. . . . And I had observed that often perfectly bright children went off to school and . . . then just had trouble learning. I could never understand why that was.[24]

Acting on these concerns, she read more about education, attended talks, and sat in on school board meetings. She agreed with Rafferty that children were not acquiring the basic skills they needed to get excited about learning; they were also not exposed often enough to inspirational, patriotic heroes of history. Gilbert threw herself into the Rafferty campaign and became a savvy political organizer. She worked with other women out of a shared interest in education and common patterns of everyday life. "Our main basis and ground," she points out, "was the drafting of somebody to help out education."[25] Thanks largely to the efforts of Parents for Rafferty and similar groups, Max Rafferty won a landslide victory in 1962. That same year California reelected liberal governor Pat Brown, but Rafferty organizers demonstrated the power of grassroots conservatives to turn out their voters.

Perhaps more important, Rafferty's campaign highlights some of the burning education issues that fomented conservatives and embroiled women in the movement. Many activists focused on school politics because they thought that American educators were too liberal, that their labor unions were too powerful, and that their progressive teaching methods were downright socialistic. Although most educators considered John Dewey's philosophy of progressive education passé by mid-century, conservatives warned that the liberal overtones and experimental spirit of progressive education still lingered in the public schools. Rafferty and others championed phonics and back-to-basics techniques over the latest "new math" and "look-say" reading methods.[26] Also, many conservative parents were politicized by John Stormer's *None Dare Call It Treason,* published in 1964. Stormer cautioned them that American children were learning to think like communists through the presentation of U.S. history "as a class struggle."[27] He charged that many widely used textbooks downgraded American heroes, the U.S. Constitution, and religion.[28] For similar reasons, Robert Welch urged John Birch Society members to take over their PTAs.[29] He warned that liberalism's twin by-products were social upheaval and centralized government and both eventually led to communism. Trends like premarital sex and experimentation with drugs, moreover, were threats to the social order that invited revolution. Max Rafferty, who shared these views, described the University of California at Berkeley as a "four year course in sex, drugs and treason."[30] This rhetoric played no small role in his 1962 election and that of Governor Ronald Reagan in 1966.

The Gledhill Elementary episode illustrates how women took the lead on school board fights and in Parent Teachers Association debates. Some of these imbroglios brought female agitators into the local spotlight. In 1963, Emily Philips of

Sepulveda, president of the local PTA, gained many supporters and notoriety because of the strong stance she took against communism, even though her protests eventually landed her in a Van Nuys courtroom. Philips was tried for, and cleared of, two counts: loitering and trespassing. The thirty-five-year-old mother interrupted a dance in the school gymnasium, charging that the Latin number's sexual overtones were inappropriate for youths. On another occasion she refused to release the hand of a five-year-old boy whom she encountered running away from school. She insisted on waiting for the boy's mother instead of turning him over to school administrators, believing the child might have good reasons for running away.[31]

Philips had long been a thorn in the side of the San Fernando Valley school officials and Parent Teachers Associations. For three years she had been speaking to groups, railing against the 31st district PTA, the Community Chest, the San Fernando State College Welfare Council, and other social agencies that she linked in a "mysterious advocacy of Socialism."[32] Tired of her accusations, the Sepulveda school principal took advantage of Philips' trespasses and called the police. The prosecutors made no effort to conceal the principal's real purposes. "You can't hit her and you can't shoot her," said the Deputy City Attorney, "so we've done the only other thing we can do—bring her to trial."[33] If San Fernando Valley educators thought Emily Philips was a crackpot, legions of concerned parents around Los Angeles believed she was dead right. A group called the Valley Association to Preserve Freedom sponsored a talk by Philips in the Woodland Hills American Legion Hall.[34] Three hundred came to hear her lecture that evening about how public schools propagated the welfare state.[35] Two months later she gave that talk twice at the Encino Community Center, both events sponsored by the same Valley Association group, and both drawing crowds of over four hundred.[36] Jim Collins, one of the event organizers, urged parents to spread the word because "it would take Emily a hundred years to go to every house in Woodland Hills."[37]

Gender shaped Emily Philips' particular concerns about communism and influenced how others responded to her claims against the school system. Philips identified herself as a housewife and mother above all, yet spoke with authority about education. Motherhood was a major component of her political cachet. For hours at a time, parents sat in community centers and churches to hear her talks.[38] Women only rarely ran for high office in the early sixties, but they did run for PTA president and frequently won. Though Philips never made an issue of gender, the media did so with verve. Philips' Hollywood-style beauty and tailored suit outfits made her a wholesome-yet-titillating news story. Local newspapers called her "personable" and usually mentioned that she was a mother of five.[39] Although a common enough description of women at that time, the mother-activist image evoked a set of connotations: selflessness, good intentions, and genuine concern, among them. Philips' homemaking credentials helped make her a martyr. The *Los Angeles Times* called her a "Crusader."[40] "She had the cloak of a saint," reflected one of her lawyers.[41] No doubt many Angelenos read "hysterical housewife" between the lines, but Philips won admirers, enough to become a local celebrity among conservatives. Just a few weeks after the trial, a Los Angeles Young Republicans unit passed a resolution commending her and her attorney "for their successful defense against harassing legal charges."[42]

Marion Miller, often described as "mother of three children and a former FBI spy," was another recognizable anticommunist housewife who ran for a seat on the Los Angeles school board in 1963.[43] "Most of you have heard her speak on her experiences as an undercover agent for the FBI," advertised the Beverly Hills Republican Club in their January meeting announcement, "Many of you have read her revealing book, *I Was a Spy*. Now she comes to us."[44] Miller's work in espionage made her a popular lecturer even though she never was a paid agent. "While never an employee of the FBI," confirmed J. Edgar Hoover to the *Los Angeles Times* in 1965, "Mrs. Miller did furnish information in a confidential capacity regarding security matters."[45] Miller lost the election, but the spy-mother-housewife image won her a following. She represented a blend of global and local knowledge. Miller's FBI resume gave her claim to expertise on the international communist threat and she offered community-based solutions to meet that threat. During her school board campaign, Miller echoed Max Rafferty, promising to return Los Angeles City Schools to the three R's and phonics and vowing to inculcate an "appreciation of our American Heritage."[46]

Emily Philips and Marion Miller became notable community mobilizers in Los Angeles; their concerns as parents guided their activism. Volunteerism, though far less powerful than paid political office, was more valuable in grassroots politics. Neatly dressed, well-mannered women caught school officials off guard when they went to war against "communism" in public education.

As Parents for Rafferty, Marion Miller and Emily Philips entered the political scene in Los Angeles, while other southern California parents ignited similar battles over textbooks, teachers unions, and school prayer. The San Fernando Valley's Parents for Education (PBE) declared war on the California Teachers Association in 1962, charging that the union's "powerful hierarchy" undermined local control of schools.[47] Two years later, Hollywood-based Project Prayer enlisted the celebrities Pat Boone, Susan Seaforth, Dale Evans, Ronald Reagan, and John Wayne in the campaign for a Constitutional amendment to legalize religious expression in schools.[48] In 1965, Mrs. Virginia Zebold of Granada Hills took her textbook research on the road, appearing before a variety of L.A. clubs to demonstrate how the "irresponsible and rebellious" behavior among students at U.C. Berkeley derived from "indoctrination [through] schools, books, movies and television."[49] The next year, *Land of the Free*, a history textbook adopted by L.A. schools, unleashed a torrent of protest. Parents in Protest of Sierra Madre and the Textbook Study League in San Gabriel complained that the book's author, John Caughey, not only refused to sign a loyalty oath in 1950, but portrayed anticommunists as witch-hunters, characterized slavery as a "shortcoming of the free enterprise system," and depicted the radicals Sacco and Vanzetti as victims.[50]

This parental activism was a reflection of the "family-centered" culture often associated with the 1950s, but that continued for many Americans well past the end of "Ike's America."[51] Although mothers and fathers shared concerns about education, women, as full-time parents, usually assumed leadership and extra responsibility in this realm. In many cases, as with Parents for Rafferty, women were more effective organizers; many groups even played up the social value accorded their gender. In 1964, the San Fernando Valley organization "Women for America, Inc." billed itself as "an organization dedicated to the defeat of totalitarianism using education as a weapon."[52] They raised money for "patriotic" libraries and sponsored "Americanism" quizzes for college students in Los Angeles.[53] Some clubs, like the Liberty Torchbearers, the Network of Patriotic Letter-Writers, Facts in Education, Inc., and the Encino Legislative Research group, were women's organizations not in name, but certainly in numbers and usually in leadership as well.[54]

Many conservative ideologues saw great potential in the deep-rooted moral outrage that drove mothers and housewives to enlist in the fight against communism. One popular anticommunist speaker in Los Angeles, Paul Neipp, wrote a manual for conservative study groups in 1962 called *Let's Take the Offensive!* Neipp highlighted housewives as a special group of "common people" who often demonstrate uncommon resolve. "These are the very ones who could do a lot," he emphasized in the manual's "Call to Housewives" section.[55] Neipp, a Lutheran minister, claimed responsibility for helping to start over five hundred study groups around the country and attributed part of his success to women's heightened sense of awareness to the communist threat. In another of his pieces, a leaflet called "For Women Only," he warned recalcitrant housewives that "if we are to survive, it must come through the women of our country . . . our men are too busy to be concerned. They are too selfishly occupied with making money."[56] Presidential candidate Barry Goldwater was another conservative who recognized homemakers and mothers as an important grassroots force. Women were important vote-getters and their support affirmed his vows to reverse the nation's moral and spiritual decline. Citizens for Goldwater-Miller, the grassroots arm of his campaign, went so far as to form a separate organization, Mothers for Moral America, that appealed directly to women's maternal instincts and sense of moral righteousness. They launched the organization in Nashville, Tennessee, two months before the election, hoping for "a spontaneous, public movement—carefully coordinated with and through the Citizens committee."[57] A Mothers unit formed in the San Fernando Valley in October and Orange County's Carol Arth Waters became the organization's national coordinator.[58]

Gender was clearly an operative force in conservative politics—organizing the division of labor, influencing why men and women entered politics, and determining how they would assert themselves—but "women's" and "men's" issues never drove the debates. Women organized together out of political necessity; men were simply not as available most hours of the day. Whether they chose to acknowledge gender or not, though, a distinctive women's political culture emerged out of their concentrated spheres of activism. While cowboy conservatives Barry Goldwater and Ronald Reagan captured the national spotlight with their masculine, western populist personas, women concentrated their own feminine style of politics on the grass roots. In these ways, they expanded the reach of the conservative movement, as well as their own political domain, well beyond school boards and PTAs.

By the 1960s, women had long been mixing domesticity and politics, mainly through political clubs. In fact, many conservative women started their activist careers in the California Federation of Republican Women, California's first club formed in Los Angeles in 1920 as a wedge for GOP women into the male-dominated world of partisan politics. Over the next few decades, clubs proliferated in California and fashioned a distinctly feminine style of political organizing for themselves in the process.[59] By 1954, there were 123 Republican women's clubs in southern California and 234 statewide.[60] Their political luncheons and coffees, get-out-the vote drives, and monthly newsletters eventually became the bread-and-butter practices of more conservative grassroots organizations in the postwar era. Republican women's clubs also popularized study groups which, as Paul Neipp was well aware, often inspired housewives to intensify their political involvement.

Over the 1950s, right-wing activist women increasingly adopted the study group model as a way to foster a more militant conservatism that went beyond Eisenhower's "Modern Republicanism." Women in these groups volunteered to research a particular issue and make themselves experts on current topics like the United Nations, mental health legislation, or school integration policies. Meeting at a regular time, often with a scheduled outside speaker, group members updated each other on political developments and often wrote letters to senators and representatives together. One of the most visible and active study clubs in Los Angeles, for example, was American Public Relations Forum. Headquartered in Van Nuys, the forum spun out of a Catholic women's church group and grew rapidly. They were "wives and mothers . . . vitally interested in what is happening in our country," declared president Stephanie Williams at the founding meeting in 1952.[61] The forum received national notoriety in 1956 when they organized a letter-writing campaign that held up passage of the Alaska Mental Health Bill, a measure, they claimed, that would have empowered psychiatrists to institutionalize political dissidents gulag-style in Alaska.[62]

A sizable force of citizen-housewives and political organizers emerged out of this decade of study, research, and correspondence and the conservative movement spread quickly through their extensive networks. The Tuesday Morning Study Club (TMSC) of Pasadena is a case in point. The club originally met as a group of friends, reading pending legislation and discussing politics in one member's home overlooking the Rose Bowl. However, several of the TMSC women eventually went in their own directions, applying their copious study to different grassroots projects. Jane Crosby, for example, formed an early Birch Society chapter in South Pasadena. She also helped establish the United Republicans of California (UROC) and participated in the conservative takeover of the Republican Party in the early 1960s.[63] When Crosby's husband, Joseph, became chairman of UROC in the mid-1960s, she managed the UROC office on Wilshire Boulevard as a full-time volunteer. "My husband bought me this beautiful air-conditioned home," remembers Crosby, "and I was down in that hot headquarters. I used to think about that."[64] Another outgrowth of

TMSC was the Network of Patriotic Letter-Writers (NPLW). The purpose of NPLW, which formed in the late 1950s and lasted into the 1970s, was to "shape trends through letter writing."[65] By 1959, the network was mailing its newsletters to subscribers all over the country, two-thirds of whom were women and one-half of whom were non-California residents.[66] NPLW bulletins routinely praised FBI Director J. Edgar Hoover and the House Un-American Activities Committee, attacked the Kennedys, demanded the impeachment of Chief Justice Earl Warren, and called for U.S. withdrawal from the United Nations.[67] The network also urged members to start their own groups. "We will be happy to help you get started," wrote chairman Gertrude Bale to subscriber Della Root, of nearby Alhambra. "This I think is the best way to get into the swing of a letter-writing group."[68]

Conservative study groups reflected not only their women's club origins, but also the new reliance on expertise in postwar American society.[69] Activists were not merely housewives, they were experts by virtue of their intense study. Technological experts built the military industrial complex; think tanks like the Rand corporation advised U.S. national security agencies; and health professionals like Dr. Benjamin Spock advised couples how to raise children.[70] In the same vein, Marie Koenig of Pasadena, self-described "housewife, researcher, lecturer," spoke out against the textbook, *Land of the Free,* but not until she finished checking every footnote.[71] Elaine Tyler May argues that "the era of the expert" diverted middle-class Americans away from political activism by advocating "adaptation" over "resistance," however many housewives cultivated their own expertise to make themselves politically adept.[72] In her own study of Queens, New York, historian Sylvie Murray observes how postwar housewife activists on the other coast also relied less often on "prescribed maternal responsibilities" and more often on "facts and figures" to speak with political authority.[73] Marion Miller and Emily Philips similarly emphasized their extensive experience with domestic communism in their lectures, one as a PTA president and the other as an ex-spy.

The study clubs of the 1950s were the means by which women politicized themselves through familiar rituals and institutions, but housewife activism came even further out into the open in the early 1960s. Around that time, women began opening patriotic bookstores and libraries in the greater Los Angeles area. "We have been lending books back and forth between ourselves so we can become informed," explained Jane Crosby when she founded the Main Street Americanism Center in South Pasadena, "now we want to come out from behind the bushes and get right out on the main street."[74] The center's fifty-odd volunteers, all mothers, made the store a comfortable, handsome space where people would want to walk off the street and sit down to read. "It had a big round oak table," remembers Crosby, "it was cozy . . . so pretty, and so patriotic-looking."[75] The Americanism Center title caught on; it implied a wholly American ideology, a counterpoint to communism. The Wilshire Americanism Center opened in 1964, promising to emphasize "the culturally important and noteworthy aspects of America's growth."[76] Promoting "faith and allegiance" to the United States was the central mission of the Long Beach Americanism Center, which opened in 1965.[77]

Poor Richard's Bookshop opened on Hollywood Boulevard as a patriotic bookstore and more. Frank and Florence Ranuzzi of Los Feliz created Poor Richard's, but Florence operated the shop because Frank was busy with the family's insurance agency.[78] In addition to books like Goldwater's *Conscience of a Conservative* and Whittaker Chamber's *Witness,* Poor Richard's stocked copies of pending bills and legislative hearings, "survival literature" for bomb shelter construction and *McGuffey* children's readers. Florence also turned the shop into a political headquarters. She and Frank designed bumper stickers, printed leaflets, and organized protests. During the 1962 gubernatorial race between Pat Brown and Richard Nixon, Florence's popular "Brown Is Pink" bumper sticker raised quite a furor.[79] Under Florence's guidance, Poor Richard's became a bookstore for the whole family, a conservative "salon" for the community. Men, women, and teenagers would drop in on Saturdays to sit around a big captain's table and hear Florence give talks about communism. "If somebody started an argument . . . she'd grab this book [and] that book," remembers her daughter, "[and] she'd say read it for yourself."[80] The bookstore was a family operation. The Ranuzzis gave away political materials at their own expense. The store never turned a profit. As a result, Frank continued to work at the insurance agency to support the family's activism. Their daughter, then a teenager, cooked and cleaned their home because Florence worked at the store six days a week. Mary also became a "Goldwater Girl." Like a cheerleader, she waved pompoms and shook bottles of gold water (ginger ale) at political rallies.[81]

The Americanism Centers and Poor Richard's provided conservatives in Los Angeles with a sense of community. Poor Richard's, for example, served as a local think tank for speakers and writers in the area. Corinne Griffith, former film star turned anti–income tax lecturer, shopped there for her speech material. So did John Wayne, spokesperson for Project Prayer.[82] Similarly, the South Pasadena center became an information clearinghouse. People called the store volunteers for references on everything from local anti-pornography initiatives to Christian histories of the Constitution.[83] The center also rented out audiovisual materials and sold copies of JBS's *American Opinion* magazine.[84] Patriotic bookstores embodied the new image of conservatism in the early 1960s; they were wholesome, upbeat, and intellectually alive.

Women activists, including the bookstore volunteers, also took the rough edges off of militant conservatism with their feminine warmth and hospitality. Some exerted this same influence through books and music. For example, two southern California women, Patty Newman and Joyce Wenger, wrote a paperback parody of President Johnson's war on poverty in 1966 called *Pass the Poverty Please!* The back cover promised readers, "Two American mothers bring you this exciting story which will make you gnash your teeth at the facts while you laugh along with their adventures."[85] Newman and Wenger's smiling head shots, along with the book's light and satiric tone, softened what was actually a heavy-handed indictment of civil rights and anti-poverty programs. The publisher identified the authors as wives and mothers to pitch *Pass the Poverty Please!* as a practical, down-home guide to politics, grounded in real life, for all levels of readers.

Janet Greene, anticommunist folk singer, was another conservative spokesperson who made femininity and domesticity a part of her popular image without talking about gender outright. Greene performed at Fred Schwarz's anticommunism rallies, often with her two daughters. Billed as "a new and effective anti-Communist weapon," the June Cleaver–looking Greene offered a wholesome alternative to the bohemian left-wing folk icons of her time. Greene fit a central organizing strategy of the Christian Anti-Communist Crusade—to fight fire with fire, to turn leftist movement tactics back on itself. "The communists have been using folk-singing for years," they advertised, "now the tables have been turned."[86] Janet Greene was the Joan Baez of the Right. The Crusade's Long Beach office sold Greene's songs, "Fascist Threat," "Commie Lies," "Poor Left-Winger," and "Comrade's Lament" as fund-raisers. "One billion conquered should reveal," she sang, "the danger that is very real. The greatest fascist threat, you see, is the Communist conspiracy."[87]

Singing, writing, operating bookstores, mailing letters and giving lectures, politically active conservative women reveal another 1960s. For the legions who built effective and meaningful political lives for themselves in the conservative movement, their roles allowed them to be activists as well as mothers and wives. For them, the late 1960s did not give birth to a new and exciting era of movement politics and culture, as it did for American leftists. Like second wave feminists, these activists fought hard to expand women's role in politics, but not by attacking hierarchies of gender. They embraced an entirely different vision of women's political advancement, one that conformed to the traditional social order. The activism of middle- and upper-class Los Angeles women shows that their lives were highly conducive to grassroots political work well before the women's liberation movement. While their own movement underwent major changes in the 1960s, its emphasis on family issues, especially education, remained a powerful force in U.S. political culture. So did conservative women in California and around the United States.

Mary C. Brennan

WINNING THE WAR / LOSING THE BATTLE: THE GOLDWATER PRESIDENTIAL CAMPAIGN AND ITS EFFECTS ON THE EVOLUTION OF MODERN CONSERVATISM

Barry Goldwater's 1964 presidential campaign was an essential step in the evolution of postwar conservatism. Building on earlier efforts to gain influence on the national level, conservatives used Goldwater's popularity to gain power in the Republican Party. The Arizona senator won the support of many Americans by addressing issues dear to the heart of the 1950s Right: the necessity for limited government, the evils of communism, and the glories of America. Goldwater won more supporters as the African-American civil rights movement and the escalating conflict in Vietnam complicated the political scene, causing some Democrats to rethink their traditional loyalties and some Republicans to embrace their party's right wing. Although these new supporters were not numerous enough to defeat Lyndon B. Johnson, they did secure conservatives' power within the Republican Party. In other words, conservatives lost the battle but won the war.

Conservatives learned important lessons from the 1964 campaign. After Goldwater's defeat, conservatives moved in a new direction. The core issues remained the same, but the specific causes changed. Conservatives continued to argue that the government was too big and too partial to special interests. While in the 1950s, however, the Right complained about labor's influence over national policy, in the 1960s, conservatives targeted what they perceived to be the increasing power of minorities to affect the federal government. As a result of these shifts in emphasis, Goldwater and some of his followers found themselves on the outside of their own movement, grateful to have succeeded in playing a role, but slightly confused as to the new priorities.

Perhaps 1950s conservatives accepted their ambiguous place within the 1960s conservative movement because it had taken them so long to achieve any kind of political influence. Various types of divisions had kept them out of power since 1932. In addition to fighting the "Eastern Establishment," Republican conservatives found themselves at odds with one another.[1] Basic theoretical disagreements among right-wingers proved most problematic. During the postwar era, American conservatives generally followed one of two strands of thought: traditionalism or classical liberalism. Traditionalists believed that morality should be the guiding principle of human existence; consequently, government had an important role to play in community life because in the end political questions were "religious and moral problems." This belief contrasted sharply with the views of classical liberals and libertarians who preached the gospel of laissez-faire economics, libertarianism, and limited government.[2]

Socioeconomic and demographic differences compounded these ideological disagreements during the 1950s and would continue to be a political problem into the 1960s. Even when conservative farmers, oilmen, academics, suburbanites, and intellectuals shared the same basic philosophies, their interpretation of those ideals sometimes clashed because of their distinctive regional, social, and economic backgrounds. Western oilmen and ranchers, for example, condemned the federal government's intrusion in their businesses while southern California homemakers protested the government's interference in their schools. In addition, the growing number of conservatives in the Southwest contested for control of the conservative movement with northeasterners and midwesterners who had long dominated conservative politics in the United States.[3]

In the early 1960s, the plethora of citizens' groups representing various aspects of the conservative agenda provided ample evidence of the complexity of the movement. Citizens across the country reacted against what they regarded as the "monolithic conformity of 'liberalism'" in culture and education as well as liberal politics and economics by forming local and national groups to combat whichever aspect of liberalism particularly offended or outraged them.[4] The most significant national organization was the John Birch Society [JBS], founded in 1958 by Robert Welch. The society preached antistatism and the evils of the "International Communist Conspiracy." Many Democrats and Republicans derided the JBS as a "crackpot fringe," but members of the society used slick propaganda techniques, publications, and simplistic analyses to build up a significant following.[5]

The JBS hammered away at the cause that unified conservatives: anticommunism. They accused the Democrats of "losing" the battle against the Soviet Union abroad and its fight against communist spies at home. While most Americans feared the spread of communism, Birchers demanded a more aggressive diplomatic stance and advocated suspending individual rights in the name of national security. While the JBS was more extreme in their anticommunism than almost any other organized group, their zealous message served as a magnet drawing diverse conservative groups and individuals to their cause.[6]

The JBS was not unique. In the 1950s, conservatives took the political offensive.

They were not content to grumble behind-the-scenes, publish scholarly articles no one read, or patiently wait their turn for influence within the GOP. A newly energized right-wing press played a crucial role in this transformation. In 1955, William F. Buckley, Jr.'s *National Review* began publication; it joined existing conservative magazines such as *Human Events, The Freeman,* and *The American Mercury.* These journals instructed the public on the philosophical and practical tenets of conservatism, publicized conservative politicians, and advocated conservative public policies. In addition, a growing number of young people discovered conservatism on their college campuses, through conservative journals, or organizations such as the Intercollegiate Society of Individualists and the Young Republicans, both of which shifted dramatically to the Right in the late 1950s. In 1960, Buckley and others helped college-aged conservatives create a new nationwide organization, Young Americans for Freedom.[7]

Despite their growing movement, conservatives had spent much of the 1950s frustrated and alienated from the government and their own party. President Eisenhower preached a "Modern Republicanism" that disappointed the Right. Not only did he fail to "undo" the New Deal, but he did not liberate eastern Europe as he had promised. His difficulty in dealing with the rising nationalism of the people of Africa and Latin America intensified their distrust. In addition, developments at home further widened divisions within the GOP. The increasingly vocal and visible demands of black Americans shocked, confused, and often frightened whites across the country. Forced to uphold the supremacy of a federal court order in Little Rock, Eisenhower found himself on the side of integrationists and opposed to conservative states' rightists. In addition, the recession in 1958 reignited debate over economic issues.[8]

These tensions mounted as the 1960 presidential race neared. The Republican front-runner was Eisenhower's vice president and heir apparent, Richard M. Nixon. In some ways, Nixon was the perfect candidate for the divided GOP. His willingness to support Eisenhower's continuation of New Deal policies and to defend the Supreme Court's decision to end segregated education demonstrated his moderation. At the same time, Nixon was not a member of the eastern elite. He had first been elected to the Senate as a rabid anticommunist, and he had boldly squared off against Nikita Khrushchev in the "kitchen debate" in Moscow.[9] Right-wingers, however, were not sure they could trust him.

Their reluctance stemmed in part from their discovery of a new conservative hero: Arizona Senator Barry Goldwater. Neither a lawyer nor a member of a political family, Goldwater epitomized the successful southwestern businessman, community leader, and right-wing activist. Elected to the Senate in 1952, he had made his name as a conservative by voting against the censure of Senator Joe McCarthy and by working to limit the expansion of federal safety-net programs. Goldwater bolstered his national reputation by criticizing Eisenhower's more moderate policies in his syndicated newspaper column. As chairman of the Senatorial Campaign Committee, he was able to build up his national reputation and relationship with party workers.[10]

In addition, Goldwater led the charge against the bugaboo of 1950s conservatives: big labor. Conservatives believed that workers should control their own labor rather than submitting themselves to a collectivist organization. They thought that business owners had the right to run their enterprises without interference from government-approved collective bargaining unions. Unions, these conservatives argued, were a kind of socialism, which was just a short hop away from communism. Despite the willingness of many unions in the 1950s to eliminate their leftist elements, Goldwater and other conservatives worked to destroy union power. Goldwater's claim that Walter Reuther and the UAW campaigned against him in 1958 only served to further enhance his reputation.[11]

Goldwater's attacks on labor won him praise from the conservative press and his work with the committee solidified his position within the party machinery, but he leapt to the forefront of the conservative movement with the 1960 publication of *The Conscience of a Conservative*. With the help of L. Brent Bozell, he drew on many of his earlier speeches to set forth a credo that redefined conservatism in twentieth-century terms. Rejecting the common misconception that conservatism concentrated solely on economic theory, he insisted instead that conservatism "puts material things in their proper place." Although conservatives emphasized freedom, Goldwater explained, they also realized that "the practice of freedom requires the establishment of order." He was careful to note that the necessity for order, however, posed the twin dangers of excessive governmental controls and the use of that power for illicit purposes. In addition to domestic concerns, Goldwater discussed the dangers of Soviet aggression. He demanded no communist country be recognized by the American government, and advocated the use of nuclear weapons against the USSR to liberate "captive nations."[12]

Goldwater's straightforward language attracted a broad range of conservatives who previously had no voice in Republican councils. In addition, he influenced many people in search of a philosophy to express their discontent, and he inspired numerous young people with his sincerity.[13] Goldwater believed deeply in the right of individuals to control their incomes, properties, and destinies. He feared the growth of a tyrannical federal government that would usurp the power of communities at the state or local level to govern themselves as they saw fit. Further, Goldwater inspired many conservatives by arguing that the United States was engaged in a life-or-death battle with the Soviets for control of the world.

For Goldwater and his supporters, the 1960 presidential campaign proved to be the first step in building a new conservative movement at the national level. Although Nixon ended up winning the nomination (and then losing the election), conservatives learned from the nomination process. Most important, they discovered the untapped potential of citizens' groups to influence the national party. By the summer of 1960, "Goldwater for President" groups had surfaced all over the country. Though Goldwater had not authorized anyone to use his name or to set up such organizations for him, these groups believed that if they spoke "loud enough," Goldwater could be nominated. This network proved useful when Nixon moved to his left during the primary campaign.[14] In a powerful speech, the

Arizona senator blasted Nixon's leftward shift and challenged the Right to "grow up" and work if they wanted to set the party back on track.[15] Complaining about establishment treachery, he explained, would not help them achieve their goal. Only real effort by grassroots activists would allow them to take control of the Republican Party.

Conservatives followed Goldwater's advice and began organizing. Several political and demographic shifts worked to their advantage. Most important, the Republican Party was gaining support in the South. Although Nixon won only three southern states, his strong showing all through the region indicated the widening cracks in the "solid" Democratic South.[16] Developments over the previous forty years explained this shift. In particular, the GOP reaped the benefits of the socioeconomic transformation of the South following World War II. The creation of a significant number of defense industries throughout the South and Southwest during the war provided steady employment for many unskilled and semiskilled workers, lifting them out of poverty for the first time and into the middle and working classes.[17] Now taxpayers instead of government beneficiaries, many white southerners no longer saw the need for large-scale federal government domestic spending. More viscerally, as the Democratic Party began to offer limited support to the emerging civil rights movements, many white southerners began to rethink their political loyalties.[18]

The revitalization of the GOP in the South strengthened the conservative wing of the party. In fact, many of new conservative Republican officeholders represented southern and southwestern states. Ignoring for the moment the racists and other extremists who disliked the liberalism of the national Democratic Party, many southerners who joined the GOP embraced the classical liberal ideals embodied in the Republican Party's opposition to high taxes, federal spending, and government centralization. Moreover, southern culture revolved around a dedication to family, God, and country—values that echoed northern right-wing ideals.[19]

In addition, Republicans found that President Kennedy caught them between the Scylla of his liberal image and the Charybdis of his conservative policies. On the one hand, he talked like a traditional Democrat who accepted the New Deal framework. On the other hand, he embraced Cold War diplomacy and adopted a conservative approach to civil rights and government-business relations, while taking care not to alienate his liberal constituents. This made it difficult for Republicans to criticize his administration effectively, and widened the gaps between conservatives and the rest of the Republican Party by forcing their differences into the open.[20]

President Kennedy's effective courtship of corporate liberals produced an important, though not immediately evident, change in the power structure of the GOP. The business contributions to the Democrats deprived liberal Republicans of funds at the same time that the growth of Southern Rim industries increased donations to conservatives. These circumstances helped conservative activists to gain control of the Republican Party. By creating an alternative financial structure dependent on southwestern and rank-and-file money, conservative Republicans obviated the Republican Party's dependence on corporate financing.[21]

Two other issues greatly increased conservative opportunities within the GOP and the nation as a whole. The first was the African-American civil rights movement exploding throughout the South. Building on the momentum of earlier leaders and organizations, Martin Luther King, Jr., his Southern Christian Leadership Conference [SCLC], and the Student Non-Violent Co-ordinating Committee [SNCC] succeeded in focusing the nation's attention on the evils of segregation. Many southern whites resisted the challenge to Jim Crow by voting for segregationist politicians, supporting police attacks on demonstrators, and using economic pressure and even violent means to stop the movement toward racial equality. As Kennedy and the Democrats acted (albeit reluctantly at times) to protect the rights of black Americans, some white southerners looked with hope to the Republican Party. In particular, they liked the sound of the states' rights arguments made by many conservatives. As early as 1963, journalists noted the beginnings of a "white backlash" against the civil rights movement in the North, boding well for conservatives in that region.[22]

The changing Cold War also helped the conservative movement as a whole, but would eventually undermine the Goldwaterites. As the situation in Europe remained at a standoff, Americans increasingly worried about the revolutionary potential of the emerging nations in Africa and Asia. Policy differences over these developing countries exacerbated the divisions within and between the political parties. The Kennedy administration, by supporting anticommunist leaders who, policymakers believed, were strong enough to defeat the revolutionary forces, frequently ended up backing men who abused power and misused American aid. As a result, such policies often did not work abroad or at home. Liberals disliked the association with dictatorships while conservatives wanted to move more aggressively against the communist hordes. Thus, Goldwaterites found an enthusiastic audience as they criticized the Democratic foreign policy. These new battles, however, shifted the nation's attention from the U.S.-Soviet conflict and complicated the foreign policy picture.[23]

Conservatives took advantage of the fact that the rise of the civil rights movements as well as the changing nature of the Cold War confused and frightened many middle- and working-class Americans. Many of these citizens longed for the old days when the causes were familiar and the answers simple. Liberal politicians, caught up in the new issues and rethinking old assumptions, misunderstood this discontent and fear. Seeing only racism and extremism, they dismissed the frustration expressed in missives to their offices and printed in newsletters. Conservatives, on the other hand, listened to people like columnist Alice Widenor who, in the *ACA Newletter,* explained that the middle class disliked funding a government that gave them nothing in return. Emphasizing that the nation could not be "saved at Washington, but at home; not from the top down, but from the bottom up," conservative activists sought to funnel this middle-class dissatisfaction into an organized movement.[24]

Increasingly, conservatives believed that the senator from Arizona was the key to conservative victory in the GOP and at the polls. They formed organizations all over the country. In the long run, most of these early organizations joined forces with the effort to nominate Goldwater led by F. Clifton White, Ohio Congressman John Ashbrook, and William Rusher in early 1961. Bringing together conservatives from all over the country, White gradually and surreptitiously created a nationwide network of volunteers, only some of whom were connected to state and local Republican committees.[25] Instead of party officials, White concentrated on gaining influence with such vital organizations as the Young Republicans, the Federation of Republican Women, and the Republican National Committee. He reminded supporters that their "primary goal was to build delegate strength for the 1964 national convention," and to that end urged them to organize conservatives at the precinct, district, and state level. Further, he encouraged his regional chairmen to learn each of their states' rules for deciding delegate election so that they would be ready for the primary fight.[26]

Goldwater's increasing visibility and popularity aided White's efforts. In addition to his continued work as chairman of the Senate Campaign Committee, his numerous after-dinner speeches, and continued attention to *The Conscience of a Conservative,* he published another popular book, *Why Not Victory?* Released in early 1962 to favorable reviews, this book on foreign affairs, along with the publication of four favorable biographies, kept Goldwater in the public eye.[27]

Although White and his group felt that the upsurge of grassroots support justified their position that Goldwater could win the nomination as well as the election, they had difficulty convincing Goldwater that victory was possible. Goldwater proved to be a very reluctant candidate. Despite evidence of the strength of the network they were building, Goldwater remained uncertain that anyone, especially a western conservative, could beat President Kennedy. He worried about the impact undertaking a race would have on his Senate seat. Most important, as Goldwater told everyone who asked, because of the impact the campaign would have on his life as well as his self-doubts, he did not *want* the nomination.[28]

Goldwater refused to acknowledge White's group and announced that he did not seek the nomination and would not accept a draft. That announcement produced a crisis for White and his committee. They finally decided, in Indiana member Bob Hughes' words, to "draft the son of a bitch . . . anyway." Consequently, White and his crew easily set up a new National Draft-Goldwater Committee (NDGC). The NDGC established committees in each state, organized signature drives, and sought support from the National Federation of Republican Women, Republican governors, and the Young Republicans.[29]

A number of factors aided the long-term growth of the movement. Because White and his Chicago group began operating in secret, they prompted little opposition at the early stages of development when they had neither the funds nor the support to withstand it. Their effort to build from the bottom up ensured that conservatives had a sturdy foundation of people throughout the country actually running the party on the state and local levels. In addition, Goldwater's genuine reluctance to work for the nomination meant a broad group controlled the movement, not Goldwater. As a result, Goldwater's defeat in November 1964 did not cripple the movement; a powerful grassroots operation remained in place. Moreover, the successful draft movement encouraged conservatives to believe that they could have an impact on national politics and ensured that they would continue rather than give up after 1964.[30]

All of White's efforts would have been in vain, however, without Goldwater. To the relief of many, by the fall of 1963, the Arizona senator began to consider making the run. The amount of support, both in money and in delegates, produced by the draft committee allayed some of his fears and doubts, while New York Governor Nelson Rockefeller's burgeoning campaign raised new concerns. During the summer of 1963, Goldwater invited his most trusted Arizona friends and advisers to Washington to discuss his options.[31] Goldwater told them he was leaning toward a run.

Goldwater reconsidered after the assassination of John F. Kennedy. The tragic events of 22 November 1963 deeply affected him; he viewed the president's death as "a great personal loss." Although some members of the Goldwater Draft Committee believed that Kennedy's assassination had not substantially changed things in regard to the election, others, including Goldwater himself, concluded that Lyndon Johnson, a southerner with a conservative reputation, made Goldwater's candidacy more untenable. Complicating matters further, Kennedy's death in a conservative southwestern city caused many people to blame the Right for the murder. In the end, however, Goldwater could not disappoint the thousands of people, especially the young volunteers, who had worked so hard for him. Reluctant and convinced that he could not win, Goldwater formally announced his candidacy on 3 January 1964, at his Arizona home.[32]

The new candidate faced a tough primary battle even though there was no single, obvious opponent. The leading moderate or liberal candidates succeeded in eliminating themselves from the race through miscalculations, misplayed hands, and misspoken words. Richard Nixon and Michigan Governor George Romney both prematurely announced their candidacies while Nelson Rockefeller focused his efforts on California only to lose by a very slim margin.[33] A last-minute campaign by Pennsylvania Governor William Scranton might have stopped the Goldwater drive if he had made up his mind sooner and concentrated on the issues. Instead, he painted Goldwater and, by implication, all conservative supporters as extremists who represented "a whole crazy-quilt collection of absurd and dangerous positions." Scranton succeeded only in further dividing the convention and in reinforcing among the national electorate the eventual nominee's extremist image.[34]

Goldwater's campaign was dogged by accusations of extremism and mudslinging. Goldwaterites complained that they struggled to keep ahead of the distortions propagated by the Johnson people. The Arizona senator's lack of national campaign experience, his often naive honesty, and his insistence on keeping his Arizona cronies in charge of the campaign made a counterattack difficult.[35]

All these problems contributed to Goldwater's overwhelming defeat. Though he garnered almost twenty-seven million votes, he carried only Arizona and the five states of the Deep South. The rest of the party went crashing down along with him. The Democrats won a 68 to 32 majority in the Senate and a 295 to 140 margin in the House.[36]

Despite the magnitude of the defeat, conservatives learned valuable lessons from the Goldwater effort. They used the campaign to present their political arguments to a national audience, and created a foundation on which they could build in future years. On a practical level, the 1964 effort showed conservatives what they could accomplish working outside the traditional pattern. Although Goldwater received significant donations from conservative eastern businessmen such as the DuPonts and the Pews as well as from Texas oilmen and ranchers, 72% of the Republican individual contributions came in sums under $500. Many of these donations resulted from the direct mail efforts by his staff.[37] Similarly, Goldwater received support from a few Republican bigwigs—most notably Eisenhower and Nixon—but only limited help from many of the state party committees. In fact, a few Republicans actively worked to undermine his efforts. The actions of Romney and Rockefeller were particularly damaging.[38]

In the end, Republican recalcitrance hurt Goldwater in November, but aided the movement in the long term. By forcing White and then the Goldwater staff to work outside normal party apparatus, the Republican establishment compelled conservatives to build a strong network of volunteers, trained and ready for the next fight. Having learned the value of grassroots activism, right-wingers continued to cultivate associates at that level by direct mail techniques developed during the campaign.[39]

Most important for the long-term growth of the movement, the 1964 campaign provided Goldwater and the conservatives with a platform to present their arguments to a national audience. Especially early in the campaign, Goldwater promised to "chart a new course of peace, freedom, morality, and constitutional order." Emphasizing that "progress comes from work, initiative and investment," he recommended expanding the free-enterprise system by reducing taxes and balancing the budget. Highly critical of the extension of the federal government into what Goldwater felt were unnecessary areas, he advocated making many governmental programs, such as farm price supports and Social Security, voluntary and encouraged the development of individual initiative and corporate-sponsored programs. Goldwater was quick to assure people that he did not intend to destroy these programs and leave the needy stranded, but that he believed an expanded economy and a strong dollar ultimately would prove more helpful than all the Democratic "give-away" programs.[40]

Goldwater did insist that the government be actively involved in providing for the national defense. Promising to "take a firm stand against Communist aggression," Goldwater declared that he intended to follow Eisenhower's peace-through-strength defense policy by maintaining military superiority over the Soviets. Though he trusted military more than civilian authority in defense and security matters, he promised not to rely solely on "bombs and bullets," but instead to offer "freedom"—a term he only vaguely defined—to the world. Goldwater frequently chided Johnson for his lack of commitment to a free world.[41]

Conservatives were so thrilled at finally getting their views heard that they ignored contradictory elements within Goldwater's proposals. Many Americans agreed that the federal government had become economically and bureaucratically bloated, but they feared Goldwater's emphasis on military superiority could lead to a garrison state that would destroy American freedom. His oversimplified economic policies ignored the complexities of the world market and the power of the modern corporation. How, some Americans wondered, could he protect their jobs from foreign competition, keep prices low, and maintain economic stability by relying solely on individual initiative and the open market? This view seemed either naive or ignorant as did his insistence that a balanced budget would cure all economic problems. Goldwater's emphasis on education and individual responsibility as answers to the problems of the poor overlooked the realities of their lives and their place in the social hierarchy. Just as experts began to discuss the "culture of poverty," Goldwater hearkened back to a nineteenth-century model of blaming inadequacies in the poor for their economic situation.

Goldwater's platform also divided his own conservative movement, favoring anticommunists and the classical liberals at the expense of the traditionalists. In fact, every time the traditionalists accused Johnson or a member of his staff of immorality, the Goldwater staff shut them down. When traditionalists produced a short movie emphasizing the seamier aspects of the Johnson administration, Goldwater headquarters refused to use it in the campaign. Although they hoped that a Goldwater presidency would return America to the mythical "good ole' days" when everyone knew their place and stayed there, traditionalists (called social conservatives by the early 1970s) were left out of the Goldwater platform. Ironically, the social turmoil of the 1960s would make the traditionalist constituency a powerful element in the American electorate in the last half of the twentieth-century.[42]

Finally, new issues that arose during the campaign altered the conservative agenda. In particular, the civil rights movement and the conflict in Vietnam changed the political debate. Goldwater's domestic platform addressed the issue of the expanded federal government in terms of New Deal-style programs like Social Security and farm price supports. After the successful passage of the 1964 Civil Rights Act, black activists nationalized the civil rights movement, confronting northern white racism. In the North, whites resisted ending de facto segregation in schools, housing, and employment that contributed to African-American frustration and led to race riots. Many northern whites joined southern whites in thinking the federal government was doing too much for "those people." LBJ's "war on poverty" now not only offended limited government classical liberals; it also infuriated middle- and working-class whites who resented their tax dollars going to rioters, protestors, and "malcontents." Alabama Governor George Wallace's success in a few northern Democratic presidential primaries in 1964 demonstrated the "backlash" vote.[43]

Similarly, the intensifying conflict in Indochina transformed what had seemed a consensual foreign policy into a political fight. For conservatives, the Vietnam conflict had always been clear: the communist threat was evil and must be destroyed.

They saw the conflict in Vietnam as a Soviet plot. Conservatives wanted LBJ to "fight or get out." Many right-wingers believed that if only the president would turn the war over to the military and use all of America's firepower—in other words, really fight—the hostilities would end. If he was not willing to do that, then conservatives felt the effort was useless and America should withdraw. At the same time, increasing numbers of students, liberals, and left-wing Americans questioned American involvement in Vietnam and its threat of communism. Conservatives now not only disliked what they perceived to be LBJ's weak military policy, they also resented his inability to stop the protestors.[44]

As a result of the shifting circumstances, many Americans began to move to the Right. Conservative domestic policy meant more than just retreating from social welfare programs. By the mid-1960s, it included an emphasis on states' rights and limiting national interference in desegregating schools. Similarly, many Americans, frustrated over the stalemate in Vietnam and angry at antiwar protestors, joined conservatives in pushing for more defense spending and greater attention to domestic order. They could not comprehend how a country that had defeated both Germany and Japan could not subdue the Vietnamese.

Goldwater, ironically, did not benefit from this conservative upsurge. He had been pushed out of the Republican Party by the moderates and liberals. His gradual ostracism from the party began in early 1965 and was almost complete by June 1965, when he was the only major Republican not invited to speak at the Ohio jamboree, celebrating the appointment of a new Republican National Committee chairman. During the 1968 Republican national convention, his name was omitted from the official program. In 1972, his invitation to participate arrived only a week before the event. Despite Goldwater's help in gaining the nomination for Richard Nixon in 1968, the new president excluded the Arizona senator from some White House events and seemed to ignore his phone calls. Even more upsetting to Goldwater was the attitude of some of the conservatives who abandoned him in favor of more successful right-wing candidates. In later years, he discovered that some of his old supporters even questioned his conservatism.[45]

In contrast to Goldwater's struggling political career, the movement he had helped to create surged forward. Ignoring the implications of Goldwater's defeat, supporters, determined to exploit the potential inherent in twenty-seven million votes, sought to continue the momentum from the campaign by enlisting and training new conservatives. Beginning in 1965, former YAF leader Richard Viguerie expanded the grassroots fund-raising technique utilized during the campaign. Drawing names from such varied organizations as the American Economic Foundation, the Committee of One Million, and the newly formed, intellectually oriented Philadelphia Society, he created the first mailing list "containing most of the active Conservatives in the US." Viguerie sold these lists to right-wing organizations who used them to expand their membership and raise money.[46]

So many conservative groups came out of the Goldwater campaign that they competed with one another for the limited time and money of grassroots conservatives. William Rusher complained in early 1965 about the "alarming proliferation of conservative fund appeals." Rusher worried that this trend would end up "emptying" conservatives' pockets and "disillusioning contributors." In addition, some on the Right feared that such a large number of groups divided right-wingers just when they needed to be most united.[47]

Conservatives also worked hard to build a following among the nation's youth. Although left-wing youth groups got almost all the press, a significant number of such young conservative groups existed in the 1960s. Conservatives dominated the Young Republican National Federation and continued to do so throughout the 1960s. Many future elected officials cut their political teeth during the Goldwater campaign as volunteers from the Young Republicans. For their part, Young Americans for Freedom struggled to buck the radical trend on college campuses by holding public rallies in favor of Vietnam and by utilizing radical methods for conservative ends. Another more specialized conservative group was the World Youth Crusade for Freedom which sent nine volunteers to several Asian countries to preach the virtues of capitalism and democracy.[48]

Another outgrowth from the 1964 campaign was the attention mainstream Republican politicians paid to the Right. In particular, Richard Nixon, astute politician that he was, moved rightward as he prepared for the 1968 election. Although he was a centrist rather than a conservative, Nixon "spoke conservatively" enough to win the respect of Reagan supporters such as Donald Lukens, who realized that the candidate emphasized many of the themes Goldwater had advocated during his campaign. Moreover, Nixon's search for the "center" had always been conducted from the Right. He moved Left when he believed it was necessary to build coalitions or to achieve broader goals, but that shift was usually temporary and the extent of the shift was usually quite limited. Clearly, he felt most at home on the Right side of the middle of the road.

In addition, Nixon respected the organization that Clifton White had created from 1960 to 1964, and he attempted to emulate it. In fact, Nixon employed White's techniques and many of his co-workers, including Draft Chairman Peter O'Donnell, Finance Committee member Jeremiah Milbank, Jr., and Head of Field Operations Richard Kleindienst. To make certain that he spoke conservative fluently, he hired Pat Buchanan as speechwriter. Adding to his conservative credentials, Nixon won endorsements from Goldwater and South Carolina Senator Strom Thurmond.[49]

Despite this support, Nixon faced stiff competition from the rising star of the conservative movement: Ronald Reagan. Reagan had made his debut as a conservative spokesman in a highly acclaimed speech supporting Goldwater in 1964. In that address, Reagan demonstrated, as Nixon noted, that he had what Goldwater lacked—"the ability to present his views in a reasonable and eloquent manner." Almost immediately, conservatives encouraged Reagan to run for the governorship of California in 1966. Espousing ideals as conservative as Goldwater's, but presenting them in more attractive form, Reagan kept the California party united as he easily won his race by a large margin. Talk of a Reagan presidency began soon after his gubernatorial victory. The *Houston Post* reported that Reagan represented "a hope for the future" for right-wingers who saw him as a "conservative with enough mass appeal to win a national election."[50] His continued popularity as he dealt with many of the controversial issues of these years reinforced this view.

Reagan delayed becoming a formal candidate for the nomination, however, because he had pledged during his 1966 gubernatorial campaign that he would not enter the race in 1968. As a result, though he went around the country making appearances and articulating his positions on the important issues of the day, his constituents were never certain whether or not he would shed his favorite son status to become a real candidate. In the end, he miscalculated and lost the nomination to Nixon.

Nixon's victory over Reagan did not mean that right-wingers surrendered their influence or abandoned their conviction that conservatism represented the future of the party. In fact, the Right played a crucial role in the campaigns of all the major contenders for the nomination. Since right-wing pressure ensured that Rockefeller really did not have a chance of winning, the main battle ensued between conservatives supporting Nixon and those backing Reagan. Even more significant, the two groups fought over the conservative southern delegations that had been crucial to the nomination of Goldwater in 1964.[51]

In the end, the competition between Reagan and Nixon did not represent a contest between conservatism and liberalism; rather, it was a battle between various types of conservatives. Reagan had grassroots support, but Nixon had the conservative political leaders and that was enough in 1968. In fact, at the time, few Republicans recognized the Right's role in deciding the nomination of 1968. It would be years before the real depth of conservative control of the GOP was realized and even longer before grassroots activists would be able to make their preference known and their power felt. Still, right-wingers' influence in 1968 indicated their political maturity and the party's recognition of their power.

In the meantime, events reinforced the new definitions of conservative goals. In 1968, following the Tet Offensive, millions more Americans lost faith in President Johnson's Vietnam policy.[52] Conservatives were especially frustrated by Tet. For years, they had been pushing Johnson to "fight and win or get out" of Vietnam. They argued that either the military should be allowed to use America's full firepower potential to achieve victory or the whole war should be abandoned. Increasingly their position made sense to growing numbers of Americans.

Other events in 1968 strengthened the conservative movement. After the assassinations of Martin Luther King, Jr. in April and Robert Kennedy in June, Americans feared social breakdown. The 125 riots that followed King's murder greatly intensified those fears. A majority of Americans saw the upsurge of violent antiwar protests on college campuses as one more sign of moral decay created by a too-permissive, too-liberal society. In April 1968, a student protest at Columbia University escalated when militant students took over several university buildings and held them for over a week before the police removed them, sometimes brutally. Other campuses across the country were wracked by similar violent confrontations. Across socioeconomic lines, Americans were disgusted by what they perceived as spoiled, naive student protestors.[53]

Finally, by the late 1960s, the long post–World War II era of economic prosperity was beginning to break down. Lyndon Johnson had promised that he could win the war on poverty and the war in Indochina without straining the American economy. He was wrong. By 1968, the economy was in trouble: a growing trade deficit, volatile international financial markets, and rising inflation. Politicians complained about the overheating economy until Johnson agreed to a 10% income tax increase. Many Americans concluded that they were paying more taxes so that welfare recipients could have bigger checks. In their view, the higher taxes went straight into the pockets of those who were threatening to burn down the cities and increasing the violence on the streets. This analysis, although simplistic, made perfect sense to people eager to see the interconnections of taxes, race, and law and order.[54]

As a result, by spring 1968, Johnson and his liberal policies had lost the support of the American people. The ideas Barry Goldwater had been promoting on a national stage since 1964 no longer seemed "extreme" to many. When he argued that the country was a "morass of indecision, weakness and bankruptcy," people listened. More and more Americans joined what one Michigan constituent called the "revolt" of the "people who are paying the taxes and bearing the brunt of inflation." These unhappy voters turned increasingly to the Right.[55]

The rapid series of social, political, and economic shocks that occurred in 1968 helped strengthen conservatives' power in the Republican Party. Though some people wanted to read the conservative faction out of the party after the 1964 disaster, conservatives had learned from their mistakes and refused to give up their power base. During the 1968 nomination process they proved their determination and political sophistication. Refusing to be carried away by emotion, they successfully backed the most ideologically conservative candidate who could win the nomination. For most, that candidate was Nixon (other conservatives backed Reagan). Conservatives played key roles in the campaign. No longer outsiders in their own party, conservatives now held much of the party machinery in their hands.

Though Nixon won the nomination, Governor Reagan proved crucial to the continued growth of the conservative movement. From the conservatives' perspective, Reagan possessed all the good points of Goldwater without any of his weaknesses: he believed deeply in the principles of conservatism, communicated them in a reasonable manner, and knew when to compromise with moderates. Reagan was a master of the soft-sell. Though he was not the 1968 nominee, the loyalty he engendered among conservatives during the 1968 campaign hinted at the strength he would have in future years.

While Nixon's victory and Reagan's emergence were crucial to the conservative movement, they took on added significance in the context of the changing circumstances of the country. As cities burned and young people fought with the police, many Americans felt their way of life slipping away. Anger and frustration at the political awakening of minorities and at the government's seeming unwillingness to condemn dissidents had caused many white, middle-class citizens to reexamine their faith in Johnson's liberal policies. As political scientist Kevin Phillips predicted in *The Emerging Republican Majority,* white America's response to socioeconomic changes in the black community would eventually result in permanent Republican strength. Phillips added that the movement of the population south and west played a significant role by shifting the locus of power away from the East Coast.[56] Conservatives had a strong institutional and popular base already in the South and Southwest, making it all the easier to bring new converts into the conservative movement.

Barry Goldwater had helped to build that regional and even national framework. Despite his defeat in 1964, his effort served as an important transition stage in the evolution of conservative Republicanism. On the one hand, he provided common ground on which various right-wing groups could meet, exchange ideas, learn about one another, and, for a time at least, agree. Goldwater's campaign united conservatives and showed them that they could win political power. More important, because of the way in which conservatives had gone about securing the nomination for Goldwater, they had created a nationwide grassroots network dedicated to building on the promise of 1964. Far from despairing after Goldwater's defeat, these newly trained conservative converts joined professional politicians in providing the cadres necessary for affirming right-wing control of the GOP.

On the other hand, Goldwater's campaign also proved to be both the last hurrah of the old-line conservatives and the birthplace of more modern conservatism. Fifties'-styled conservatives had supported Goldwater because he voiced their concerns about the continuation of New Deal era programs in the Eisenhower administration, the dangers of the increasingly powerful union movement, and Ike's failure to reduce the budget. Most important, Goldwater had understood, as they did, the dangers of communism both at home and abroad. These men and women, many of whom had stood by Senator Robert Taft in 1952, saw Goldwater's victory at the convention as a reward for their years of work. Caught up in the moment, they failed to recognize the shifting sands beneath them. For even as the old timers celebrated, younger conservatives, determined to learn from Goldwater's defeat, were usurping the elders' power. These new right-wingers understood that a broader base could be built by changing conservative rhetoric to fit the issues of the 1960s: anti-New Deal became anti-Great Society; a dangerous labor movement morphed into a rioting civil rights movement; and anticommunism transformed into a call for a stronger military response in Vietnam as well as an indictment of antiwar protestors at home. In their quest to establish long-term control of the GOP, these new modern conservatives used the American public's alienation from the Johnson administration to gain supporters.

In an ironic twist, 1960s conservatives secured control of the GOP by building on the successes of the 1950s conservatives while eliminating some of the older leaders and redefining the issues. Certainly, the older conservatives remained dedicated to the cause of conservative Republicanism even if they did not always use the catch phrases of the new generation or understand the new causes. Goldwater himself, after an initial period of isolation, returned to the Senate and Republican leadership. Still, he, like many of the 1950s conservatives, did not always fit in with the new right-wing leaders as they worked to consolidate their position within the GOP.

Jeff Roche

COWBOY CONSERVATISM

I don't believe that either Reagan or I started a conservative revolution because for most of our history the majority of Americans have considered themselves conservatives. They have often not voted that way because they were offered no clear choice. I began to tap, and Reagan reached to the bottom of, a deep reservoir that already existed. He came along at the right time and in just the right circumstances to lead a real surge in conservative thought and action.   —Barry Goldwater[1]

One of the most important developments in postwar American political culture was the articulation of "cowboy conservatism." Emerging full-blown in the 1960s, this type of politics, characterized by an intertwined set of ideas that celebrate individual freedom and community responsibility, entrepreneurial capitalism and traditional family, Protestantism and patriotism, has found popular expression using the symbols and myths of the frontier West. Cowboy conservatives crafted a political ideology that managed to stress the importance of individual freedom from government restraint—especially in the form of taxes and regulation—even while promoting the supremacy of their community-shared values—especially in issues of race or morality. Prevalent throughout the West, this ideology was perhaps most unmistakable in the Texas Panhandle, a postwar conservative stronghold. The process of articulating and implementing a cowboy conservative ideology in Texas reveals much about the ways that conservatism emerged across the West and the nation.[2]

The articulation of this conservatism happened in stages. As the decade opened, Cold War anticommunism dominated conservative thinking. Like a sledgehammer, anticommunism, as an ideology, was crude, but powerful. It enabled conservatives to both criticize national liberalism and provide a language that projected their community values. Couching a political philosophy in anticommunist terms forced Americans to define what it meant to be an American in opposition to communism: if communists were atheists, then Americans were churchgoing Protestants. If communists believed that the state should run the economy, then Americans supported unbounded free enterprise. If communists sought a world with no borders, then Americans must preserve all boundaries—individual, family, town, state, national. It was the defense of these boundaries that transformed 1950s anticommunism into 1960s conservatism.

Anticommunism, as a basis for a conservative political philosophy, however, demanded of its adherents a steadfast belief in the abstract threat of an eventual communist takeover of the United States. The conservatism that emerged by the late 1960s, on the other hand, required only the recognition of the very real challenges to the status quo. Historians have clearly acknowledged that, on a national level, rights revolutions, the liberalization of American social policy under the Great Society, antiwar protest, the radicalization of the civil rights movement, the rise of a drug-using counterculture, and the impact of rising street crime, all helped to stimulate a conservative movement. Few, however, have examined these national trends on a local level. Those recent studies of the 1960s, which have shifted the focus away from Berkeley, Madison, and New York and to Middle America, have shown that perhaps the best way to examine the decade is by tracing the transformations that sixties radicalism brought to local political culture.[3] In this essay, I demonstrate the crucial shift from anticommunist crusades to contemporary conservative attitudes by examining the impact that SDS activism, Black Power advocacy, busing, and prairie counterculturalists had on local politics.

Importantly, cowboy conservatives forged their ideology during local battles to define and defend local values. The language of anticommunism proved particularly adept at articulating these beliefs. As was the case across the nation, public education was a crucial site of contestation. In Texas, fights over textbook adoption proved particularly fierce and revealing. Texas provides free textbooks to all students. Public school teachers choose books from a pre-approved list created by a state textbook committee made up of lawmakers and educators. In 1960, Panhandle historian and rancher J. Evetts Haley, a sort of right-wing spokesman-for-hire, and other members of his Texans for America (TFA) politicized the textbook selection process when they burst unannounced into committee meetings. Haley, speaking to the press as much as the committee, charged that too many Texas schoolbooks contained a subtle communist message. He warned that the TFA would, from that point forward, monitor all approved texts to ensure that the schoolbooks used by Texas schoolchildren would reflect only Texas and American values. "Until they [schoolchildren] are old enough to understand both sides of a question," Haley argued, "they should be taught only the American side."[4] The next year, after yet another interruption by Haley and his group, a group of politically motivated Texas legislators demanded statewide hearings on textbook selection.

For Texas conservatives, these hearings provided a public, state-sanctioned forum to broadcast their views on the crucial contest between centralized power and local tradition. Choosing textbooks, as one woman commented, really represented the will of the people against the power of the "self-appointed elite." At the Amarillo hearing, witness after witness agreed that local communities, not some far-off bureaucratic institution, should determine the values to which their children were exposed. One woman went so far as to suggest that textbook companies send door-to-door representatives to each family, so that parents could determine which books their children would use.[5] On the premise of promoting Christian values, one woman denounced a book because it had a favorable mention of Albert Schweitzer, who, she explained, had denied the scientific possibility of the virgin birth and resurrection of Jesus Christ. Couched in the language of anticommunism, the most potent linguistic and political weapon available to conservatives, most witnesses demanded that the state refuse to adopt any textbooks that referred to "world government" or "collectivism." Citing chapter and page, witnesses objected to books that contained any positive reference to those people, ideas, or institutions they deemed un-American, including: the income tax and Social Security, the New Deal and Fair Deal, integration and civil rights, the League of Nations and United Nations, John Dewey and George Marshall. Still others rejected textbooks that did not, in their estimation, do enough to praise patriotism and Protestantism, Joe McCarthy and Douglas MacArthur, big business and laissez-faire economics, or Herbert Hoover and J. Edgar Hoover.[6] As witness and Conservative Club of Amarillo president Mildred Shively put it, "[o]ur real battle [against communism] is not so much of bullets but of wills not of space but of spirit."[7]

At the textbook hearings, Texas conservatives conflated the protection of local values with anticommunism. Not content with simply fighting instances of potential internal communist subversion, most of the witnesses also demanded *their* values—their Americanism—a still largely inchoate amalgam of Christian fundamentalism, patriotism, small-town pride, and frontier individualism be taught to the schoolchildren of Texas.

Anticommunism was more than rhetoric for many conservatives. When they saw the massive and confusing changes in postwar American society—the emergence of the Cold War, a growing youth culture (exemplified by rock and roll), the intensifying civil rights movement, an acceptance of a welfare state—they interpreted these cultural and political shifts as "evidence" of a Soviet conspiracy. Honestly fearing a communist takeover of the United States, they began to look for opportunities to halt what they believed was the disintegration of American values. They sought out the like-minded and determined to save their society. With few outlets to vent their frustration, these conservatives flocked to the anticommunist Christian crusades of Billy James Hargis or to groups like the TFA. The most significant conservative organization in Texas, however, was the John Birch Society (JBS). Although the JBS's national membership was small, and its leader the frequent subject of derision (even in conservative circles), in the Texas Panhandle, the JBS fundamentally altered the tenor of local politics. Convinced that the Kremlin had already penetrated the highest levels of American government and that the communist plot to corrupt America from within was well under way, Massachusetts businessman Robert Welch formed the JBS in 1958 to inform Americans about the dire threat of the communist influence. He attracted thousands of Americans looking for an organization that took communism seriously. Welch recruited regional organizers who formed small local organizations of twenty members; when one group grew too large, it split into two or more groups. With membership rosters secret and local cells virtually independent of a national agenda, the JBS permitted like-minded conservatives an opportunity to organize around a set of local issues.[8]

Not coincidentally, Texas conservatives flocked to the JBS shortly after the Kennedy inauguration. In Amarillo, *Daily News* editor Wes Izzard invited several prominent locals to organize the first Panhandle chapter of the JBS. The former commander of the Amarillo Air Base, General Jerry Lee, then serving as JBS regional coordinator, gave a short talk and then screened a two-hour film featuring Robert Welch. JBS cells multiplied rapidly.[9] Panhandle Texans, nourished for a decade on a steady diet of anticommunism and Americanism in their local newspapers, radio and television news programs, and in civic organization meetings, greedily devoured the JBS philosophy.[10]

Although Panhandle *members* of the John Birch Society were relatively few, the organization was regarded with respect by many for taking the communist threat seriously. As Hop Graham, the folksy editor of the *State Line Tribune* (Farwell, Texas) who was not a member and who depicted Robert Welch as a pompous blowhard, wrote in 1962: "I am pro-John Birch in the sense that I think this group has an important place in helping form American opinions . . . it has done a tremendous and amazing job at stirring people to inquiring into national and international events." Local Birchers, he posited, "are not fanatics. They don't wear arm bands, salute Robert Welch, or burn homes. Like any other movement they have a few over-enthusiastic and misguided souls. But the Birch movement on the whole is not the lunatic fringe it has been made out to be. It is made up mostly of people who reason."[11]

A common joke among Texas politicians was that in the Panhandle one had to join the John Birch Society to gain the "middle-of-the-road" vote. In 1961, that vote elected a Bircher mayor of Amarillo. Jack Seale not only defended the JBS after his victory, but also worked to implement government policy based on Bircher principles. He turned down a federal grant that would have helped the city build a new waste sewage facility. Twice during his tenure, he refused to recognize United Nations Day—a quasi-national holiday. Instead, he proclaimed United States Day. (The Junior and Senior Teenage Republicans used the event as a fund-raiser and sold American flags.) He welcomed right-wing hero General Edwin Walker to the city, proclaiming the visit "American Patriots Day."[12] Seale also lent the city's official welcome to a pantheon of right-wing legionnaires including: Billy James Hargis, Clarence Manion, Dan Smoot, and Tom Anderson. Seale's mayoralty marked a crucial shift in the evolution of conservatism in the 1960s; conservatives had entered the political arena and begun to formulate public policy based on their newly articulated political philosophy.[13]

Despite his successes as mayor, Seale failed in his bid to unseat Democratic Congressman Walter Rogers in 1962. Although Rogers made Seale's JBS membership the centerpiece of his campaign—he consistently warned voters that "a vote for Seale is a vote for the dictatorial John Birch Society"—ultimately the race was more about party politics than ideology. Rogers was a popular and very conservative

Democrat running against an upstart, ultraconservative Republican in a region with almost no Republican infrastructure.[14] Seale resorted to accusing his opponent of fraternizing with the effete Harvard easterners of the New Frontier at the expense of the good folks back home. Although the incumbent Rogers won the election, Seale (one of several Birchers running for Congress that year) still won six of the district's twenty-eight counties and 41% of the votes.[15]

The John Birch Society represented a crucial step in the maturation of cowboy conservatism; it permitted the like-minded, trapped within one-party Texas, to organize at the grass roots and weave their ideas about community, individualism, government, and responsibility into the political system. Buoyed by the success of the Seale mayoral election and even by his failed attempt at Congress, Birchers across the Panhandle engaged the political process. Increasing numbers, usually operating secretly, worked to take over Parent Teacher Associations or school boards. Getting conservatives elected to public office meant organizing beyond a coffee klatch or sandbagging a PTA election, however. Most looked toward taking over the weak local Republican Party.

Just as the John Birch Society attracted a host of ultraconservatives into its folds, another group of conservatives, less concerned with the dangers of internal subversion than with what they saw as the redistributive liberal economic policies of the New Frontier, labored to create a working Republican Party in the heart of Democratic Texas. The men and women who originally built the Panhandle GOP welcomed, often with reservations, the more strident Birch element into the party. For the Birchers, the Republican Party offered an institutional tool to implement a fierce anticommunist ideology. For the organizers of the Republican Party, their organization meant an alternative organization that more closely reflected the political attitudes of the Panhandle. Richard Brooks, former chair of the Randall County Republicans, was determined to build a legitimate, ideologically based two-party system in Texas—regardless of individual candidates. He and his fellow Panhandle Republicans worked, as he put it, "to get that done at the local level."[16]

With only the barest skeleton of a party in place, Panhandle conservatives built the local GOP in their own image. And since conservatives already dominated the Texas Democratic Party, ultraconservatives came to control the Panhandle GOP. Creating and organizing a new party, however, meant that they had to more clearly define conservatism and offer a constructive formula for change. The successful 1961 campaign of Republican senatorial hopeful John Tower helped many elucidate their brand of electable conservatism.[17] Tower's victory demonstrated the potential for political change. What they needed, however, was a national leader who personified their brand of conservatism who could inspire conservative Democrats to join the Republican Party.

In 1964, Texas conservatives found their candidate—Arizona Senator Barry Goldwater.[18] Emerging as the conservative leader of the Republican Party after the death of Ohio's Robert Taft, Goldwater espoused a rugged, western conservatism based less on small-town sensibilities and midwestern isolationism and more on frontier traditionalism and a gunslinger foreign policy. His public persona, a careful blend of the Old and New Wests, lent itself to this new style of conservatism. The grandson of Arizona pioneers, he cultivated a "cowboy" image, often appearing in public wearing boots, jeans, and a Stetson. His Native-American art collection and his photographs of a vanishing West were world-renowned. But Goldwater also represented the vibrant New West; he owned a successful department store, flew jets (he once commanded the Arizona Air National Guard), and was an accomplished white-water rafter. His consistent, strident criticism of postwar liberalism and constant warnings about the danger of communism echoed the voices of that new generation of conservatives coming of age in southern California, the suburbs of Phoenix and Dallas, and the plains of Texas.[19]

Crucial to his popularity among western conservatives was Goldwater's focus on community values and traditions. His book *The Conscience of a Conservative* (1960), widely read among Panhandle conservatives, echoed the message that many in the region had been preaching since the 1930s. Goldwater promoted values, tradition, responsibility to the poor, and local authority. Conservatives, Goldwater argued, "look[ed] upon politics as the art of achieving the maximum amount of freedom for individuals that is consistent with the maintenance of social order." "The Conservative," he explained further, "is the first to understand that the practice of freedom requires the establishment of order."[20] Local GOP leader Richard Brooks called the book a "rallying" cry. Goldwater echoed the ideas of Panhandle conservatives who believed in an individual's responsibility to community welfare, but rejected the federal big government approach.[21]

Goldwater's western conservatism uprooted the term "conservative" from its historical roots. For well over a century, when people thought about "conservatives" they thought of wealthy eastern bankers or industrialists—the sort of silk stocking crowd that appeared in Thomas Nast's cartoons. Goldwater conservatives, on the other hand, were likely to be western, middle-class entrepreneurs or middle-management suburbanites. They were anticommunists who believed in a hard-line foreign policy, especially where the Soviet Union was concerned and had little patience for a policy of coexistence. They, like Goldwater, asked *Why Not Victory?* They agreed with the Arizona senator that it was long past time to dismantle the bureaucracy of the New Deal and abandon the philosophy of big government. Goldwater conservatism closely presaged the political beliefs of Panhandle Texans. In just six years, the percentage of voters who described themselves as "conservatives" would jump from thirty-eight to eighty-two.[22]

Lyndon Johnson, of course, won the 1964 presidential election, even in the Panhandle. Goldwater, however, took eight counties (half his Texas total) and 47% of the region's vote. "Conservatism" still did not resonate with enough voters for a right-wing Republican candidate to defeat a popular native Democratic Texan for the presidency. What Goldwater accomplished, however, was to infuse the local Republican Party with enthusiasm and membership.[23]

After the Goldwater effort, Republicans had an infrastructure in place in the South and Southwest, even in locales long considered Democratic bastions. Equally, Goldwater conservatism was, for many voters, a meaningful stage in the articulation of a new political ideology. Ultimately, however, the brand of politics preached by Goldwaterites required a fairly substantial leap of faith; one had to believe, even in the midst of economic expansion and unprecedented American power, that liberalism would lead to socialism and eventually to a communist takeover of the United States. Put another way, for most, the threats of an expanding Soviet Union, a federal government run amok, and hurtling down the slippery slope of liberalism were just not real enough.

*   *   *

Over the next few years, the chaos of the rights revolutions, antiwar protests, and an emerging counterculture persuaded a majority of Americans to seek out candidates who promised a return to a set of bedrock values understood by all. It was this cultural emphasis that marks the crucial shift in conservative ideology; the growing force of conservatism in the mid- to late sixties was not necessarily a "backlash" against liberalism as much as it was the next step in the formulation of a long-standing core political philosophy. Many of the voters who turned to Ronald Reagan or a host of other conservative candidates (especially at the local level) sought protection for a status quo that had rarely been threatened in their lifetimes. These Americans sensed danger close to home. While the television news brought antiwar protesters, Black Panthers, rioters, Yippies, feminists, and hippies into their living rooms, it was their reaction to local challenges to local society that provided the final and vital step in the articulation of conservatism. Protecting community values became much more than omitting obscure passages in an eighth-grade history book; it meant defending Christianity, family, whiteness, capitalism, and tradition.

Between 1968 and 1972—characterized too often as the "winding down" of the sixties—the civil rights movement, the counterculture, student protests, and antiwar demonstrations moved into the heartland. Panhandle Texans confronted, for the first time, homegrown Black Power advocates, SDS members, Vietnam War protesters, and hippies. Primed by years of watching protests on television, Panhandle Texans had a pretty good idea of how radicals—whatever their form or issue—should be treated. Authorities had little tolerance for those who might challenge the status quo. Still, it was a shock to see local young men and women in tie-dye flashing peace signs and marching down small-town streets to protest the war or advocate civil rights.

Before any protests had erupted at Panhandle colleges, local residents had figured out how college administrators should deal with student troublemakers—they should throw them off campus. One man, when asked in a 1966 survey about student unrest, suggested that "kooks and longhairs be inducted into the army immediately and sent to Vietnam." Another wrote his state senator, "I believe that all students should be expelled and all teachers dismissed at once when they participate in these actions [protests]." Commenting on African-American demonstrations at the University of Houston, one man called the protesters "communists" and suggested that "these outlaws" be "deport[ed] to Africa." The sympathetic recipient of many of these letters, Panhandle State Senator Grady Hazelwood, once wrote: "If you want a real eye-opener—a real education—one on morals, perverts, and queers, you ought to come down here [to Austin] and observe. I am about to believe that there are about as many hippies teaching at the university as there are students."[24] At a meeting of the Muleshoe Rotary Club, former gubernatorial candidate and Plainview attorney Marshall Formby summed up the feelings of most Panhandle Texans when he pointed to college campuses as harbingers of dangerous trends in American society:

> In recent years, the liberal press and the liberal t.v. and the liberal teachers, especially the liberal college teachers, have been teaching our children some things that we don't agree with down here in this Rotary District. They've been teaching our children to be ashamed of their country; they've been teaching our children to be ashamed of their parents, they've even taught our children to be ashamed of our old, dirty, evil capitalistic profit system. . . . They're being taught to be ashamed of America's role at home, and our role in the world. . . . Maybe the stinking sixties, that's what they'll be known as—the period of time when we decided we'd just start obeyin' the laws that we wanted to and not obey those that we didn't want to.[25]

The morality of college students was of particular concern. Grady Hazelwood, mindful of his constituency, waged war on campus liberalism throughout the 1960s. After Hazelwood delivered then published a speech condemning the "Texas Student League for Responsible Sex Freedom," Panhandle Texans praised him. One man congratulated him for his courage to "take a stand for old fashioned morals." Another woman agreed and lamented the changes on campus. "In years gone by there was always that teeny minority [of different-minded folks]—but we both ignored them and ridiculed them and that was the last we heard of them." Another man commented: "I realized a number of years ago, when our government was allowing the communists access to our files and science departments, that we were in for heaps of trouble, but I couldn't imagine an institution of higher learning and culture, tolerating such a sickening thought as [sexual freedom]. It's unbelievable that Universities would allow the uncouth [and] immoral the liberty of degrading [educational] principles," he concluded.[26] Hazelwood complained privately, "Either I am going 'crazy' or this world has left me far behind. I cannot for the life of me understand the spineless, wishy-washy and mealy-mouthed conduct on the part of [state educational] leaders. . . . We have such a shameless lack of leadership in some spots that these minorities are completely taken over."[27]

When local college students began to question American society and the war in Vietnam, reaction by university officials, local law enforcement, and the conservative hierarchy was swift and harsh. Student protest centered on the tiny campus of West Texas State University (WT) and around a group of students who formed a chapter of Students for a Democratic Society (SDS). Hardly the revolutionaries that other SDSers had become by the late 1960s, the WT SDS primarily advocated students' rights, lamented the plight of the working class, and tried to raise campus consciousness on issues of American social policy, race, class, gender, colonialism, and the Vietnam War.[28]

Regardless of their relatively "mild" agenda, university administrators thwarted every attempt to charter the group. Only in spring 1969, after an American Civil Liberties Union lawyer stepped in, were they able to meet publicly and recruit on campus. Even then, they were ostracized by fellow students, harassed by administration officials, spied upon by local police, FBI agents, and army officers from military intelligence, and condemned as dangerous revolutionaries by the local press. The Amarillo *Globe-Times* warned that SDS sought nothing less that the "destruction of the university and the whole social structure of this country." It continued, "although the number of SDS member on any on campus is small (maybe about three dozen undergraduates at WTSU [the actual number of members was never greater than eight]), without the official sanction of the administration, their outside support and revolutionary activism increase their danger out of proportion to their size."[29]

WT administrators, similar to their counterparts across the nation, confronted not just protest, but a massive influx of new students and faculty during the 1960s. Over the course of the decade, fueled by baby boom growth and an explosion of students seeking college draft deferments, WT's enrollment increased by almost 150%. Moreover, the faculty doubled in size and many new professors from outside the region did not share the conservatism of the community.[30] The administration knew that if students became a disruptive influence, the school's relationship with townspeople, alumni, and regents would suffer. As the Dean of Students Paige Carruth put it later: "We were just scared to death that the same thing going on in Berkeley would go on in Canyon."[31] Consequently, local law enforcement, university officials, and town leaders kept a tight rein on any likely student protest.

The most potentially volatile issue was race. Like the rest of the nation, the evolution of the civil rights movement from nonviolent protests against the de jure mechanisms of white supremacy in the South to questioning the economic and social structure of the United States to promoting a scary (to most whites) form of racial nationalism changed the ways that local whites thought about race. When African Americans challenged the status quo, reaction was quick and, initially, proactive. It was the assassination of Martin Luther King, Jr. that spurred WT's black students to action: "We raised our fists," one WT student remembered, "and for the first time, Whites began to fear us . . . and listen." Students and faculty organized a march down Canyon's main street to commemorate King. The Chief of Police, reluctant to even allow the march, ordered marchers to walk two by two and had a deputy film them as they passed. Later that spring, WT's African Americans demanded black organizations, a black student union, and an end to campus racism. Working with the local SDS chapter, several black students organized a successful campus-wide protest of the Kappa Alpha fraternity's "Old South Day"—an annual event celebrating the Confederacy. In response, university officials appointed a special commission to investigate complaints of racist behavior. [32]

The next spring, black power rhetoric grew strident on campus. During a talk by Amarillo NAACP president, Dr. R.W. Jones, in which he urged black students to include whites in their upcoming Afro-American Week celebration, Franklin

Thomas, known for his dissatisfaction with the racial attitudes of the region, jumped up and demanded: "How can we celebrate our heritage by including the white students?"[33] Six weeks later, on the opening night of the Afro-American Week festivities, Bobby Watkins, from Dallas, declared that African Americans' most pressing need was to free black history and identity from the "cultural terrorism" sponsored by whites. The next day, Frank Wyman, president of the Black Student Union at North Texas State University, urged black separatism and self-sufficiency.[34] The actions and words of angry students from SDS and at Afro-American Week convinced many Panhandle Texans that WT was becoming another Berkeley or Columbia. Their conservatism began to reflect their fears of losing control of their own communities from these outside forces. WT was a constant source of tension in the Amarillo press and the university's president began cracking down on troublesome faculty and students.

The shifting political landscape is perhaps best revealed in the popularity of California Governor Ronald Reagan and segregationist firebrand George Wallace among Panhandle conservatives in 1968. The High Plains were Reagan Country long before pundits coined the phrase "Reagan Democrats." As local young people smoked dope, questioned authority, and challenged every moral and racial more, Panhandle conservatives turned to the man who had taken on the Black Panthers, Haight-Ashbury hippies, and Berkeley radicals.[35]

When five-term Democratic State Senator Grady Hazelwood, a lifelong progressive legislator, endorsed Reagan for president in April 1968, he created a ruckus that aptly demonstrates the position of local politics. The Panhandle Democratic hierarchy, mortified by Hazelwood's endorsement of "an extremist candidate," demanded his resignation.[36] Panhandle voters, however, rushed to Hazelwood's defense. Hazelwood received hundreds of letters supporting his decision and only three criticizing his endorsement. The letter writers clearly shared his opinions about the state of American politics. They too feared the growing power of government and the leftward tilt in both political parties. Distrustful of a new generation of civil rights leaders (exemplified by the changing tone of black students at WT) and horrified at the corrosion in American morality, they sought a return to a more simple, just, and orderly America. They justified Hazelwood's endorsement of Reagan by pointing to the shifts in the American cultural landscape. One woman told Hazelwood, "someone has got to stop these anarkists [sic]. Someone has got to use more judgments in these poverty programs. People should work for a living, as I have to do. I resent being robbed (by force) to support more able bodied people than I am." Mrs. Wayne Maddox agreed: "I am fed up with these demonstrators, draft card burners, marchers and all of those who deliberately set out to cause trouble. . . . Personally I used to feel sorry for the Negro, and I still admire those who will get out and work for a living, but I am fed up to HERE with the troublemakers."[37]

Hazelwood's independence mirrored his constituents' shifting partisan loyalties. Echoing many of the letters Hazelwood received, one man applauded Hazelwood's decision: "I was born and raised a Democrat . . . but long ago I put my love of country ahead of my party or any party." Yet another added, "party plat-forms and party labels have become meaningless."[38] Local GOP chair Dick Brooks later commented that Hazelwood's endorsement of Reagan while remaining a Democrat made more of an impact than it would have if he had changed parties.[39] Free to express their vision for America within their new two-party system, facili-tated by a willingness by men and women like Hazelwood to support candidates from the "opposing" party, the number of self-described conservatives continued to grow.

After Ronald Reagan failed to receive the Republican nomination, many Pan-handle conservatives, including some powerful members of the local Republican Party, threw their support to the other "outsider" in the election—George Wallace. As Ed Gill, Thirty-First District Wallace for President chair, commented: "We've had several people coming into our headquarters today who tear off Reagan stick-ers and get Wallace stickers to put on their cars." He added, "I believe the American people are getting tired of the federal government being in everyone's business. . . . And the people are tired of the police being prevented from prosecuting effectively to the full extent of the law. Wallace's platform is so clear and so strong that the common class of people are now looking to him for a change."[40] Clearly Wallace's appeal lay as much in his antagonism toward federal liberalism as his racial atti-tudes. An elaborate study prepared by a political scientist working in the Panhandle confirms the basic conservatism of Wallace's Panhandle supporters.[41] An analysis of hundreds of Wallace voters reveals that they were not simply blindly lashing out against African Americans; instead they were engaged in a political metamorphosis triggered both by abstract national events and changes within their own society. Although angry, disaffected, oriented toward the extreme right-wing, anti-intellec-tual and anti-elite, Wallace voters were still committed to the democratic process.[42] They expressed their ideas in the voting booth.[43]

What attracted many to the Wallace campaign was his position on the Vietnam War—win or get out. The Vietnam War (and the antiwar demonstrations that ac-companied it) proved the final catalyst for most Panhandle voters to join the Re-publican Party and firmly and finally adopt the conservative label. Like other events of the decade, war and protest made its way slowly into Panhandle Texans' con-sciousness. Patriotic Americans, they supported the war effort, but were dismayed at the seeming lack of will shown by Johnson and then Nixon. Bucking national trends, most were willing to not only continue to fight until U.S. forces had won the war, they were also willing to increase the war's scope. In 1970, Panhandle Con-gressman Bob Price, speaking to an enthusiastic crowd in Pampa, said that he would introduce a measure in Congress recommending the use of nuclear weapons in Southeast Asia. "Four hundred of our atomic weapons would annihilate North Vietnam and turn it into a sandy beach," he promised as the crowd leapt to its feet. Two years later, a Panhandle poll revealed that a clear majority of Panhandle Texans justified increasing bombing of North Vietnam: 75% believed that bombing in-creases were necessary to protect U.S. troops, and 70% felt that increased bombing was the best way to force the North Vietnamese into serious peace talks.[44]

In this hawkish atmosphere, a few brave students, ministers, and professors began to speak out against the war. At WT, concerned faculty organized an October 1969 Moratorium Day protest. Interested students, faculty, administrators, staff, and townspeople watched Bernard Fall's film *Last Reflections on the War* followed by a heated discussion over Vietnam. Later that evening, faculty and students held panel discussion of the U.S. role in Southeast Asia.[45] At nearby Amarillo College, a young history professor, John Matthews, almost lost his job for participating in a similar event. Attending a moratorium gathering at a local park, Matthews mildly suggested that it was okay for Americans to discuss military policy in Vietnam. That evening, a local television news program rebroadcast Matthews's words. Overnight, he became the face of local protest. His department head, the dean, and the president all pulled him aside and warned him to stop publicly criticizing the war. When he continued to speak out, the administration punished him by taking away his summer classes (a traditional way for professors to make extra money) and forcing him to teach three night classes the next fall.[46]

After the October protests, the local power structure worked to prevent any further demonstrations. WT administrators even forbade faculty and students from using campus buildings for another moratorium event in November. Even in the heat of 1969, as protests spread across the nation, officials at WT clung desperately to the illusion of an apolitical campus.[47] When enough faculty protested the administration's recalcitrance, the event went forward. Ostensibly, to prevent the "rednecks" from disrupting the demonstration, the administration invited local law enforcement to not only maintain a visible presence, but to secretly tape-record the proceedings. Local police, campus security, and even undercover military intelligence officers from the Amarillo Air Base attended and took note of the participants.[48] State Senator Grady Hazelwood promised school officials that he would make sure that the National Guard would be available in an emergency.

The actions of WT administrators clearly reflected the attitudes of the majority of Panhandle Texans. An October 1969 poll revealed that although close to half of Panhandle Texans agreed that protesters raised "real questions" that should be discussed, 80% believed that the protesters were "giving aid and comfort to the Communists" and that Richard Nixon was right in asking them to stop protesting the war.[49] Local newspaper editors agreed; they called for the dismissal of the faculty who organized the moratorium. WT administrators, after debating whether or not to fire the professors involved (one had tenure), decided that unwanted publicity would only bring negative national attention to the campus.[50]

It was not simply increases in black militancy or student protest that scared many Panhandle Texans; their sons and daughters began to defy local conventions while still in high school. Across the region in the late 1960s locals school administrators quickly enacted new rules concerning hair and dress for students. In Amarillo, male students were not allowed to grow sideburns, mustaches, and beards or wear their hair below their collar. All women (students and faculty) had to wear skirts or dresses that hung below the knees; pants of all types were strictly forbidden. Another local principal explained the need for his school's dress code: "Long hair has come to classify an unhealthy, irresponsible subversive un-American reactionary attitude and personality." In Canyon, the dress code rationalized: "There is a strong relationship between how one is dressed and how one acts. Our student body has long been recognized for being generally appropriately dressed—and our student body has a good reputation for behavior." Teachers also forbade art students to create "peace" signs and those students who wore black armbands to protest the war were expelled across the region. Many school administrators handed out striped red, white, and blue armbands for their students to wear on Moratorium Day.[51]

Crackdowns on "hippies" expanded. Young men with long hair who stopped to buy gas or eat on their way to California or Oregon were often arrested and given a jail haircut. Whenever they spied hippies, Amarillo merchants would call for police to arrest longhairs for violating vagrancy statutes. Before dropping the charges, the police took the young people downtown and, on the pretext of preventing lice, put them in a barber's chair and shaved their heads.[52] In Lubbock, Texas Tech administrators even banned the sale or distribution of the local underground newspaper from campus. In the lawsuit that followed, Tech's attorney blamed *The Catalyst*, which had taken special pains to jab Tech administrators, for increased drug use and radicalism on campus.[53]

The appearance of hippies, student radicals, and black militants in the Panhandle shocked the local citizenry. Besides their attempts to crack down on behavior deemed inappropriate and stifle changes to the status quo, local voters turned to national candidates whose rhetoric promised quick and decisive actions to stem the tide of change. Panhandle Texans, like so many other Americans, were still the type of people who believed in an America where a neighbor could and should be judged by how nicely they kept their yard; "you just know these people pay their bills and have a proud and healthy attitude," commented newspaper editor Tommy Thompson on his neighbor's well-manicured lawn. In the 1972 presidential election, given an opportunity to express their feelings in the voting booth, these lawn-mowing Americans responded with vigor.[54]

Most Panhandle Democrats could not understand George McGovern. How could a man whose positions on the major issues were so different from their own could be the nominee of *their* party, they asked. Polls taken through the fall revealed that Panhandle Texans found McGovern cowardly, addle-minded, indecisive, deceptive, and impractical. Seventy-five percent gave the candidate a negative rating—over half gave the candidate the worst possible rating. Close to 50% agreed that a McGovern victory would be the "worst thing" that could happen to the United States.[55] They might not ever love Richard Nixon, they might not even like him, but they understood him and he understood them. By 1972, they were no longer fighting abstract threats of internal subversion or balancing on the precipice of liberalism; in Amarillo, black militants threatened to burn the city; at West Texas State, some hippie had defaced the ROTC building with a peace symbol; Lubbock teenagers could read the reviews of the latest drugs in the city's underground newspaper. Richard Nixon won 78% of the Panhandle vote. The last presidential candidate to win such an overwhelming majority was also elected during a time of national and local crisis—Franklin Roosevelt.[56]

Since the sixties, conservatism, reflecting changing national issues, has continued to evolve. Conservatives have had to articulate their positions on feminism, abortion, the environment, pornography, affirmative action, gay marriages, national health care, campaign finance, the global economy, stem-cell research, and a myriad of other issues. In the 1970s, many social conservatives found solace within evangelical and fundamentalist Christian churches. The burst of evangelical religion into American culture has also added a dynamic component to the conservative movement. Fundamentalist religion has helped many conservatives find answers in their ongoing spiritual and moral quest.[57] The Republican Party has, since the 1960s, proven a flexible enough vehicle to absorb economic conservatives, social conservatives, and evangelicals. And even the Democratic Party has, in recent years, been dominated by "New Democrats," men and women who combine economic conservatism and a more liberal social agenda. The conservative movement built by ordinary Americans, people like those in the Texas Panhandle, has proven to be one of the longest-lasting political coalitions in American history. The political infrastructure conservatives created in the 1960s to transform philosophy into action has enabled them to respond to four decades' worth of issues quickly, powerfully, and nationally.

"A GREAT WHITE LIGHT": THE POLITICAL EMERGENCE OF RONALD REAGAN

Shortly after being sworn in as governor of California in January 1967, Ronald Reagan delivered his inaugural address. After a few obligatory populist comments about the "simple magic" in the orderly transfer of gubernatorial authority "by direction of the people," Reagan focused on a cornerstone of his speech: freedom. "It is not ours by inheritance," he maintained. "[I]t must be fought for and defended constantly by each generation, for it comes only once to a people." Reagan's use of the word "freedom" differed greatly from the broadly unifying use of the word during World War II and the early Cold War. He used the word mainly to attack liberals' insistent demands that government in the United States had to pursue greater equality and opportunity for its citizens.[1]

Reagan had been honing this sort of rhetoric since the mid-1950s, when he was hired as the celebrity spokesperson for General Electric Corporation. Then, he had defended American freedom from the encroachments of Soviet communism. By the early 1960s, he was accusing the "misguided" liberal architects of "big government" in Washington, D.C., of imperiling freedom at home. In the mid-1960s, Reagan charged urban rioters, "radical" protesters against the Vietnam War, and civil rights activists as the greatest threat to freedom and civility, and that argument swayed California voters in his 1966 gubernatorial campaign. As governor of the most populous state in the nation, Reagan gained a powerful platform from which to promulgate his views. Championing individual freedom and assailing liberals and their redistributive government policies, the charismatic governor became the key crusader of a conservative political movement that reached its apogee with Reagan's 1980 election to the presidency.[2]

Reagan did not enter political life as a conservative. In the 1930s and 1940s, he had supported President Franklin Roosevelt's liberal New Deal social programs.

Enamored of the president, he memorized portions of Roosevelt's speeches and even did FDR impersonations for friends.[3] In 1948, Reagan, a registered Democrat, displayed his liberal stripes by campaigning for liberal Democrat Hubert Humphrey in his first bid to represent Minnesota in the Senate. In 1950, he backed another New Deal-styled Democrat, California Congresswoman Helen Gahagan Douglass, in her unsuccessful U.S. Senate race against her congressional colleague, Richard Nixon. In 1952, the Los Angeles County Democratic Central Committee declined to recommend Reagan as a potential candidate for an open congressional seat because committee members considered him "too liberal." Yet, by 1960, Reagan supported Nixon for president over Democratic senator John F. Kennedy. In a letter to Nixon, Reagan, still a registered Democrat, maintained that "[u]nder the tousled boyish [Kennedy] haircut it is still old Karl Marx—[ideas] first launched a century ago. There is nothing new in the idea of a government being Big Brother to us all."[4]

Though Reagan transformed his political perspective in the 1950s, he later maintained that his politics had changed very little: "I did not move away from the Democratic Party," he asserted. "The party moved away from me."[5] His anticommunism was the critical factor behind his change in parties and perspective. In his 1965 autobiography, Reagan declared, "I was a near hopeless hemophiliac liberal" during the 1930s and World War II, and "not sharp on communism." His naivete about communism, he contended, even led him to join certain groups with communist connections. He began his move to the right in the late 1940s—along with millions of other Americans—when he came to believe that communists planned to take over the Hollywood film industry to establish "a world-wide propaganda base." During this time, Reagan became active in Hollywood politics as president of the Screen Actors Guild (1947–53) and began to associate liberal government not with the altruistic social programs (and antifascism) of the New Deal, but with the "planned economy" attendant to socialism. His antistatism grew in the 1950s with his anticommunist fervor, which was further fueled by his growing dedication to the corporate capitalism championed by his new employer, General Electric.[6] His objections to government bureaucracy and "encroachments" on freedom in the aftermath of the Roosevelt and Truman years were not unusual, but, by the early 1960s, the vehemence of that opposition put him squarely in the ranks of the Goldwater conservatives, who were often derided as "extremists" by their liberal and moderate opponents.[7]

It would take the social tumult of the 1960s to transform the political perspective of enough white middle- and working-class voters for Reagan's views, and conservatism in general, to find firm footing on the American political landscape. Even then, most conservative political aspirants, including Reagan, tempered their criticisms of "big-government" economic policies and offered support for middle- and working-class entitlement programs, such as Social Security, which other conservatives had long criticized. Barry Goldwater learned that lesson the hard way in 1964, when his attacks on Social Security and other popular "liberal" programs contributed to his extremist image and landslide loss to Lyndon Johnson. When Reagan ran for governor two years later, Democratic strategists thought they could effectively portray him as an extremist as well, but they misunderstood both Reagan and the rapid change in California's (and the nation's) political climate. Reagan understood, however, that a majority of Californians believed that the extremists who threatened the "American Way of Life" were not Republican conservatives, but campus radicals, lawless rioters, and their liberal apologists. Reagan's adroit transfer of the extremist label marked a crucial turn in 1960s political culture.

In part, Reagan proved successful in this effort because he, unlike Goldwater, did not come across as a dangerous maverick. Indeed, as biographer Lou Cannon has noted, "Reagan inspired where Goldwater tended to terrify." This talent was first displayed to a national audience the week before the 1964 presidential election. Reagan defended Goldwater by attacking the "socialistic" and "dictatorial" policies of Lyndon Johnson. Reagan described Johnson as a well-intentioned liberal but weak-kneed appeaser. Goldwater, and conservatives in general, he stated, were made of stronger stuff: "We must have the courage to do what is right, and this policy of accommodation asks us to accept the greatest possible immorality." Reagan concluded his speech by offering two starkly different choices: "We can preserve for our children this, the last best hope of man on earth, or we can sentence them to take the first step into a thousand years of darkness."[8]

While the political Reagan was rhetorically brazen yet eloquently reassuring, Reagan the actor had spent a career being simply reassuring. He had turned his natural charm into movie stardom. A fan magazine from that era accurately described Reagan's all-American appeal:

> [Reagan is] the clear-eyed, clean thinking young American in uniform. You can see a montage of American Background when you look at him—debating teams, football, ski parties, summer jobs in a gas station [a lifeguard, in Reagan's case], junior proms, fraternity pin on his best girl's sweater, home for Christmas, home for Easter. Your mother would approve of him. Your dad would talk politics with him while you dressed.[9]

Reagan used this same charm to give shape to his political persona. In his 1966 gubernatorial campaign, Reagan's managers focused on his image as an industrious, self-made young man, cut out for leadership. Campaign brochures informed voters that he had been "President of the [Eureka College] Student Body"; "Captain [of the] swimming team"; and had "Worked [his] way through college."[10]

The best years of Reagan's film career were behind him by the time his outspoken conservative views began to attract attention. To the extent that he was still a celebrity, it was due to his television work, not the movies. As GE's spokesperson, he hosted *General Electric Theater,* which dominated the Sunday-night ratings from the late 1950s to the early 1960s. During this time Reagan also appeared in advertisements for GE, including a three-minute TV ad in which he and his wife, Nancy, gave a tour of their GE-equipped dream house. Perhaps the most visible individual promoter of conspicuous consumption, Reagan, *TV Guide* opined, was America's ambassador "of the convenience of things mechanical."[11]

Despite *General Electric Theater*'s success, the company cancelled the show in 1962 in no small part due to Reagan's increasingly scathing and visible denunciations of government in private and company-sponsored speaking engagements. Coinciding with his change of political registration to Republican, the media commonly referred to him as an actor *and* "prominent conservative spokesman." Reagan later claimed that when GE cancelled its show, speaking tours as far ahead as 1966 had to be cancelled as well, though he maintained private engagements with "[p]eople [who] wanted to talk about and hear about encroaching government control."[12]

In 1965, Reagan, in his natural role of the easygoing good guy, began his last stint as an actor when he hosted, and occasionally starred in, the weekly television series *Death Valley Days,* which chronicled the trials and travails of settlers—both good and bad—in the desert West. An appropriate terminus for Reagan's acting career, *Death Valley Days* was one of the many westerns dominating mid-1960s American television at this time. The western genre reflected essential elements of Reagan's worldview: the wide-open, untamed space of the West represented the boundless opportunity and unbridled freedom that beckoned generations of pioneers—past and present. It also provided a popular cultural crucible for the melding of myth and nostalgia into history by touting the predestined triumph of "civilized" white America in the "wild" West. Commenting in this vein on the popularity of the western, Reagan observed in his 1965 autobiography that the "post–Civil War era when our blue-clad cavalry stayed on a wartime footing against the plains and desert Indians was a phase of Americana rivaling the Kipling era for color and romance."[13] Reagan's romantic view of this bloody period of American history was not unique. However, it portended a pattern in his political life in which he repeatedly glossed over and distorted both disturbing historical events and controversial current affairs.[14]

Reagan's romantic view of the American experience began with his small-town upbringing in the Midwest, which, as he described it, was "one of those rare Tom Sawyer–Huck Finn idylls." That he held on to and purveyed this idyllic perspective during and after the turmoil of the 1960s proved crucial to his political success. In an adroit analysis of Reagan's persona, historian Garry Wills compared Reagan's life to Mark Twain's, noting a distinct similarity: Even later in his life, the then-cosmopolitan Twain "liked to present himself as the untutored voice of the 'natural man'. . . and pretended to less acquaintance with high culture than he possessed." In the glamour and glitter of Hollywood, Reagan, "by the roles given him—as the voice of Midwestern baseball, as the best friend of the star, as the plain-spoken hero of horse epics—was also repeating [this] American instinct to claim a simplicity his circumstances belie, to remain with the innocent at home even as he escaped his [Midwestern] home." Wills observes that with Twain "the pretense was artful, highly conscious, [and] used for cultural satire. With Reagan, the perfection of the pretense lies in the fact that he doesn't know he's pretending."[15] Exuding boy-next-door charm without cynicism, while touting simple virtues in an increasingly complex and chaotic world, Reagan, by the mid-1960s, became the leading conservative romanticist on the "way we were" and "the way things ought to be" in a country increasingly divided over its history, heritage, and place in the world.

By early 1965, many conservatives viewed Reagan as the best person to carry on the conservative movement in the wake of the disastrous Goldwater campaign. The actor cheered California conservatives when he angrily declared after Goldwater's defeat that the California Republican Party "will have no more of those [liberal] candidates who are pledged to the same socialist philosophy as our opposition." [16] Still, he gave no indication that he would run for governor in 1966, and in fact had no desire to do so. But, as he later noted, after his Goldwater campaign speech, "groups and people . . . were just very insistent that I should be the gubernatorial candidate" because he was the best hope "to bring the party back into something viable."[17] In the process of deliberating whether to run for governor, Reagan delivered speeches throughout the state warning of the need to battle the "enemy at our gates" but retreated from his earlier diatribe against "liberal" Republicans and their "socialist" inclinations. Instead, he sought to unite his party: "This is the time for every Republican to look very deep into his own heart and say 'is there possibly any difference I have with another Republican more important than the responsibility of the challenge that faces us in this day?'"[18] Reagan eventually decided to run for governor and tackle that challenge head-on. Believing for some time "that government [had] gone beyond the consent of the governed," Reagan realized that "now I was going to be in a position to deal with it instead of just talk about it."[19]

In early January 1966, the actor-turned-politician announced his formal candidacy for governor in—appropriately enough—a half-hour prerecorded television film. During a live question-and-answer session after the film, Reagan warned against the encroaching control of the federal government. He refused to condemn those described by others as the "radical right." "There is a place in any party," he contended, "for anyone who feels they can support the goals of that party." As if somehow seeking to rise above the usual fray of the political arena, Reagan declared that he was a "citizen politician," and as a Republican would "campaign on the basis that the opposition is the [Democratic] administration in Sacramento." In stating, "I will have no word of criticism for any Republican," he helped maintain party solidarity and largely limited the criticism of his Republican opponent, George Christopher.[20] While Christopher criticized Reagan's lack of political experience, Reagan's campaign staff countered with a "citizen politician" image—a variation, in a sense, on the popular Jimmy Stewart film, *Mr. Smith Goes to Washington* (Sacramento, in this case). "The founding fathers of this country were not professional politicians," Reagan observed. "They were citizen politicians." Ignoring the complexities of running a modern state government, especially one the size of California, he contended that individuals outside the realm of government service should "make their talents available to help solve the state's problems that baffle professional politicians."[21]

Among those vexing issues, civil rights, which had become intertwined with property rights, was subjected to heated debate. Almost all the conservatives in

Congress (including southern Democrats) had opposed the landmark 1964 Civil Rights Act, which they believed conferred privileges to minorities at the expense of the rights of others. Reagan shared and espoused this belief. During a campaign appearance at the state convention of the National Negro Republican Assembly, Reagan was asked how black Republicans could "encourage other Negroes to vote for you after your statement that you would not have voted for the civil rights bill?" Defending his opposition to the bill, Reagan responded that he favored the aims of the act but could not support "a bad piece of legislation." Attending the event with Reagan, Christopher made clear that he had supported the bill and contended, "[u]nless we cast out this image [of not supporting civil rights legislation] we're going to suffer defeat." To the surprise of most everyone, the normally unflappable Reagan shouted, "I resent the implication that there is any bigotry in my nature. Don't anyone ever imply that I lack integrity." He then stormed out of the hall. Believing his opponent had inferred he was a racist, Reagan, after returning, apologetically told the audience, "[f]rankly I got mad."[22]

The actor clearly did not see himself as bigoted in any way, which he made clear in his 1965 autobiography. Repeatedly equating his life with that of ordinary Americans (his Hollywood years notwithstanding), Reagan recalled that his father taught him "that all men were created equal and that a man's own ambition determined what happened to him after that." As a movie star, he participated in productions that assailed the Ku Klux Klan and racism in general. In December 1945, Reagan spoke at a southern California rally against the discrimination many Japanese-American veterans experienced after World War II. "America stands unique in the world," he declared, because it is "a country not founded on race, but on a way and an ideal."[23] Despite his many declarations against racism, Reagan believed that the quintessential American ideal was individual freedom, and the chief individual virtue, in keeping with the words of his father, was ambition unfettered by government interference.

Defending his largely laissez-faire view of race relations in a 1980 interview, Reagan proclaimed, "I will weigh my fight against bigotry and prejudice against that of the most ardent civil rights advocate, because I was doing it when there was no civil rights fight."[24] Though he inflated the magnitude of his actions, he was no racist. Yet at the time of his 1966 campaign he prominently displayed civic awards in his home from Orval Faubus and the unreconstructed racist Ross Barnett, two southern governors who had resolutely blocked federally mandated integration in public education institutions in their respective states. Though Reagan professed on the campaign trail that "freedom can't survive in a nation that tolerates prejudice or bigotry,"[25] he apparently simply saw what he wanted to see in Faubus and Barnett: two dedicated defenders of states' rights. He proved smilingly resistant or oblivious to anything ignoble about individuals or causes he liked when these undesirable realities threatened the foundations of his worldview and politics.

Having had little success in depicting Reagan's views on civil rights as out-of-step with the Republican "mainstream," Christopher charged that Reagan's ideological swing from Left to Right occurred so quickly "it might indicate instability of some sort."[26] Reagan's move to the Right was neither rapid nor as extreme as Christopher had suggested, and certainly did not indicate emotional instability. Other influential conservatives had in fact journeyed much further along the ideological spectrum. For example, a number of former members of the American Communist Party could be found among the editors of the stridently conservative *National Review*. Several of these men defended the western conservative tradition with a Christian moral angst, integrating reason with faith in God.[27] In moving from New Deal liberalism to Goldwater conservatism, without discarding his admiration for FDR, Reagan skimmed the intellectual surface of liberal and conservative theory. He had neither the desire nor the capacity to plumb the theoretical depths of his convictions like his cohorts at the *National Review*. Nevertheless, at the outset of Reagan's primary campaign, the *Review's* editor, William F. Buckley, the conservative movement's celebrity intellectual, pronounced Reagan a "true conservative, who recognizes limits of political action." This "true conservative," still exuding the charm of the boy-next-door and transcending his intellectual limitations with a flair Goldwater sorely lacked, defeated Christopher by a wide margin.[28]

Reagan's opponent in the general election, Democrat Edmund "Pat" Brown, Sr., was seeking a third term as governor and, unlike Reagan, had decades of political experience. Beginning his political career as a Republican, Brown switched his registration to Democrat in 1934 and became a party activist. Elected as San Francisco's district attorney in 1943, Brown, in 1950, successfully ran for state attorney general. He defeated conservative Republican William Knowland, the minority leader in the U.S. Senate, in his 1958 campaign for governor. Brown's liberal vision for California accommodated the state's great postwar population and economic growth. His master plan for state-supported higher education and efforts to improve state infrastructure and water projects were widely commended. In 1962, Brown defeated an even more formidable opponent, former Vice President Richard Nixon.[29] With two impressive electoral victories behind him, it did not seem likely that Reagan, the political neophyte, would pose much of a challenge. By 1966, however, Brown seemed to be caught in the undertow of liberalism's waning current, as social upheaval in California (and elsewhere in the country) cast doubt and scorn on liberal programs and politicians. These sentiments strengthened the gubernatorial candidacy of the conservative Democrat Sam Yorty, who had been elected mayor of Los Angeles in 1961 and reelected in 1965. Yorty, a one-time New Deal liberal, echoed Reagan in charging that the governor had become beholden to "left-wingers." Brown in turn called Yorty a right-wing "fright-peddler." Nevertheless, the mayor's popularity with conservative Democrats garnered him almost one million votes in the June primary. Brown won by 300,000 votes, but the fact that Yorty, "a transparently hack politician," as one Brown aide later observed, could mount a serious challenge to the governor revealed the latter's political vulnerability.[30]

Brown's greatest weakness was his inability to find the middle ground on a host of fast-moving political issues. In part, the governor's problems grew out of his strong support for the Rumford Fair Housing Act in 1963, which, with limited exceptions, extended the ban on discrimination in the sale or rental of all private dwellings. The Democrat-controlled California legislature, at the behest of Brown and behind the legislative leadership of Jesse Unruh, passed the act in the final days of the 1963 session. Powerful opponents of the bill sought to repeal it through a referendum in 1964, and that effort gained broad support among voters. Reagan and other notable Republicans vigorously backed the measure, while Brown called the petitioners for the referendum "the shock troops of bigotry."[31]

Reagan predicated his support for the repeal on the "sacredness" of property rights and individual freedom, and other individuals and groups followed suit. These groups distributed red, white, and blue pamphlets, emblazoned with "FREEDOM," which trumpeted the right to "rent or sell to whom you choose" and featured sketches of happy, white, middle-class families outside their cherished suburban homesteads.[32] The message seemed clear: The Rumford Act threatened lily-white suburban life. At the polls in November 1964, Californians—including many white Democrats—voted by a two-to-one margin to repeal the Rumford Act, but the issue remained contentious.

Further fueling the debate on race and rights, three weeks before the 1966 primary elections, the California Supreme Court ruled the repeal of the Rumford Act unconstitutional. Reminding voters that Brown had referred to petitioners for the repeal referendum as bigots, Reagan declared that all "of us are losers if we allow this precedent [against the rights of voters—and property owners] to be established."[33] In an attempt to counter Reagan's assault on the court's action, Brown's advisers released documents showing that the actor had signed a "Caucasion-only" race covenant for a home he had purchased in 1941. Reagan countered by reiterating his standard denunciation of "the sickness of prejudice and discrimination," but maintained that, in a free society, citizens have a "basic and cherished right to do as they please with their property. If an individual wants to discriminate against Negroes or others in selling or renting his house he has a right to do so."[34]

In addition to championing property rights, Reagan focused on the "law and order" necessary to quell civil unrest. Initially targeted at student unrest in Berkeley, his law-and-order theme gained wider application after the devastating August 1965 riots in Watts, a culturally vibrant but impoverished African-American section of south central Los Angeles. The riots had left thirty-four dead and reduced parts of Los Angeles to rubble. The harrowing images of the riots, along with a near-riot there in March 1966, made "arson and murder" in Watts a salient issue for Reagan, who connected the riots to the liberal social policies touted by Brown, and to his lack of leadership. An increasingly desperate Brown charged Reagan with "riding the white backlash." Despite his frequent public condemnations of "Negro unrest," Reagan claimed that it had never been his intention "to attempt to capitalize on such tragedy [as Watts] for political purposes." He maintained that the race issue reflected "nothing more than the concern people have for . . . extremists in the civil rights movement" and portrayed himself as simply trying to bring order to the social and moral chaos wrought by failed liberal policies. Criticizing the nascent "black-power" movement, Reagan expressed his hope that the "more responsible elements of the Negro community" would repudiate African-American leaders who had abandoned the "orderly process of appealing wrongs through legitimate channels."[35]

Another potent issue, campus protests at Berkeley, provided Reagan with a matrix through which he ably exploited and intertwined the key issues of antiwar protests, race relations, and morality. In so doing, he touched a nerve among the many working- and middle-class parents whose children attended or planned to attend Berkeley or other California colleges and universities. Brown could not afford to vehemently attack campus antiwar activists given the rising opposition to U.S. policy in Indochina among his left-leaning Democratic constituents, including numerous activists in the influential California Democratic Council. Reagan therefore gained an advantage in terms of unabashed patriotism, for he freely castigated those dissenters. Not lacking help from his supporters in this regard, Reagan experienced a powerful campaign moment in the small town of Lakeport, when a uniformed G.I., his face scarred by a shrapnel wound, placed a California flag in the candidate's arms and exhorted: "You go get yourself some of those Berkeley Cong, Mr. Reagan."[36] Blending salient issues more subtly, the actor further inflamed the controversy over a black-power rally scheduled at UC for late October, declaring, "we can not have the university . . . used as a base to foment riots from." Concerns about sexual immorality on campus provided Reagan with another potent UC issue, particularly when he spoke of "sexual orgies" there, "so vile I can not describe them to you."[37]

Meanwhile, Brown's political base grew increasingly fractious. Reagan's emphasis on "moral decency" played well with some traditional but socially conservative Democrats, particularly with labor union members tired of Brown's tolerance of "the filthy long-haired . . . scum at Berkeley" and his "whitewash of the Negroes" arrested for rioting. On the other hand, labor groups on the left, such as the International Longshoreman's and Warehouseman's Union, urged Brown to end his retreat from liberalism and "fire the imagination" of the many people "who were once your most ardent supporters," specifically, labor, minorities, and liberal and "middle-of-the-road" groups. Polls revealed that Brown's labor support had dipped dramatically. He had won 78% of the labor vote in 1958, when he defeated William Knowland, the right-to-work candidate; but that support dropped to 57% by the fall of 1966.[38]

In a campaign memo, one of Brown's political operatives maintained that Reagan was engaged in a right-wing "conspiracy" to "divide and conquer . . . the working people . . . by using the race issue."[39] Though not a conspiracy in any strict sense, the memo accurately identified a trend-setting conservative strategy that grew out of Goldwater's electoral success in the South. Due to the broad Democratic support for the 1964 Civil Rights Act and the 1965 Voting Rights Act, both of which were touted by Lyndon Johnson, the "race issue" was now clearly tied to the Democrats. The party's vocal left wing, led mainly by affluent individuals with college degrees, largely controlled the activist element within the party.

As historian Lisa McGirr has noted, the "issues they championed were not the traditional economic majoritarian bread-and-butter New Deal ones that had ensured the loyalty of lower-middle-class white ethnic voters to the party, but a rights-based liberalism that championed the interests of African Americans and the poor."[40] One of Reagan's veteran campaign managers later highlighted the opportunity that this new emphasis created: "It was the first time we came up with the category 'white conservative Democrats'. . . . we really went after them." In fact, Reagan spent so much time wooing these voters that some of his "grassroots" Republican supporters complained of being neglected when Reagan's campaign team turned down speaking invitations from them. Seeking to placate a disgruntled California Republican Assembly (CRA) chapter president in a letter, Reagan said he understood "all the people in your group thinking they've been abandoned," but "we [now] must count on our friends while we turn our attention to getting those Democrats who voted for Yorty."[41]

The occasional disgruntled Reagan disciple notwithstanding, Reagan's charismatic candidacy stirred his many ardent supporters. Angeleno Jud Leetham, a prominent Republican activist, proclaimed: "There's a messianic thing about [Reagan]—a great white light."[42] Reagan enjoyed the adulatory support of conservative grassroots organizations such as the CRA and the even more conservative United Republicans of California. While the foot soldiers of the Republican Right maintained their vigilant commitment to Goldwater's principles, their tactics became less obstreperous. As a Republican state party official explained, during the Goldwater crusade the senator's workers "would ring a doorbell, and if the man answering it said he didn't like Goldwater they had the impulse to grab for his throat."[43] That changed with Reagan's candidacy. Bellicose zealots surely remained, but by and large, the Republican Right, effectively emulating its new star, had learned the virtue of the softer sell. Even the purported "kooks"—such as John Birch Society members—seemed to realize the need to maintain a low profile and for Reagan to remain more than arm's length from their activities and statements. "They saw Reagan as more electable, more genial than Goldwater," historian Matthew Dallek has observed. "If they had to endure a few slights, they would do so for the larger cause."[44]

Reagan clearly understood the importance of party unity and tempered rhetoric. In a letter to fellow conservative and friend George Murphy, Reagan expressed optimism that Republicans would remain "glued together, if only we can keep some of the kooks quiet." In Reagan, of course, right-wing Republicans had found a candidate with that long-sought balance between electoral popularity and ideological commitment, the prototype of the new conservative populist. He proved to be a "goddamned electable person," as one "citizen advisor" put it.[45] Rewarded for his citizen politician role by receiving strong support from a broad spectrum of white voters, Reagan defeated Brown in a landslide. He led California Republicans—and conservatives in particular—back to Sacramento. In a letter to Goldwater that subtly signified the passing of the torch, Reagan saluted his erstwhile mentor and the principles he had espoused in 1964:

You set the pattern and perhaps it was your fate to just be a little too soon, or maybe it required someone with the courage to do what you did with regard to campaigning on principles. I have tried to do the same and have found the people more receptive because they've had a chance to realize there is such a thing as truth.[46]

Reagan downplayed his own appeal with typical modesty, but, as one of his biographers has stated, Reagan, unlike Goldwater, succeeded in good part because he was "a thundering conservative without being thunderous."[47] He often used blunt and alarming language to delineate the forces of good and evil in his speeches; yet references to the "poet Belloc" or the "great French philosopher Alexis de Tocqueville" gave his oratories an element of erudition that combined with his mellifluent delivery and pervasive charm to make him a compelling figure to a wide audience. Though Reagan received criticism for his "Kiwanis Club" oratorical style, it helped distinguish him from shriller voices on the right, such as George Wallace and his anti-civil rights assaults on "welfare chiselers" (a coded reference to blacks). Historian Dan Carter noted that Wallace "thrust himself forward as the authentic defender of the 'common man'" with a raw energy that the "soothing" and "avuncular" Reagan lacked.[48] Carter is quite right; but the appeal of Reagan's "soothing" message was in those very feel-good encapsulations of the politics of resentment, which enabled him to capitalize on those resentments with a greater number of voters than Wallace, the abrasive racist, could ever hope to win over.

Having predicated his campaign on moral decency and fiscal responsibility, Governor Reagan in 1967 promised to make every effort to ensure that the state's colleges and universities "buil[t] character on accepted ethical and moral standards," and to "seek solutions to the problem of unrealistic taxes."[49] As a member of the University of California Board of Regents, he pleased conservatives when he led the successful effort to oust UC president Clark Kerr, whom conservatives accused of "coddling" campus demonstrators, and he continued to be a fervent adversary of left-wing demonstrators at UC and other state campuses. Nevertheless, while his rhetoric remained that of a populist conservative throughout his gubernatorial years, his actions often differed from his oratory, though the latter helped mask his deviations from right-wing principles. Despite the governor's desire to curtail state spending, he discovered that due to California's rapid growth and the unavoidable costs of most state programs, many of which were mandated by law, he would have to substantially increase the state budget. In fact, he soon found himself in the awkward position of having to "bite the bullet" and sign the largest tax increase in the history of any state up to that time. Reagan's refusal to challenge these budget hikes and attendant tax increases angered fiscal conservatives. He also dismayed many supporters who anchored themselves to right-wing social issues when, under pressure even from members of his own party, he signed the Beilenson Bill, which enacted the most liberal abortion law in the nation. Overall, Governor Reagan's actions in 1967 reflected the fact that governing as an ideologue proved far harder than campaigning as one. He therefore moved closer to the pragmatic center.[50]

Another major disappointment for conservatives came during the 1967 legislative battle to once again repeal the Rumford Fair Housing Act after the state Supreme Court invalidated the initial repeal of the act by California voters. Reagan did not endorse a Rumford repeal bill until William Bagley, a moderate Republican assemblyman, added significant amendments that watered the bill down so much it displeased not only conservatives *and* liberals in the legislature, but also the powerful California Real Estate Association (CREA). Given that Reagan's support, even for the amended bill, was tepid, and that opposition to the bill had grown after the amendments, the legislation died. The governor's position on the bill vexed both opponents of the Rumford Act, who believed Reagan had abandoned them, and proponents. "I don't believe the governor knew what he was doing," claimed the act's author, former Democratic Assemblyman Byron Rumford, an African-American businessman from Oakland. Reagan later claimed to have reversed his position on the Rumford Act after meeting with "members of the minority community" with whom he had little contact during the campaign. "When I realized the symbolism of [the act]. . . and how much it meant morale-wise [to blacks]. . . I frankly said no" to the repeal. Bagley, however, vividly recalled receiving a phone call from Reagan aide Phil Battaglia, asking Bagley to devise a way to "kill" the repeal bill so that Reagan, with the 1968 presidential election looming, wouldn't have to face the political consequences of having the bill on his desk for his signature or veto.[51] In September 1967, speaking to the annual CREA convention, Reagan renewed his pledge to fight for the repeal of the act during the next legislative session, but he never earnestly renewed that fight.[52]

While Reagan proved ambivalent about civil rights, his view of liberal welfare programs—another racially charged issue—bordered on outright contempt. In his 1966 campaign, Reagan was reluctant to criticize welfare, thinking that it "might be a dangerous subject, something like Barry [Goldwater] and Social Security." He soon discovered, however, that reducing welfare rolls was a concern among the audiences he addressed, and he responded accordingly.[53] By 1968, this issue grew more salient, as reflected in the popularity of buttons and bumper stickers that declared: "I Fight Poverty: I Work!" or "Join the Great Society: Go on Welfare." Increasing his speaking engagements across the country in early 1968, Reagan told an audience at the University of Pittsburgh in January that the Great Society "is a complete failure" and that "we [must] stop being our brother's keeper and become our brother's brother so he can take care of himself." He blasted liberals who sought to "institutionalize" the poor by "keeping them in poverty and degradation."[54] He acknowledged that certain welfare recipients were truly needy, but the image of the black "welfare queen" (supplanting Wallace's "welfare chiseler"), which became a mainstay of Reagan's diatribes in the late 1970s and during his presidency, sprang from resentments and depictions that first surfaced in the 1960s. Similar to his views on crime, the governor maintained that welfare "dependency" could be linked to a "loosening of morals, a drifting away from tried-and-true principles" and individual responsibility.[55]

Reagan believed the public worried most about the decline in morality, which weakened the country's binding social fabric,[56] and he carried that message to the Republican National Convention in Miami where he unsuccessfully sought his party's presidential nomination. After turning back Reagan's challenge in Miami, Richard Nixon went on to win the presidency—albeit narrowly—largely by campaigning on Reagan's issues: the values of "decent" Americans, the wrong-headedness of antiwar "radicals," anarchy on college campuses, and government heavy-handedness on civil rights.

Not long after his return from Miami, Reagan found himself embroiled in another battle in the nascent "culture war" after a group of Berkeley students invited the controversial black nationalist, Eldridge Cleaver, to teach an accredited course on racism. Reagan adamantly opposed this invitation. Cleaver subsequently led a crowd of 5,000 in Berkeley's Sproul Plaza in a repeated chant: "Fuck Ronnie Reagan!" After Cleaver challenged Reagan to a duel, Reagan chose the weapons: words of more than four letters each.[57]

Militant demonstrations against the Vietnam War and in support of minority academic programs continued into the following year at Berkeley and San Francisco State University. Reagan responded in accordance with the widespread public disapproval of these demonstrations, declaring that campuses would be kept open "by bayonets if necessary." Reagan also warned that conservative students, such as members of the Young Americans for Freedom, might be provoked to "counterviolence" against left-wing campus militants.[58]

In the summer of 1969, at the Woodstock Music Festival in New York, Reagan was firmly etched into the counterculture's demonology. Folksinger Joan Baez and her band dedicated a song to Reagan in which he was depicted as a racist redneck, indeed, as "the head of the Ku Klux Klan."[59] Reagan certainly did nothing to soften his image in dealing with campus unrest when, in an April 1970 speech to the Western Growers Association, he averred, "If it's to be a blood bath, let it be now." He later said that the statement was just a figure of speech, but he continued to attack the counterculture—the "Woodstock Nation," in popular parlance—and campus protests as his reelection campaign geared up.[60] Addressing the annual convention of the California Republican Assembly in 1970, Reagan lamented that when "poverty-stricken mothers" have to watch "shaggy dropouts" use food stamps to buy steaks, "[t]he Age of Aquarius smells a little fishy." In another speech, the governor stated, the "academy . . . is not to be a privileged sanctuary for those who would destroy society; it must not be used as a staging area for insurrection."[61] Even though Reagan never broke the control of the liberals who dominated the UC system, and Berkeley radicals declared victory over the governor in a prominent local conflict, both liberals and radicals were "astonished" by Reagan's popularity and "drastically underestimat[ed] the force of conservative impulses" in California and across the country. Reagan ultimately emerged from this long confrontation a "winner," historian W. J. Rorabaugh has noted, because his "contempt for liberals and opposition to Berkeley radicals helped him . . . [win] the White House" in 1980.[62]

His contempt for and opposition to liberals and radicals, along with his simple advocacy of "good government," helped Reagan win reelection as governor in

1970. His opponent, Jesse Unruh, the former powerful speaker of the state assembly, tried to finesse Reagan's politicization of campus demonstrations and curricula into a campaign issue, but found little traction with that argument because Reagan represented the majority of Californians. Unruh tried to portray Reagan as a "tool of the rich." To make his point, he held a Labor Day press event in the driveway of the Bel-Air mansion of prominent Reagan supporter Henry Salvatori. He lambasted Reagan's failed attempt to create the "Henry Salvatori tax relief fund." Although Reagan's tax plan (which had failed by only one legislative floor vote) did have significantly more breaks for wealthier taxpayers than those in lower brackets, the public held little interest in the arcane details of the now-dead plan. Reagan responded to Unruh's charge that he was beholden to his rich backers by asserting that the "only thing they [his wealthy supporters] ever told me they wanted was good government."[63]

Reagan campaigned on his good-government theme, citing his citizen-politician record and vision for the future, with jabs at obstructive Democrats. "When you get your property tax bill this year," one campaign ad stated, "remember—it could have been cut." Tax relief, the ad vowed, "would be the first order of business next year" for Governor Reagan.[64] Reagan also pledged to clean up California's "welfare mess" and claimed that Americans "had never been more determined to bring decency and order to the world." Echoing Reagan shortly before election day on behalf of Republicans in races across the nation, President Nixon declared: "The time has come for the great silent majority of Americans of all ages to stand up and be counted against the appeasement of the rock throwers and the obscenity shouters."[65] Despite Nixon's plea, Republicans fared poorly in 1970, but Reagan emerged victorious, albeit by a slimmer margin than in 1966.

Just as anticommunism gave Reagan an explanation for and an alternative to his declining Hollywood career in the 1950s, the turmoil of the 1960s provided him a sense of purpose for his political career that would take him to the presidency.[66] In 1976, Reagan challenged President Gerald Ford for the Republican nomination by campaigning against the socially corrosive effects of 1960s liberalism. During a nationally televised address shortly before the Republican convention, he declared, "[F]or too many years a philosophy of government has dominated Washington . . . that works against the values of the family and the values that were so basic to the building of this country. I believe this is the central issue of this campaign and of our time." He narrowly missed taking the nomination from Ford, but his message on values (and taxes) resonated with many voters. In his 1980 speech accepting the GOP presidential nomination, he pledged "to renew the American spirit and sense of purpose," and "to carry *our* message to every American . . . who is a member of *this* community of shared values"[67] (emphasis added). During Reagan's 1984 reelection campaign, his ads trumpeted the theme of renewal, primarily through this declaration: "It's Morning Again in America." The ads hailed not only the recovery of the long-slumping economy, but the renewal of the values that embroidered Reagan's main-street past, that community of "shared values." Though this "renewal" often divided Americans as much as it unified them, the Reagan "revolution" pushed liberalism, which had reached its apex in the 1960s, to the margins of American political life. Ironically, the sixties proved crucial to the conservative movement by providing the cultural milieu that served as a springboard for its success.

No one played a greater role in the movement's success than Ronald Reagan. After he entered the political arena, he adroitly rode the crest of a wave of conservative public opinion that had initially been shaped by the Cold War, and then by resentment of the welfare state and the counterculture's assault on the "American way of life." When Reagan ran for and won the presidency, those resentments still resonated with voters, and they ultimately put their hopes in a man whose values and ideals wistfully aligned with their own.

Donald T. Critchlow

CONSERVATISM RECONSIDERED: PHYLLIS SCHLAFLY AND GRASSROOTS CONSERVATISM

In 1959, writing in the first issue of the conservative magazine, *The Freeman,* the editors declared, "In terms of labels, *The Freeman* will be at once radical, liberal, conservative and reactionary. It will be radical because it will go to the root of questions. It will be liberal because it will stand for the maximum of individual liberty. . . . It will be conservative because it believes in conserving the great achievements of the past." So too, they concluded, would the journal be reactionary if this meant reacting against reckless efforts to destroy "our great economic, political and cultural heritage in the name of alleged 'progress.'"[1]

A few years after this proclamation, political scientist Clinton Rossiter, in his insightful and at times persnickety dissection of the conservative tradition, *Conservatism in America: The Thankless Persuasion* (1962), exclaimed, "I must confess that when I came across this statement, I considered throwing my notes to the wind and taking up botany, a science whose practitioners have come to some agreement on terminology."[2]

If Rossiter found himself perplexed by the rhetoric of postwar conservatism, he was not by any means alone among those historians and social scientists who grappled with coming to grips with the sudden emergence of a growing right-wing movement in the late 1950s and early 1960s. The ascendance of the political Right in the Republican Party, leading to the nomination of Barry Goldwater in 1964, caught many commentators by surprise. Hard right-wing conservatism did not seem to fit easily into the American liberal tradition that had been so carefully delineated by scholars who had come of age during the New Deal and World War II. Reflecting on their own political outlook, this generation of scholars constructed a paradigm that equated the American political tradition with liberalism.[3]

In this liberal paradigm, conservatism had little, if any, place in American political thought. Thus, literary critic Lionel Trilling could write in his classic study, *The Liberal Imagination* (1950), "liberalism is not only the dominant but even the sole intellectual tradition" in America; and while he conceded that a reactionary impulse could be found, it expressed itself only in "irritable mental gestures which seem to resemble ideas."[4] This perspective that the Right stood outside the American political tradition, and the corollary that conservatives frequently displayed psychological disorders, set the tone for much of the scholarship on conservatism until the early 1980s. The ascendancy of conservatism in the 1980s led scholars to reexamine its place in American history.[5]

A new narrative of American politics that fully incorporates this new scholarship on postwar American conservatism remains to be written. At the same time, the history of conservatism itself needs further exploration, both empirically and conceptually. As a consequence, questions remain as to the ideological roots of conservatism, organizational and political differences within the conservative movement, and the general development of American conservatism over the last half-century. In short, we need to accept Clinton Rossiter's ironic suggestion that we dissect American conservatism as a social movement to determine its etiology, taxonomy, and development.

This essay offers an exploration of some of these fundamental questions of the origins and course of American conservatism through the early career of Phyllis Schlafly before she organized the Stop ERA movement. While best known for her leadership in defeating the Equal Rights Amendment in the 1970s, she began her involvement in conservative Republican politics in the late 1940s and continued this work as a Republican candidate for Congress in 1952, president of the Illinois Federation of Republican Women, anticommunist crusader, and author of the best-selling *A Choice Not an Echo* in 1964. In addition she co-authored with Admiral (Ret.) Chester Ward a number of widely read books on defense policy and strategic balance that outlined the Right's critique of arms reduction treaties and "peaceful coexistence" with the Soviet Union. Her activities in the late 1960s and 1970s played a decisive role in the revival of a dormant conservative movement that led to the election of Ronald Reagan in 1980.

Schlafly's political outlook in the pre-Reagan, post–World War II era is reflective of the major strains in postwar American conservative thought. In her political outlook she—like much of the conservative movement—combined a libertarian espousal of the virtues of private enterprise and individual responsibility with a Burkean approach that expressed a profound faith in tradition, social custom, and Divine authority. These two strains—libertarianism and traditionalism—were held by the conservative movement in uneasy and, at times, volatile contradiction to one another. More concretely, as Schlafly's political development reveals, the origins of postwar conservatism can be found in Cold War anticommunism, which activists saw as a worldwide conspiracy directed from the Soviet Union, in hostility to the New Deal welfare state, and in American globalism embodied in the United Nations. Religion played an essential role in the anticommunist movement, especially traditional Roman Catholicism and evangelical Protestantism.

Furthermore, postwar conservatives, including Schlafly, showed greater concerns about communism and statism, in general, than they did about race relations. Although there were some anti-Semites and segregationists on the Right, most conservative leaders frequently pointed out that it was a common ploy of the communists to play on racial and social divisions in American society.[6] Robert Welch, founder of the John Birch Society, in his three-day seminar on communism, devoted an entire lecture to how "three-quarters" of racial and religious division in the world is stirred by 'the Reds.' "[7]

Schlafly's successful writing career in the 1960s demonstrates another critical aspect of postwar conservatism. Too much importance has been placed on the role of intellectuals in forming this movement. Conservatives writing their own histories of the movement are given to Richard Weaver's asseveration that "ideas matter." Intellectuals, even of the conservative persuasion, tend to emphasize their own importance in shaping social movements, but, as Lisa McGirr astutely observes in her recent book on grassroots conservatives in Orange County, California, *Suburban Warriors,* grassroots activists were less influenced and motivated by Jay Nock, Friedrich von Hayek, Russell Kirk, Eric Voeglin, Leo Strauss, or William F. Buckley than they were by books such as Barry Goldwater's best-seller *Conscience of a Conservative* (1960), John A. Stormer's *None Dare Call It Treason* (1963) that claimed sales of 7 million, or Schlafly's *A Choice Not an Echo* (1964), which sold 3 million copies, or her *The Gravediggers* (1964), 2 million copies sold, or *Strike from Space* (1965), with a modest 200,000 plus copies sold.[8] Yet, while great attention needs to be given to popularizers such as Schlafly and Stormer in defining the conservative movement, it should be noted, in order to avoid an invidious dichotomy between the two, that popular authors relied on and drew their inspirations from the work of intellectuals such as Buckley, Burnham, and Frank Meyers, who hammered out the basic propositions of the conservative movement. Also, it is worth noting that Goldwater's *Conscience of a Conservative* was wholly written by Brent Bozell, Jr., who was Buckley's brother-in-law and a senior editor of *National Review*.[9]

This brings us to the taxonomy of conservatism. Those writing about postwar conservatism have tended to view conservatism as a continuous spectrum ranging from the racist and anti-Semitic Right to the so-called "Responsible Right." Yet this spectrum does not tell us very much about the composition of the Right and is in many ways misleading. As Lisa McGirr notes, William F. Buckley was touted in *Life* magazine in 1965 as a leading "extremist," while "Barry Goldwater was often labeled a dangerous extremist by his contemporaries, but more recently these individuals have been regarded as representatives of 'responsible' conservatism, despite the fact that their politics did not change significantly during the past decades."[10]

Furthermore, differences between grassroots anticommunist groups and mainstream Republican organizations in this period were minimal. Both anticommunist groups and Republican Party organizations used much of the same language in denouncing communist infiltration of the federal government, trade and cultural exchanges with communist countries, and peaceful coexistence with the Soviet Union.[11]

Any hard-and-fast categorization of "responsible" conservatives and "extremist" is belied by the career of Phyllis Schlafly. Phyllis Schlafly served, at the same time, as research director of the vehemently anticommunist Cardinal Mindszenty Foundation, a radio commentator for the Daughters of the American Revolution, and as president of the Illinois Federation of Republican Women; she was also the Republican candidate for Congress in the 24th district of Illinois in 1952.

Schlafly's involvement in women's groups such as the DAR and the National Federation of Republican Women indicates another significant feature in the taxonomy of the Right: the importance of women in the movement.[12] Female activists provided the ground troops for many conservative organizations, but also played leadership roles in the early movement through their own organizations such as the Daughters of the American Revolution, with a membership of approximately a quarter-million women in 1965 and the National Federation of Women with a half-million members in 1967. Women continue to play an important part in the conservative movement: Schlafly's Eagle Forum claims a membership of approximately 80,000 women; Concerned Women for American has an estimated 300,000 members; and the National Conference of Catholic Women has 500,000 women. The Women's Independent Forum, based in Washington, D.C., has recently proved to be an important intellectual voice among conservatives.

Arguably, these activist women can be seen as bringing to the modern political arena a tradition of volunteerism not unlike that of female civic activism in the nineteenth century. Like their nineteenth-century counterparts, female conservative activists were mostly white, Christian, and middle class.[13] Sharp ideological and religious differences over the meaning of reform, progress, and modernity separated female activists in the nineteenth century from those in the late twentieth century. These conservative female activists, proclaiming the virtues of the traditional family, believed that women had important roles to play in upholding and protecting the values of the American Republic. Many of these women were homemakers, but many also pursued careers outside the home. They were not opposed to women working outside the home, but they held that a mother's primary role should be that of caring for their children. They did not seek independence outside the home for its own sake, but instead believed their primary responsibility lay in the preservation of traditional family values, often meaning conservative Christian values of family.

Phyllis Schlafly's deservedly famous campaign against the ERA in the mid-1970s grew out of her activism within the conservative women's movement. This tradition of activism proved critical to the fortunes of the conservative movement in the 1970s. The election of Richard Nixon in 1968, initially supported by many conservatives, including Phyllis Schlafly, subsequently left the conservative grassroots activists disappointed and in disarray. By 1974, the conservative movement had reached its nadir—perhaps as low as the Goldwater defeat ten years earlier. This campaign showed the potential for mobilizing evangelical Christians and gave conservatives their first victory since Watergate. This effort coincided with the founding in this period of the Heritage Foundation, the *American Spectator*, and other conservative organizations that laid the basis for a political infrastructure. These organizations and the ERA battle set the stage for Republican congressional victories in the midterm elections of 1978 and Ronald Reagan's election two years later.

Schlafly brought to the anti-ERA campaign the skills of a longtime activist in the Republican Party and the anticommunist movement. All of her activism expressed a passion derived from her religious adherence to Roman Catholicism, as well as her commitment to grassroots mobilization against the liberal elites and Eastern Establishment, which she and others believed were running the country to the detriment of the nation's interest and traditional values.

Phyllis MacAlpin Stewart was born on August 15, 1924, and grew up in a devout Roman Catholic family in St. Louis. During the Depression, she learned the values of hard work, education, and the importance of family. Although the family voted Republican and both her parents were vehemently anti-New Deal, it was not a political family. During the Depression, the family focused on financial survival, not larger social or political issues of the day. When her father, Bruce Stewart, lost his job as a heavy-equipment sales engineer for Westinghouse in 1930 (he was fifty-one at the time), her mother, Odile, was forced to take a job outside the home, first as a teacher and then as the librarian of the St. Louis Art Museum, a position she held for the next twenty-five years. Throughout their lives, the Stewarts lived in rented apartments and never owned their own home. A graduate of Washington University in St. Louis, Odile instilled in her two daughters the importance of education and cultural refinement.[14] Both parents, although traditional in their religious faith and in their views of the family, believed that girls should not be any less educated than a boy.

Phyllis and later her younger sister attended the Sacred Heart Academy, one of the most prestigious Catholic girls' high schools in the city. To pay for the school, Odile Stewart volunteered her time in the evenings and the weekends to catalogue the school's library. "All my school years were most happy and most full," the sixteen-year-old Schlafly recorded in her diary.[15] Sacred Heart Academy emphasized daily Mass, Christian doctrine, and a classical education. She graduated highest in her class, with honors in classical languages and French.[16]

After graduation, Phyllis Schlafly received a full scholarship to Maryville College, a local Catholic school run by the Religious of the Sacred Heart. The school reinforced her piety as a young Roman Catholic, but within a year she concluded that she was not getting the education she wanted.[17] She enrolled in Washington University, taking a full-time job working the night shift at a local ordnance factory as a gunner testing ammunition by firing rifles and machine guns. "Phyllis the gunner" made her commitment to the war effort from 1942 to 1944, sometimes sleeping only three or four hours a night.[18]

She completed her political science major in two years, graduating Phi Beta Kappa. She then pursued a Master's degree in political science at Radcliffe College.

She excelled at Radcliffe, earning her Master's degree in June 1945 with straight "A's" in all her classes. At this point in her life, her politics remained ill-formed. As a high school student in 1940 she had worn a pin for Wendell Willkie, but she had not taken much interest in partisan politics. Her term papers at Harvard reveal a gifted graduate student able to write well-researched, well-argued, and academically objective papers on narrow administrative topics.[19] Encouraged by Pendleton Herring, one of her professors at Harvard, she sought a government appointment, either with the Tennessee Valley Authority or with the Bureau of the Budget.

She decided that the best way to land a job was to move to Washington, D.C. She arrived in the nation's capital on 2 September 1945, in a city in which she knew only about two people and lacked political contacts. As she would write later in life, she was never an outgoing person and only "by the most painful effort emerged from a natural shyness."[20] She was determined to find a job, but often found herself competing with returning veterans who were given preference in hiring. Taking her lament to the press, she won a readers' essay contest sponsored by the *Washington Daily News,* in which she declared, "The cards are stacked against the enterprising and ambitious person and in favor of the mediocre adults or the unqualified veteran."[21] The essay did not help her land a government job. Finally, answering an ad in the paper, she found work as a researcher at the newly organized American Enterprise Association (AEA). Established in 1945 by the president of Johns Manville Corporation, Lewis H. Brown, the American Enterprise Association asserted that "the tide of radicalism may be receding momentarily, but this certainly does not mean that America has returned to sound fiscal policies, put an end to deficit financing, to economic experimentation, and stopped making utopian plans for the future."[22]

Her year at AEA changed her politically. When she arrived, her politics were generally centrist, maybe even a bit to the left, although she considered herself a Republican. In Washington, she joined a local chapter of the United Nations Association, attending meetings and receptions and taking a speech class offered by the local chapter. By the end of the year at AEA, she emerged a conservative, devoted to free enterprise, antistatism, and the preservation of American liberty. Her religious faith as a Roman Catholic, now combined with well-formed conservative ideology, created a moral passion that would shape her lifelong politics.

In 1946, she returned to St. Louis to rejoin her parents. She found work at the First National Bank and the St. Louis Union Trust Company, dividing her time as a librarian and speechwriter for the bank and as a researcher for Towner Phelan, a trust officer who wrote a conservative monthly newsletter, *The St. Louis Union Trust Company Letter*. The newsletter, generally libertarian in its outlook, expounded free enterprise and warned of "creeping welfarism" and communist influence in Washington and the external Soviet threat.

In her capacity for the trust company, Schlafly gave lectures targeted to women on the need for estate planning and financial investment. Referred to in the local newspaper as the "blond banking expert" and a "forceful" speaker, Schlafly told her female audiences that they needed to plan for their financial future. Her message was direct and encouraging: "When women have been able to get adequate information and experience in investing, they have done as well as men."[23]

In 1946, she volunteered to work as a campaign manager for Claude Bakewell, Republican candidate for Congress in St. Louis. In this role as manager, she wrote press releases, scheduled events, and drafted all of Bakewell's speeches. Running against an incumbent Democrat Joe Sullivan in the Eleventh District, a district with a heavy labor and black vote, Bakewell attacked the Democratic administration for its failure to provide housing to veterans; called for the end of price controls; spoke of the need for a volunteer army to replace conscription; and championed free enterprise and warned of the dangers of centralized, bureaucratic government in Washington. In one of his set speeches written by Schlafly, he called for racial tolerance, declaring that "religious and racial intolerance is the very antithesis of the principles of which this great American Republic was founded. . . . No man is either good or bad because of the color of his skin or the Church he attends. . . . There is a decency and a fineness of character in every man, which recognized and given a chance to develop, will grow and expand, not only throughout our country, but throughout the world." And to answer charges that Republicans were antilabor, he answered, "The right of labor to organize for the purpose of advancing its own interest is an inherent right of the working man." Bakewell did not make anticommunism a central theme of his campaign, but he warned of "moral laxness" in the nation and charged the Democratic administrations of Roosevelt and Truman with allowing communist infiltration into government.[24] In a fiercely fought election, Bakewell won 41,202 to 39,879 votes. He profusely thanked Schlafly for the essential role she played in his victory.

Schlafly found other avenues for volunteer work as well. In October 1948, she made the front page of the *St. Louis Post Dispatch* when her thirty-page booklet on slum clearance was published by the Citizen's Council on Housing and Community, a local community group of ministers, businessmen, and civic officials. Her proposal included a $16-million bond issue for urban renewal between the Market Street and Olive area. In order to halt white urban flight to the suburbs, she called for the public funding of apartments, hotels, public buildings, and parks. The booklet declared, "There are 280,000 residents of St. Louis living under slum conditions. They account for crime and disease out of all proportion to their numbers and depreciate property values in the rest of the city." The bond issue failed in the November elections.[25]

In 1949, Phyllis Schlafly was twenty-four, unmarried, and independently supporting herself. She dated frequently, but had not found a man who met her high expectations. Then she met Fred Schlafly, a thirty-nine-year-old attorney in Alton, Illinois. Fred Schlafly came from a distinguished family in the St. Louis area. He was politically conservative and Catholic. Phyllis's politics and religion—and her intelligence—attracted his attention. Their courtship proved unusual. They dated only once a week and the rest of the time exchanged poetry and letters. These letters were highly intellectual, discussing theological and political questions, written in a style seemingly intended to prove to one another how clever each was. Responding to a copy of a speech he was to give, Phyllis wrote, "I have never been able to sympathize very much with Republican campaign oratory about Roosevelt's statement in regard to sending our boys to fight in foreign wars. . . . He did not send any boys to fight in foreign wars until after Pearl Harbor, and then it certainly was our war." At another point she told her suitor, "I noted with pleasure that you did not use the old argument about the order in the universe as proof of the existence of God. I think this is a fallacious argument." Fred Schlafly had found his match. They married October 20, 1949. Phyllis moved across the Mississippi River to Alton, Illinois, to begin her new life as a homemaker, mother, and political activist.

As the wife of one of the leading attorneys in Alton, Phyllis became involved in community life in Alton. She joined the board of the local YMCA, headed a Red Cross drive, and became president of the St. Louis Radcliffe Alumnae Club. In 1950, they had their first son, John. Over the next fifteen years, five other children followed.[26] As a mother she had set principles in raising her children and running the home. She breastfed all her children. Later she wrote articles and gave speeches to women's groups and conservative organizations on the benefits of breastfeeding, maintaining that "nursing baby are such happy babies" and "they have never interfered with any speaking or social engagement. I have taken my nursing babies everywhere." "Last year," she declared, "I took my youngest, who was then three months old, on a two-week lecture tour of Illinois."[27]

She insisted that her family eat healthy food, waking up an hour before everyone else each day to cook hearty Roman wheat porridge for them. She did not allow her children to eat refined sugar, white or any commercial bread, cakes, pies, candy or gum, soft drinks, or fried foods. She bought organic vegetables and unpasteurized milk and fertile eggs from local farmers and a local health food store.[28] She taught her children how to read before they went to school (an experience that convinced her that phonics was the only way to teach reading). She home-schooled all of her children before sending them to second grade in the local Catholic parochial school. When the children began school she packed them healthy lunches of organic peanut butter sandwiches on whole wheat bread, carrots and other vegetables, while the other kids ate their baloney sandwiches and Fritos.

Fred and Phyllis Schlafly formed a political team, often working together in anticommunist projects sponsored by the American Bar Association and later the Cardinal Mindszenty Foundation, a Catholic anticommunist organization they founded to teach the public about the dangers of the communist "conspiracy." They shared the same politics: Republican, conservative, and fiercely anticommunist.

In the early years, Schlafly's political work was done at their home in the evenings, after she put the children to bed. She traveled little in the first years of her marriage until she became president of the Illinois Federation of Republican Women in 1959. When she did accept speaking engagements—always without an honorarium (indeed, she only accepted her first honorarium in 1975)—she tried to make it a point of returning home in the evening. Fred Schlafly's legal practice allowed his wife the financial freedom to pursue her political work.

Fundamental to Schlafly's work was a belief that grassroots activists were essential to political change. In a frequently given speech, "The Big Things Are Done by Little People," she declared that "when Jesus selected His Apostles, He did not go to the great university of the day. . . . He did not try to convert the world overnight by picking a large number of well known men. He chose a dozen plain, insignificant men. . . . But the big things in life are not usually done by heads of big groups, but by little individuals; not by handsome, healthy people, but by handicapped people; not by highly educated people, but by self-taught people."[29]

Schlafly was active in the Republican Party, the Illinois Federation of Republican Women, and the Daughters of the American Revolution. Much of her work focused on anticommunism, although she spoke on a broad range of other issues including foreign policy, strategic balance, mental health, civil liberties, and education. Often, though, these issues related to the internal and external threat posed by what she perceived of as the communist conspiracy.

In the early years of the Cold War, the grassroots anticommunist movement was composed of disparate organizations operating through local organizations with little coordination between them. Fred Schwarz's Christian Anti-Communist Crusade, incorporated in 1953, offered a national focus to the movement, but it is worth noting that this operation primarily consisted of Schwarz and one assistant.[30] Similarly, the Cardinal Mindszenty Foundation remained a Schlafly-family-run organization, without a paid national membership. Billy Hargis's Christian Crusade, based in Tulsa, took in huge amounts of money through the sales of its publications, but failed to organize local chapters. Other anticommunist groups included Kent and Phoebe Courtney's Conservative Society of America, Edgar Bundy's Illinois-based Church League of America, and the Life Line Foundation, sponsored by H. L. Hunt in Texas, which produced publications, but did not maintain memberships. Although attempts were made to bring these organizations together, they had little organizational contact with one another.

Grassroots activists read the same authors and heard the same speakers.[31] Nonetheless, the grassroots anticommunist movement remained fragmented organizationally. As a result, both the anticommunist movement and the larger conservative movement were, in effect, local movements that shared similar anxieties about the communist threat. These groups differed as to organizational focus and often disagreed as to whether communism posed more of an internal threat or an external threat. The founding of the John Birch Society (JBS) by candy manufacturer Robert Welch in 1958 provided the first anticommunist organization with a nationally based membership and a centrally directed program. Nonetheless, many conservatives and grassroots anticommunist activists shied away from the JBS after it was revealed that Robert Welch had accused President Eisenhower of being a conscious agent of the Soviet Union. As a result, in the 1950s there was not a conservative movement per se, but, in a certain sense, only conservative movements. The modern "conservative movement" only came of age with the Goldwater presidential campaign of 1964.

In the 1950s, anticommunist activists offered political support to Joseph

McCarthy's and House Select Committee on Un-American Activities (HUAC) investigations into communist infiltration of the government, the movie industry, and
the schools, but much of their time was given to the study of communism.[32]
Through educational seminars and local reading groups, activists studied Marxist
doctrine, the history of Bolshevism, and communist strategy and tactics. As one
anticommunist tract declared, "Brains and moral courage are needed to stop the
Communist, not brawn and lung power. The remedies we suggest are undramatic.
. . . First study Communism."[33] Another brochure advised: "Only an expert can tell
who is a Communist." Avoid reckless charges as well as racial, religious, social and
economic intolerance because "it not only is unfair, but intolerance plays directly
into the hands of the enemy."[34] Emphasis was placed on individual commitment in
the battle against communism.[35] Self-education was touted in pamphlets, brochures, and newsletters as the first step in the confrontation with this global conspiracy. As a result, study groups were organized to read government reports and
books such as Schwarz's *You Can Always Trust the Communists (to be Communists)*,
W. Cleon Skousen's *The Naked Communist*, Herbert Philbrick's *I Led Three Lives*,
and a myriad of other anticommunist books. In addition, long before Alexander
Solzhenitsyn's *One Day in the Life of Ivan Denisovich* appeared in 1962, a powerful
memoir literature had emerged that reinforced recognition of the evil and treacher-
ous nature of the Soviet Union and other communist regimes.[36] As a result of their
common reading, grassroots anticommunist activists developed a unique subculture, based on radically different assumptions about the nature of communism and
the possibilities of negotiating with communist regimes. Although this subculture
remained in many ways insular, its outlook was not very different from Republican
Party statements concerning the domestic communist and Soviet threat.

Schlafly emphasized education in her own work in the Illinois Federation of Republican Women, the Cardinal Mindszenty Foundation, and as state chairman of
the national defense committee for the DAR. Within each of these groups she organized anticommunist study groups. At the same time, her husband Fred Schlafly, who had served on the American Bar Association Committee on Communist
Tactics, Strategy, and Objectives, participated in a number of Fred Schwarz's seminars across the country. In 1958, after one of Schwarz's schools on communism,
Fred and Phyllis Schlafly and her sister-in-law Eleanor Schlafly organized the Cardinal Mindszenty Foundation as a Catholic counterpart to the Christian Anti-
Communist Crusade.

The Cardinal Mindszenty Foundation, named after Hungarian Roman Catholic Cardinal Mindszenty, brought a moral enthusiasm to its efforts to educate
American Catholics about domestic communism and the oppression of Christians
in communist countries. Working with a small volunteer staff under Eleanor
Schlafly, with most of the writing being done by Phyllis, the foundation quickly
emerged as a prominent anticommunist organization in Catholic circles. Although
not officially endorsed or formally affiliated with the Catholic Church, the advisory
board was composed only of priests with "direct" experience with communism—
many of them had been imprisoned under communist regimes before joining the

Mindszenty Council.[37] The foundation's message was that the struggle against communism was just not a battle between two economic systems, but between communism and Christianity.[38] To fulfill its mission, the Mindszenty Foundation conducted seminars and organized local study groups to "safeguard our Church and our country."[39] The foundation offered a ten-week study program involving group discussion and individual homework based on an extensive reading list of government documents. Remember, the Mindszenty Foundation told its students, "to be an effective Freedom Fighter you must spread your knowledge with tact and with facts. Don't argue generalities, but calmly present specific facts."[40] At a time when many Roman Catholic Masses ended with prayers being said for the conversion of the Soviet Union, this program attracted wide attention.

By 1961, the Cardinal Mindszenty Foundation was sponsoring more than 3,000 study groups in forty-nine states, as well as study groups in Canada, several Caribbean countries, and Mexico. Attendance in its seminars ranged from a hundred to several thousand. In Houston, a four-day seminar in 1960 drew a total audience of 10,500 and more than 20,000 pieces of free literature were distributed and 1,600 books and pamphlets were sold. A monthly newsletter *The Mindszenty Report,* written by Phyllis Schlafly, reached tens of thousands of subscribers. In 1961 alone, the foundation distributed over 125,000 copies of the American Bar Association's report, "Communists Tactics, Strategy, and Objectives." That same year the foundation began sponsoring a fifteen-minute radio talk program, "The Dangers of Apathy," which ran in twenty cities coast to coast and is still running.[41]

Schlafly also took her anticommunist message to a receptive Daughters of the American Revolution, which she had joined shortly after her marriage. Following a national resolution by the DAR urging its members to "take up the study of Communism for the protection of our country and our freedom," Schlafly, who had been appointed chairman of the National Defense Committee, organized DAR study groups across the state. She told Illinois DAR members, "Our Republic can be saved from the fires of Communism which have already destroyed or enslaved many Christian cities, if we can find 10 patriotic women in each community."[42] She developed a ten-session program to be used by each study group. She also began writing a National Defense Report in the monthly state bulletin. She reported that of the 113 chapters in Illinois, 110 reported having active national defense committees in their chapters. She urged these DAR study groups to become involved in community activities by sponsoring writing contests in local high schools on American history and freedom; donating anticommunist books to local public and school libraries; and hosting well-known anticommunist speakers at public forums. Moreover, chapters were encouraged to write letters to Congress. Schlafly reported in 1961 that state DAR members had written 9,003 letters in defense of the McCarran-Walter Immigration Act; 454 letters opposing foreign aid; 293 letters against Khrushchev's visit; and 1,021 letters in support of the Connally Amendment against our participation in the World Court.

To further this program, the state DAR began sponsoring a radio program, "Wake Up America," hosted by Schlafly. The program originated when a DAR member who owned a radio station in Sterling, Illinois, donated tapes and fifteen minutes of public time for the program. The weekly program was eventually picked up by about twenty-five radio stations across the state. The format usually included a thirteen-minute talk by Schlafly, but occasionally guest speakers, such as Clarence Manion, Herbert Philbrick, and other national figures, were interviewed on pressing political issues of the day.

Schlafly's involvement in DAR and the Mindszenty Foundation paralleled her involvement in Republican Party politics. Her activity in anticommunist organizations such as the Mindszenty Foundation and the Republican Party fell within the general ambit of conservatism. Indeed, resolutions passed by the Illinois Federation of Republican Women (IFRW), as well as the National Federation throughout the 1950s and early 1960s, expressed equally intense anticommunist sentiments and opposition to trade and cultural exchanges with communist regimes, U.S. participation in the World Court, Kennedy's Nuclear Test Ban Treaty, and other policies perceived as being "soft" on communism.

Schlafly found an avenue for her activities in women's organizations. In doing so, she believed that women activists made a critical difference in shaping politics and policy. Speaking before the IFRW women in 1960, she declared, "The time is past when women of the Republican Party are merely doorbell pushers. We have earned our right to participate in the making of policies at the top which spell the difference between defeat and victory."[43] Furthermore, she maintained that "women are slowly but steadily winning recognition on the policy making and administrative level."[44] Schlafly expressed the belief of many women Republican activists. Schlafly's support of the Republican Party remained steadfast for the next fifty years, even while others spoke of forming third parties. Her time-consuming commitment to the party was humorously noted in a poem her daughter Anne wrote while in grade school: "Mary had a little lamb/It hoped to be a sheep/Instead it joined the GOP/And died from loss of sleep."[45]

Schlafly had drawn the attention of Republican state and national leaders because of her energetic campaign for Congress in 1952. That year twenty-nine women ran for Congress, but Schlafly—"the Alton housewife"—attracted national press coverage. In winning the primary in the 12th Congressional District, she took on the local Republican machine headed by Dan McGlynn in East St. Louis.[46] In doing so she was the first woman to run for Congress in the district, announcing at the outset of her campaign, "I feel very disturbed about the corrupt situation in politics today. I think that women should get into politics and do something about it." [47] Because of her status as a "housewife" running for Congress, the press gave plenty of publicity to "the young blond housewife with lots of brains to go with a charming personality," as she was described by one local paper. In a nasty primary campaign in which her rival denounced her as a "powder-puff candidate," she won the primary by 8,000 votes, taking her home Madison County and enough votes in East St. Louis's St. Clair County. The local newspapers announced, "Powderpuff In," with a picture of an apron-wearing Schlafly captioned, "Glamour In."

The race then pitted Schlafly against Melvin Price, an incumbent Democrat with close ties to organized labor in East St. Louis. Writing her own speeches and acting as her own campaign manager, Schlafly undertook an unrelenting speaking schedule at local women's clubs, civic and church groups, and public assemblies. At first Price, well known for being a poor speaker, refused to debate her, but as her campaign accelerated he was forced appear in a public debate with her. He proved to be little match for Schlafly on stage. The local papers reported, "They disagreed every inch of the way. . . . Price spoke casually without notes, while Mrs. Schlafly cited figures extensively, used notes, and pointed to charts, graphs, and maps set up on the stage." She charged that "Mr. Price is not a Communist. He is a loyal American. But his voting record shows he does not realize the dangers of Communism." At the end of the debate Price refused to shake Schlafly's hand. Yet, for all of Schlafly's vigor, the election was a foregone conclusion in a heavily Democratic district. Price won by a 2 to 1 margin, the same margin by which Eisenhower lost the district in the presidential election.

The 1952 campaign gave Schlafly experience running for public office and brought her to the attention of leading Republicans. During the campaign, she met Richard Nixon, Robert Taft, and Dwight D. Eisenhower. Asked to give a keynote address to the state GOP convention in Springfield, she held her audience in awe with her crisp, often eloquent, delivery with frequent applause lines. Even the often-critical *East St. Louis Journal* observed that her audience "sat at rapt attention in torrid temperature [the hall was not air-conditioned] listening to her address."[48] Further visibility in Republican circles came when she attended the Republican National Convention in 1952.

Speaking invitations across the state soared in the following years. She became one of the state's most popular Republican speakers. In 1959, when the president of the Illinois Federation of Republican Women, the largest Republican organization in the state, resigned, Schlafly was elected to replace her. She easily won reelection twice. Under her leadership in the next four and half years, membership increased a net 91%, making Illinois one of the largest chapters in the country. In 1964, in Louisville, she was unanimously elected national vice president of the organization, a position seen as a stepping-stone to the presidency.

Schlafly used her position to promote the Goldwater bandwagon following the defeat of Richard Nixon in 1960. Prior to the 1960 election, Fred Schlafly had joined a movement organized by his friend Clarence Manion to draft Goldwater as president.[49] Manion, well known in conservative circles for his radio and later television program, *The Manion Forum,* organized the draft campaign without the official endorsement of Goldwater.[50] Behind the scenes, Manion hoped for a deadlocked convention between Richard Nixon and Nelson Rockefeller, opening the way for a Goldwater nomination. If this failed, he hoped that conservatives, disgruntled with Eisenhower's Modern Republicanism, would leave the party to join forces with disgruntled Democrats, forming a Goldwater–Ernest Hollings ticket.[51] To promote Goldwater's visibility, Manion proposed a short campaign book, written under Goldwater's name, stating the principles of conservatism. After getting the senator's agreement, Manion made arrangements with Brent Bozell, William Buckley's brother-in-law, to ghostwrite the book under the title *The Conscience of a Conservative*. When the book appeared, Manion and his associates promoted it by selling tens of thousands at $3 a book. While Goldwater did not receive the 1960 Republican nomination, the book made him the nation's leading conservative politician.

In 1963, Phyllis Schlafly decided to promote another Goldwater campaign by writing her own book, *A Choice Not an Echo*. Completed in early 1964, this book summarized conservatives' views that an eastern elite, "the kingmakers," had chosen all the Republican politics since the nomination of Alf Landon in 1936. Composed of eastern financiers, newspaper publishers, and political insiders, these kingmakers had sought to impose liberal and internationalist policies on the GOP, even if it meant defeat by the Democrats. The views in her book were not new, but her argument was graphically stated in short, simple sentences intended to motivate the rank and file within the party. In April 1964, she undertook to publish the book herself in order to assure quick distribution, a tactic that had been employed by John Stormer in his widely read, *None Dare Call It Treason*.

The Conscience of a Conservative provided a model for distributing the book to the rank and file. Selecting a list of 200 friends she had made in the NFRW and anticommunist activities, Schlafly sent out a letter announcing the book and offering a discount for bulk orders. Meanwhile, Clarence Manion urged wealthy businessmen to purchase bulk orders of the book.[52] Grassroots activists found in *A Choice Not an Echo* just what they were looking for. California businessman Gilbert Durand, whom Schlafly knew through the Cardinal Mindszenty Foundation, found the book so powerful that he ordered thousands of copies to be sold to Republican precinct workers. Sales soared, reaching two million copies, by the time of the June California primary.

The book played an important part in the crucial California primary. Although Nelson Rockefeller, Goldwater's rival for the nomination, won forty-five of fifty-eight counties, Goldwater triumphed with 51.4% of the vote.[53] Observers claimed that *A Choice Not an Echo* was critical in obtaining volunteers and votes for Goldwater. Gardiner Johnson, the California Republican National Committeeman, maintained that the Schlafly book was "a major factor in bringing victory to Goldwater, against the terrific assault of the press, the pollsters, and the paid political workers of the opposition." Such attacks only convinced grassroots activists that the kingmakers were at work. In addition, Stephen Shadegg, an adviser during the campaign, noted that precincts in which the book was heavily distributed went 20% stronger for the senator than other precincts with residents with the same educational, occupational, and economic background.[54] Although Schlafly went to the San Francisco Republican convention as a strong Goldwater delegate, she played little role in the national campaign other than to urge Goldwater to focus his campaign on national defense and "the missile" gap between United States and the Soviet Union. She was pregnant with her sixth child, who was born November 16, 1964.

Goldwater's crushing defeat in the 1964 election left many conservatives demoralized and the party in disarray. The ramifications of this defeat were played out in the party as liberal and moderate wings sought to regain control of the party and its organizations. This struggle between competing factions became apparent in the NFRW presidential election in 1967 that pitted Gladys O'Donnell against Schlafly.

From the outset, political observers saw the fight as a struggle over control of the Republican Party by the moderates and the conservatives whom Rockefeller labeled "extremists." William Rusher warned in a widely distributed pamphlet that the liberal eastern wing of the party was attempting to sneak in the back door by gaining control of the NFRW.[55] Similarly, political columnist David Broder writing in the *Washington Post* declared that the temptation to dismiss the NFRW as "Mickey Mouse politics played with exaggerated emotion for minimal stakes is an error. . . . Their internal battles historically have proved accurate forecasts of succeeding convention fights. And, increasingly, senior party officials and even presidential prospects have been drawn into the fray."[56] As the battle between the Schlafly and O'Donnell forces intensified, the fight spilled over into the GOP itself, dividing the Republican leadership. Many saw the heavy hand of Ray Bliss, chair of the Republican National Committee, evident in the struggle as he sought to turn the party toward the center. Although he continued to deny involvement in the NFRW battle, Bliss had openly attacked "extremists" in the GOP when he assumed his post as RNC chair.[57]

Prior to the convention, Schlafly had been the odds-on favorite to win the election. The first signs of trouble came when the NFRW board meeting in 1965 decided to change the biennial convention from its traditional even-dated year to 1967. The board's unanimous decision to postpone the convention and move it from Los Angeles, a hotbed of Schlafly supporters, was seen by many as a ploy to keep Schlafly out of the presidency. Writing in the *St. Louis Post Dispatch,* longtime Schlafly critic, journalist Richard Dudman reported that "moderates" within the party did not want to be "saddled" with a Schlafly presidency in the 1968 election.[58]

At the following September board meeting, the NFRW nominating committee confirmed its opposition to Schlafly by nominating Gladys O'Donnell, a California activist from Long Beach. Although O'Donnell had worked in conservative campaigns for George Murphy and Ronald Reagan, she denounced "extremists" within the California Federation. Feelings were exacerbated when O'Donnell was quoted in the *Chicago Tribune* as saying that a women who is the mother of six children wouldn't have time to devote to the national presidency of the federation.[59] Charges about her six children continued to be heard throughout the fight.[60]

Schlafly declared her candidacy in a joint press conference with Maureen Reagan, Ronald Reagan's daughter, who had enlisted in the Schlafly cause. Schlafly declared, "It is high time that the Federation has a president who is a wife and a mother. . . . We must attract youth." [61] In the ensuing campaign, both sides spent ten of thousands of dollars, while exchanging bitter accusations of unfair campaign tactics and allegations. Rumors spread that Schlafly was a member of the John Birch Society and a member of the militant Minutemen.[62] The NFRW divided along regional lines, as much of the Far West, Midwest, and South threw its support to Schlafly, while critical eastern chapters including Pennsylvania, New York, and New Jersey supported O'Donnell.[63]

Acrimony within the NFRW spilled over to the mainstream of the Republican Party. The RNC reported that its office was flooded with mail, running sixty to seventy letters a day, plus phone calls. One national committee member working in the national office lamented, "It is a sad thing that this break had to come when we have an excellent chance to win in 1968. This fight is tending to split our party again." In April, an irate Goldwater telephoned the RNC claiming that this fight was "so bitter in Arizona that it might cost him winning the Senate race."[64] In Arizona, charges were made that because Goldwater had taken a neutral stand in the election, Schlafly supporters in the state were secretly supporting a more conservative candidate in Goldwater's bid to regain his Senate seat.[65] California Senator George Murphy issued a statement to the press declaring that Gladys O'Donnell was a conservative, contrary to the claims of Schlafly supporters.[66] Meanwhile, Congressman John Ashbrook (R-Ohio) denounced Bliss for trying to purge the party of conservatives by supporting O'Donnell.

When the convention met in Washington, D.C., in June 1967, both sides came prepared for battle and battle they did. In the most hotly contested election in the history of the federation, O'Donnell won by 516 votes, 1,910 to 1,494. Schlafly supporters later claimed that delegates had been denied credentials, kept waiting in lines for hours by the credentials committee, and that the credentials committee failed to issue its report before voting took place. Even more serious charges were made that hundreds of illegal votes had been cast by women bused in from Pennsylvania, New York, Michigan, and New Jersey. Furthermore, Schlafly accused NFRW official Dorothy Elston with not allowing the voting machines to be inspected by her representatives, as agreed to prior to the convention. In the end, Schlafly conceded defeat, announcing to her supporters, "The principle I work for will not die—constitutional government, individual freedom, dignity and morality, and American freedom."[67]

The convention left the NFRW bitterly divided. Over the next three years membership fell from over 500,000 members to less than half that number. Schlafly withdrew from the organization and started her *Phyllis Schlafly Report,* a monthly newsletter sent to her followers.

During the Goldwater campaign she had published her first book on defense, *The Gravediggers,* with retired Rear Admiral Chester Ward. Other books on national defense followed: *Strike from Space* (1965) and *The Betrayers* (1968). Warning that the Johnson–McNamara policy was deliberately dismantling America's nuclear arsenal in hope of securing "parity" through arms control treaties, she believed this would lead to nuclear blackmail or outright surrender by the United States. Schlafly and her co-author called for a massive nuclear buildup and nuclear superiority over the Soviet Union, a policy that was repeatedly endorsed in the Republican national platforms. She maintained that the Vietnam War was a Soviet-engineered distraction designed to weaken America's defense capability. By emphasizing the external threat posed by the Soviet Union, she was bitterly assailed by the John Birch Society, which continued to maintain that the only communist threat was internal and that the Soviet Union was economically too weak to challenge America militarily.

This concern for national defense led her, much to the chagrin of many of her followers, including Chester Ward, to endorse Richard Nixon in 1968. By supporting Nixon, she refused to join other conservatives in supporting Ronald Reagan for the nomination. At the same time, she urged her followers not to be led astray into the Wallace third-party movement. Writing in *Human Events,* she warned that "The kingmakers are hoping that conservatives will fall for this argument. . . . [T]heir constant hope is that conservatives by the hundreds of thousands will take a walk from the Republican party so as to leave the liberals in full control."[68] A delegate to the Republican Convention in Miami, she worked for Nixon's nomination, while joining forces with Strom Thurmond to place a conservative on the ticket as Nixon's running mate. (Nonetheless, she was disappointed in the selection of Spiro Agnew.)[69]

Nixon's administration left Schlafly and other conservatives bitterly disappointed. Nixon's appointment of Henry Kissinger, continuation of the Robert McNamara policies, endorsement of the Family Assistance Plan, support for environmental regulations, wage and price controls, growth of federal social expenditures, and finally the opening of relations with mainland China caused conservative activists to desert the Nixon administration. These activists found themselves isolated and demoralized. Schlafly's bid for Congress in 1970, in which she was narrowly defeated, did not offer much encouragement to the movement. Efforts by William Rusher to form a new third party failed, as did an effort by Ohio Congressman John Ashbrook to challenge Nixon in the 1972 primaries.[70] By the time Nixon resigned from office in 1974, the conservative movement was in disarray.

One of the first signs of a conservative revival came with the Stop-ERA movement led by Phyllis Schlafly. Her own involvement in ERA came about accidentally in December 1971 when she was invited to a debate sponsored by a conservative club in Connecticut. She suggested that the debate focus on national defense, but she was told that the club wanted the topic to be on the Equal Rights Amendment, then in the U.S. House of Representatives. Claiming that she did not know much about the ERA, or even that she had given much thought to the subject, she asked for material to be sent to her. The first step had been taken. The February 1972, the *Phyllis Schlafly Report* was headlined, "What's Wrong with Equal Rights for Women." A month later she received a phone call from an excited supporter in Oklahoma, Ann Patterson, who told her that the Oklahoma state legislature had defeated the ERA after her report had been circulated to them. At this point, Schlafly knew she had an issue to rally the grass roots. In September 1972, Schlafly started Stop ERA.

Schlafly entered the ERA fight as an experienced organizer with a network of supporters throughout the country. Many of the women, who had supported her in the NFRW election, quickly joined the crusade to stop ERA. Moreover, Schlafly saw the potential of mobilizing evangelical churches and their members. Few political observers believed the forces organizing to defeat the ERA stood much of a chance. Similarly, leaders in the National Organization for Women (NOW) and ERAmerica at first dismissed Schlafly and her grassroots crusade. They made a monumental mistake. By 1977, they were taking Schlafly seriously, admitting that she and not they had won over the average "homemaker."[71] Schlafly's successful leadership against the ERA was the first major victory for the conservative cause since Nixon's resignation from office in 1974; it paved the way for many more.

What can be learned from this brief narrative of Schlafly's early life? First, Schlafly's political career shows continuity within the postwar conservative movement. This suggests that we should reconsider the dichotomous nomenclature of the Old Right and the New Right. While the intensity of the anticommunist movement may have decreased by the end of the 1950s, as Michael Kazin and others have argued, this decline was one of degree, not substance.[72] Anticommunism continued to be a major concern of the Right in the 1960s, sometimes reinforced by perceived communist involvement in the civil rights movement, the antiwar movement, and the nuclear-freeze movement. Moreover, whatever distinction might be made between the Old Right and the New Right, conservatives consistently opposed the welfare state, called for a decrease in federal power and spending, and demanded a military buildup that included nuclear supremacy over the Soviet Union.

In this political agenda, race relations fell under the category of "states rights" and "property rights." By equating the civil rights movement with "communist agitation," the Right ignored race relations per se and failed to address a major problem confronting American society in the postwar period. As a consequence, charges of racism were leveled against the Right by its opponents, as well as later scholars.[73] Some well-known conservative activists such as Tom Anderson and Revilo Oliver, both council members of the John Birch Society, enlisted in the Wallace campaign, but this was not John Birch Society policy and by the mid-1970s these men had become isolated from the larger conservative movement.

This brings us to the origins of the New Right. Historians such as Michael Kazin and Dan Carter who find the origins of the New Right in the Wallace movement ignore the vast support Richard Nixon and Ronald Reagan enjoyed among most conservatives in 1968. To suggest that the relationship of race and the Right remains a complex problem that needs further exploration is not to condone the lack of a civil rights policy by the Right. By failing to condemn segregation and racism as vociferously as it condemned communism meant that the Right avoided—at the very least—addressing a critical social problem in postwar America. The growing conservative movement in the 1950s and 1960s was equally silent on other social problems that are so prominent today, such as abortion and the family.

Conservatives consistently focused on their primary issue, one that they perceived as threatening the very existence of the Republic—statism, whether in the guise of the New Deal welfare state or in the apocalyptic threat of communism, at home and abroad. At the root of their anxieties about statism lay a deep anxiety—an anguish—that American traditional values were being subverted—not because of modernity or affluence (these only set the conditions for such erosion), but by the misguided efforts of a liberal elite, arrogant in its own certainty and seemingly unaware of the communists' support of such efforts. This perception that Americans had become morally soft posed a dilemma for conservatives who proclaimed the values of the free market that produced such affluence and for conservatives who claimed to uphold the virtues of the average American. Conservatives were hesitant to consider an argument that a free market tended to destroy those traditional social values they thought bound a civil society together. Their passion for tradition blinded them to any of the social consequences of a free market.

Schlafly's own activism was shaped by a ideology influenced by her Roman Catholic faith and her commitment to a fierce anticommunist, antistatist conservatism. Ideology, not psychology, explains her politics.[74]

Schlafly's moral passion inspired other conservative women to join the battle against what they perceived as radical forces, led by eastern elites, intent on extending the welfare state, appeasing communist regimes, and subverting traditional family values. Schlafly and her conservative female activists, by proclaiming the virtues of the traditional family, believed that they could uphold and protect the values of the American Republic.

To their battle they brought a moral certainty and a ferocity that equaled that of their adversaries. This was especially evidenced in the fight over ERA ratification. Yet to see women on the Left and these women on the Right as mirror images, as some have suggested, belies the antithetical core values that separated these two groups.[75] And, any new narrative of recent American politics will have to incorporate this dialectic of opposition that found expression not just in political contention, but in a democratic culture divided by seemingly irreconcilable beliefs as to what makes for a just and good society.

Scott Flipse

BELOW-THE-BELT POLITICS: PROTESTANT EVANGELICALS, ABORTION, AND THE FOUNDATION OF THE NEW RELIGIOUS RIGHT, 1960–75

Harold Lindsell sat in his office on 21 January 1973 staring at the blank page in his typewriter. It was evening and the editor of *Christianity Today,* the flagship magazine of American Protestant evangelicalism, had spent an exhausting day on the phone, trying to confirm rumors of a forthcoming U.S. Supreme Court decision in the *Roe v. Wade* and *Doe v. Bolton* cases. When the court's decision finally came in, Lindsell was "stunned." [1] In his editorial denouncing the *Roe* decision, Lindsell flashed the type of righteous anger that would fuel later activism. "The Supreme Court," he wrote, "had decidedly sided for paganism and against Christianity." He entertained the prospect that divine judgment was imminent for an "American holocaust . . . where life was being exterminated at a rate not equaled in any war." For Lindsell, the *Roe* decision signaled that the state was "hostile" to religion and to religious values. [2] In subsequent years, he, and other contributing editors to *Christianity Today,* counseled readers to confront federal and state governments with coordinated political action. After years of political reticence, Lindsell tried to rouse evangelicals to reclaim a nineteenth-century heritage of political-moral reform. [3]

The *Roe* decision was the catalyst that fused a diverse array of religious conservatives into an active political force. The emergence of issues such as abortion, pornography, women's rights, and homosexuality in the public arena, and the state's willingness to protect individual choice in these areas, challenged the moral leadership of Protestant, Catholic, and other religious voices in the area of family life and sexuality. As the liberationist Left scored political and legal successes in the late 1960s and early 1970s, religious conservatives sought like-minded allies in an increasingly fractured cultural terrain. A surprising compact formed between conservative Protestants and Catholics to fight "below-the-belt" issues. Historically antagonistic faith traditions worked together to produce an intellectual and organizational alliance that significantly changed the patterns of American political life. Eventually, religious conservatives blended into the Republican Party, reviving that party's nineteenth-century "conscience wing" around a pro-family, anti-secularist, and anticommunist message.[4]

The emergence of religious conservatives as an active political force is a remarkable story. Dubbed the New Religious Right, it included conservative Catholics who departed the New Deal coalition, southern Protestant fundamentalists who ended self-imposed political exile, and Protestant evangelicals who sought ways to interpret and accommodate cultural and political changes without losing their theological cohesion.[5] What follows is a story of how Protestant evangelical leaders struggled to engage sexual politics and how their engagement shaped political action.[6]

Evangelical leaders, such as Lindsell, initially tried to build a compassionate, morally temperate, anti-Catholic, and politically viable consensus on sexual issues; for example, endorsing use of "the Pill," supporting the Equal Rights Amendment, and defending efforts to "liberalize abortion." When questions of public morality became matters of political debate, settled by legal dispute and grassroots political organizing, evangelical religious leaders were caught unprepared—ignored by the left and criticized by the right. In the end, a large number of evangelicals moved right, making common cause with other religious conservatives to create the "family values" political agenda of the 1980s.[7]

Entering the Debate: Protestant Evangelicals and Politics

Protestant evangelicals catapulted into sudden prominence in 1976 when Democratic Party presidential candidate Jimmy Carter, a southern Baptist, admitted to having been "born again." Protestant religious voters turned out in large numbers for Carter; some commentators credited the evangelical vote for helping Carter win a close election.[8] The public emergence of evangelicalism surprised most observers of the American political scene. The mixture of religion and politics seemed a departure from long-established secular patterns of American political history. Evangelical leaders, on the other hand, saw their venture into the public square as recapturing an older political-moral heritage given up in the 1920s. After losing battles over evolution and temperance, religious conservatives—both fundamentalist and evangelical—moved to the fringes of American politics, becoming either politically inactive or blending in with the dominant national parties. Though evangelical leaders disengaged from public life in the decades between 1925 and 1950, they devoted considerable energy building broadcasting and educational institutions and winning converts. They also nurtured long-standing grudges against mainline Protestantism, theological liberalism, and the progressive social policy they saw as growing out of it.[9]

The political rebirth of evangelicalism began in the late 1940s.[10] A new generation of evangelical leaders sought to distance themselves from the separatist strain of American Protestant fundamentalism. Though they remained conservative theologically, they believed the negativism, sectarianism, defensiveness, and isolationism of fundamentalism repelled a large share of the American public. Evangelical leaders hoped to promote interdenominational unity, produce rigorous theological and biblical scholarship, and revitalize an evangelical social ethic. Although soul winning was their primary concern, they aspired to attain a wider social and cultural influence. They labeled their movement the "new evangelicalism."[11]

From the start, the new evangelicalism sought to organize a national and interdenominational movement drawn from several disparate faith traditions (Baptist, Pentecostals, Free Church, Nazarene, Mennonite and Reformed). The task was particularly difficult; most of these traditions were deeply suspicious of one another. Nonetheless, evangelicals came together around certain faith commitments, institutional affiliations, and personal relationships. In May 1943, nearly 600 religious leaders met to found the National Association of Evangelicals (NAE). The new organization was intended to give the new evangelicalism a single voice and a national platform to launch a number of joint ventures. NAE members were drawn from across the Protestant religious landscape, from mainline Protestant denominations to small, southern Pentecostal sects. They all affirmed such basic beliefs as a high view of Scripture, aggressive missionary work, the importance of a spiritually transformed life, and salvation through faith in Jesus Christ alone.[12] Billy Graham proved a crucial figure for the new evangelicalism. He bridged northern and southern evangelicals and helped heal divisions present since the Civil War. He was also a popular figure; a wide majority of American Protestants favored his efforts "evangelizing the world."[13]

With Graham leading the way, the new evangelicalism was transformed from a small group of denominational leaders into a national movement. The cohesion of many different denominations and traditions was helped by cooperation in a growing number of radio, television, and print media, colleges and seminaries, humanitarian and missionary organizations. These included the National Religious Broadcasting Association and the National Sunday School Association, *Christianity Today* and *Eternity* magazines, Fuller Theological Seminary and Wheaton College, World Vision and World Relief, Inter-Varsity Christian Student Fellowship and Youth for Christ. Evangelical special purpose groups and organizations were a cohesive force—they stood outside the denominational structure, remained independent from denominational oversight, and sought support from those devoted to the larger cause of evangelicalism. During the 1950s, evangelicalism benefited from the general postwar growth of American religion—some of the fastest growing denominations were NAE members. The swelling membership of its denominations and organizations boosted evangelicalism from a loose association of denominations to a well-established piece of the American religious mosaic. By the 1960s, evangelicalism was poised to exert a greater influence in American religion and society.[14]

The magazine *Christianity Today* under the editorship of Carl F. H. Henry became the place in which evangelical leaders debated current theological and cultural trends. Both Henry and *Christianity Today* were pivotal figures in the new evangelicalism. Henry, a university-trained philosopher and former journalist, was eager to provide a conservative alternative to liberal theology, secularism, scientific rationalism, and fundamentalism. As editor, he followed an editorial policy that avoided the theological and denominational differences of the evangelical coalition. The magazine stressed revivalism, individual spiritual renewal, and moral reform. More important, Henry argued for the direct infusion of Christian values into the public square.[15] In a 1965 editorial, Henry argued that evangelicals needed "to use every political opportunity to support and promote just laws, to protest social injustice, and to serve humanity." He was impatient with those preoccupied with "private saintliness" and preaching the Gospel in "absolute isolation." The Gospel, he thought, stressed social engagement and public empathy. For the first time in American history, argued Henry, "evangelical Christianity stands divorced from the great social reform movements."[16]

The problem was that most evangelicals, following their fundamentalist forebears, held a negative view of politics. For most evangelicals, politics was tainted by conflict and compromise—it was not a "pure form" of activity. Henry, on the other hand, urged a more "positive attitude" toward politics. Evangelicals, he argued, should overcome their reluctance to participate in the public sphere and use politics for their own purposes. Henry recognized that a broad-based evangelical movement needed to address the social and intellectual challenges of the day within the political realm if the movement was to have an impact on American society.[17]

Henry, however, never advocated embracing political action as the best, or only, agent of social change. He was no liberal. He, and most of his northern evangelical colleagues, were conservatives closer to Republican Robert Taft than Democrat Harry Truman.[18] Henry was suspicious of any government that sought to expand its role far beyond the imposition of justice and the maintenance of basic social order. He argued that the state could not by itself eradicate social ills or improve social welfare. Any state that tried was either doomed to fail or would become "an idol." The good society could only be built through cooperation between private and public institutions. He believed that through the work of mass revivalism, individual moral reform, and voluntary associations evangelicals could help address the social problems of "aggressive warfare, racial hatred and intolerance, the liquor traffic, and exploitation of labor or management, and political naturalism."[19]

The political issue that most concerned evangelicals in the 1950s was communism. During the first decade of the Cold War, evangelical leaders shared the same strident anticommunism as groups like Fred Schwarz's Christian Anti-Communist Crusade, Billy James Hargis's Christian Crusade, or Carl McIntires's American Council of Christian Churches.[20] Evangelical leaders, however, never worked closely with these groups. The lack of coordination was due, in part, to personality and theological differences. Religious anticommunist organizations were led by fundamentalists pastors who were as suspicious of Protestant evangelicals as they were of Protestant liberals. Hargis and McIntire, for example, attacked every evangelical they thought "soft" on communism; they singled out Billy Graham and Carl Henry for their "moderate" views on civil rights and Vietnam.[21] Henry was very critical of the apocalyptic theology of religious anticommunists, who saw the Cold War as evidence of a coming Armageddon. He admonished his readers that fundamentalism had too often taken "major crises as the last chapter of world history." They were not wrong, he said, in believing in a "final consummation of history," but had erred "in assuming that this is it." Henry, along with most evangelical leaders, refused to understand political and social problems as a "Manichean" battle between socialism and democratic-capitalism.[22] Anticommunism never mobilized evangelicals to direct political action.

From his post at *Christianity Today,* Henry urged evangelical leaders to actively engage the broader culture. He believed that evangelicals could produce a distinct message for American society. His confidence was bolstered by the growing competence of evangelical academics and by the professionalization of the laity. During the 1940s, the new evangelicalism was led by university-trained theologians, pastors, and academics. This generation's children went to college and often graduate school and, by the 1960s, found homes in American universities, a network of Christian colleges, and an array of professions across the country. Evangelical academics and professionals started an array of public associations such as the Society of Christian Philosophers, the Christian Medical Society, the Society of Christians in Science, the Religious Broadcasters Association, and the National Association of Evangelicals. These public associations gave members the ability to think about social issues from a religious point of view.[23]

Henry, for one, sought to direct the growing evangelical confidence and competency toward issues of contemporary ethics. In the early 1960s, ethical discussions surrounding issues of human reproduction caught his eye. Commenting on the introduction of "the Pill," Henry noted that modern conceptions "of the good life" were often equated with eroticism and sexual pleasure. Failure to "review the new morality in light of the Scriptures," he warned, "would make the Christian view of the good life" seem dull and irrelevant to "men and women promised the richness of experience" by the "cult of eros."[24] Responding to Henry's challenge, a whole range of voices entered the debate over the proper evangelical response to both birth control and changes to existing abortion laws.[25]

They first addressed the issue of birth control. Earlier birth control advocates found allies among Protestant leaders, particularly among former missionaries and aid workers. Dire, Malthusian predictions of massive population growth combined with limited resources colored most early discussions. Evangelicals were not immune to this thinking; in fact, their positions on birth control mirrored that of the larger society.[26] Many evangelicals who commended the use and distribution of birth control were concerned that world population would outstrip food, medical, and development aid and lead to widespread starvation, disease, and social tension. Many evangelical missionaries counseled the distribution of birth control to stem global population pressure. *Christianity Today* reported in 1967 that several evangelical missionary organizations provided family planning assistance throughout the globe.[27]

Besides limiting global population, another argument in favor of birth control was the maintenance of healthy Christian marriages. As new attitudes about sex crept into the cultural mainstream, evangelical marriage manuals began to describe explicitly the joys of recreative sex. The manuals continued to view sex as proper only within the bonds of marriage, but they were effusively and enthusiastically excited about marital sex. According to Dwight Harvey Small's *Christian: Celebrate Your Sexuality,* sex provided a "sense of well-being, complete identity, joy unbounded, and perfect mutuality" for the married couple. Other books offered explicit advice on lovemaking, for overcoming sexual tension and boredom, and one manual, Marabel Morgan's best-selling *The Total Women,* even counseled women to meet their husbands at the door clothed only in plastic wrap. Most of these manuals suggested that contraceptives gave couples the ability to explore the sexual aspect of their relationship, initially putting off the responsibility of children, as they experienced "sex for recreation, renewal, and love." The use of contraceptives was an important part of the "Christian marriage."[28] Evangelical leaders gave their consent to couples using artificial forms of family planning. They backed this claim with an appeal to act in the "liberty of good conscience before God." The vision of the "good Christian life" expected married couples to have a healthy and robust sex life, but did not require them to have large families.[29]

Because the Christian scriptures never explicitly condemned the use of birth control, evangelical leaders emphasized that its use and distribution were a matter for the Christian conscience. The freedom given by the conscience, however, was never used as an excuse to promote sexual license. Even among ardent proponents of birth control, there was the recognition that the reproductive and sexual freedom they offered would lead to increased levels of divorce, adultery, and premarital sex.[30] In the ethical debate over birth control, however, such predictions were generally ignored. When an oral contraceptive (the Pill) was approved by the Food and Drug Administration, one writer in *Christianity Today* argued that evangelicals should welcome the new technology "recognizing that nothing can be uninvented and that such a major breakthrough . . . demands a better quality of living, a better type of man and women. Thus we may seek . . . to bring those within our influence to live ethically, rather than merely by the mores and usages of society."[31]

On the ethics of birth control, evangelicals never strayed far from what they thought to be the cultural mainstream. Conservative Protestant marriage-advice manuals, articles, and editorials from the 1960s all reveal their author's eagerness to navigate between changing sexual mores and traditional religious thought concerning sex and marriage. For example, in an article discussing the Supreme Court's *Griswold v. Connecticut* decision that established a right to privacy for families seeking artificial birth control, *Christianity Today* endorsed the notion that the "old Protestant laws in Connecticut" were outdated in the current climate. But more than supporting the overturn of antiquated laws, the most prominent evangelical, Billy Graham, worried that opposition to improvements in birth control technology would make conservatives Protestants "look as foolish as those who opposed vaccinations or television." Evangelicals were eager to see dispelled the "negative views that have characterized conservative Protestants."[32]

Again according to Carl Henry, such negative characterizations were largely self-inflicted wounds. For example, he believed that evangelical positions on sexuality and family life were "unintelligible" to the broader culture. Instead of grasping a unique opportunity to enter the ethical debate, evangelicals often repeated "cliches . . . that equated Victorian traditions with the Law of God." Defense of these attitudes, argued Henry, may provoke more sympathy for the "new morality." He suggested a critical appraisal of both tradition and the contemporary mood. If that is done, he predicted, "evangelical Christianity may be able to exhibit its cutting edge at the frontiers of ethical discussion" about sex and sexuality.[33]

To stimulate a "cutting edge" discussion on birth control and abortion, Henry and the Christian Medical Society gathered an international panel of twenty-seven scholars, lawyers, journalists, and doctors for a conference on human sexuality and reproduction. The conference, called "A Protestant Affirmation on the Control of Human Reproduction," was a careful attempt to produce an evangelical consensus on birth control and abortion.[34] The conference was called as a response to legislation being considered in California and New York that would liberalize existing abortion laws. The energy behind the legislation came from medical professionals who were concerned about the legal vagueness of performing abortions when medical science increasingly made the usual justifications obsolete. In the past, abortion procedures were granted to save the women's life. But, as medical science reduced the risks of pregnancy, the consensus on which circumstances constituted a risk to the mother's life evaporated. Doctors looked to government to write laws that took into considerations factors such as mental health, environment, pregnancies due to rape or incest, and cases of prenatal and genetic deformities. The American Legal Institute (ALI) drafted legislative language to protect doctors and broaden the legal scope for performing "therapeutic abortions." The language from ALI's Model Penal Code of 1961 was used in over forty state legislatures. As sociologist Kristen Luker's study of California's passage of abortion laws during the 1960s and early 1970s shows, only a few "pro-life" organizations emerged to fight the ALI Model Law in California. Most of these activists were Catholic doctors, nurses, priests, and nuns. In California, these people were overwhelmed by the voices of other doctors, lawyers, and abortion activists.[35]

The conferees considered a broad range of legal, theological, medical, and philosophical questions. They discussed such topics as the changing legal status of abortion, the morality of performing abortions in cases of genetic deformities, when the fetus gained full legal rights, and whether or not life began at conception. There was even brief discussion supporting development of a "morning-after pill."[36] The goal of the conference was to produce a final statement that reflected the best of evangelical thought on the "perplexing questions" of human reproduction. That statement placed the decision to perform abortion in the hands of a "medical team" in which the "Christian physician" was the "captain." The conferees opposed any legislative decision that "usurped the authority of the Christian conscience" and the professional judgment of the doctor. The final document also affirmed the fetus as a "developing human life," more than a "mass of cells or an organic growth." At the same time, however, the conferees recognized that in an "evil" and "distorted" world, doctors would have to perform abortions for "individual, familial . . . societal" and medical reasons.[37]

The "Protestant Affirmation on the Control of Human Reproduction" was carefully worded to affirm the gravity of abortion while placing evangelicals firmly within the political mainstream on "the abortion question." The final document did, however, commit evangelicals to support wider legal access to abortion. It supported the ALI Model Law, which the final document reprinted in full. The ALI Model Laws severely limited abortion after the sixth month but, during the first trimester, doctors were given wide leeway to prescribe abortion in particular physical, psychological, genetic, or social situations. The final document had few detractors, though one conferee warned, "Anyone who permits abortion for some reasons has opened the door to abortion for any reason."[38]

The "Protestant Affirmation" recognized the changes occurring in American politics and health care and sought to carve out a niche where ethical decisions would be made within the purview of doctors, hospital committees, families, and presumably friends, relatives, and clergy. Evangelical leaders believed that the combination of family, medical experts, and "caring professionals" would make the tough moral choices about when to prescribe abortion. They opposed "abortion on demand," but recognized the utilitarian argument that "social good" would have to be weighed when dealing with complex family situations. Given the argument that the fetus was "developing life" that did not necessarily have a "soul at conception," the decision to abort came down to weighing many moral goods at once.[39]

Immediately following the conference, *Christianity Today* published the final document and selected several of the conference papers for publication. For its readers, Henry sought to address the main philosophical question of whether the fertilized embryo was endowed with a soul at conception. Paul Jewett, a Harvard-trained theologian, reviewed biblical, historical, biological, and philosophical sources and concluded that a final statement about the "origin and nature of the soul is impossible." The fetus has value as a "primordial person" and bears the "divine image in some sense." Thus, he argues, an abortion cannot be equated with "an appendectomy." Jewett concludes that the fetus was potential life, but not fully human. It never reaches the same status as that of the mother or a born child. He conceded that abortion is morally permissible in certain situations including cases of maternal health, illegitimacy, rape, living with a deformed or mentally retarded child, and in life situations with which a pregnant woman could not cope. Jewett counseled his readers to include women in the decision of what "ought to be done" about pregnancy, saying the "males of the species" must be "humble" when deciding questions of maternal health and well-being. At the same time, he recognized that the fetus possessed enough humanity for abortion to "remain the last recourse, never to be denied out of hand, only ventured in emergency, and burdened with uncertainty."[40]

Bruce Waltke, a Harvard-trained biblical scholar, agreed with Jewett and argued that the Old Testament "did not equate the fetus with living persons." Although the Bible placed great value on a developing fetus, he argued, it did not describe it as having a soul. Additionally, Waltke pointed out that the killing of a fetus was not a capital crime in Mosaic law. These facts, he noted, made Jewish law less stringent than Assyrian laws that meted out equal punishment to someone who killed a fetus or another person. It was Waltke's conclusion that abortion was not murder because the fetus's rights did not supersede the rights of the mother.[41] The positions taken by Waltke and Jewett were shared by other evangelical scholars.[42] Their analysis was considered influential.[43]

The key point that needed clarification, however, was whether the fetus, as potential life, made a viable claim for legal protection. Most evangelical leaders agreed that at some point during the second trimester legal rights should be granted. The question was when exactly that point occurred. Both journalist Nancy Hardesty in *Eternity,* and physician Robert Visscher in *Christianity Today,* argued that a fetus was infused with a soul and with legal rights at "viability," when the fetus could survive outside the womb. Striking a logical note that augured Justice Blackman's *Roe v. Wade* majority opinion, Visscher argued that "therapeutic abortions" should be allowed until viability, because of the wide disagreement among religious and philosophical sources about when life begins. Visscher was not an advocate of abortion on demand before the sixth month, but citing both Thomas Aquinas and English common law, he believed doctors should be able to prescribe abortion for the "unfortunate circumstances" some women faced in the period of time before viability.[44]

The positions taken by the "Protestant Affirmation" and the supporting articles published in *Christianity Today* were widely applauded by a broad cross section of evangelicals. Letters to the editor supported the document. One letter objected to the word "sex" on the magazine's cover, but was nonetheless satisfied with the conclusions printed inside. Additional support came from such diverse sources as the nascent movement of evangelical feminists, "young" evangelicals, Billy Graham, and even the *Christian Century,* the magazine of liberal Protestant thought, lent its blessing.[45] Henry was satisfied with the final document and with the conference. He would later say that "on these issues [birth control and abortion] where there was little direct biblical guidance" the conference was a "meeting of the minds."[46]

The predicted consensus never materialized. Evangelical leaders, theologians, doctors, lawyers, and academics agreed with the tenor of the "Protestant Affirmation," but it did not filter down far into the rank and file. In fact, between 1970 and 1973, those who signed the "Protestant Affirmation" were assailed by a growing number of fellow-evangelicals. There was a concern that support of "liberalized" abortion laws contributed to the steep rise in the number of abortions being per-formed in places like California and New York, where the number of actual abor-tions rose 2000% between 1967 and 1970. In 1971, one out of three pregnancies in California was aborted. The number of abortions leveled off by 1974, but still, in states enacting "liberalized" abortion laws along the ALI Model Law guidelines, fully one-fourth of all pregnancies ended in abortion. The rising numbers of abor-tions shocked evangelical observers who expected doctors and hospital ethics com-mittees to serve as a responsible brake on the numbers of abortions performed. In states like California and New York, abortions were being performed without even the restrictions envisioned in the ALI Model Laws. State law gave doctors the ulti-mate authority whether or not to perform an abortion and often restricted the practice to such cases as rape, incest, fetal deformity, and maternal health. In fact and practice, physicians in California and New York rarely distinguished between the types of abortions they performed and seldom challenged the reasons why women sought them. After the passage of "liberalized" abortion laws, the proce-dure became an accepted (and expected) medical practice, insurance companies covered the procedure, and women sought abortions in large numbers.[47]

Despite the passage of "liberalized" abortion laws in almost forty states, a grow-ing legalization movement mobilized to further change state law. The legalization movement, led by the National Organization of Women (NOW) and the National Abortion Rights Action League (NARAL), argued that abortion was a "women's right" and her "individual choice." Women chose abortion, these activists claimed, to control if, when, and with whom they would have children. These decisions, they argued, involved complex personal and financial considerations that could not be weighed by even the most sympathetic physician conforming to the ALI Model Laws.[48] The legalization movement succeeded in many states. When legislative agendas stalled, activists pursued court cases and argued that access to abortion should be constitutionally protected based on the "right to privacy" found in the *Griswold* decision of 1965. Legalization forces refused to compromise and sought to make access to abortion a constitutionally protected right. Their success hinged on their use of key symbols of American democracy, protection of individual rights and liberty, and their well-organized and compelling campaign of popular protest.[49]

Evangelical leaders were shocked at the dramatic rise in the number of abor-tions. They were also caught unprepared for the early successes of the legalization movement, finding it difficult to respond to its grassroots political campaign. The problem was twofold: evangelicals were not organized politically and they had dif-ficulty with women's calls for abortion rights when couched in terms of personal autonomy. On the first issue, evangelicals possessed few resources and could not contest political issues at either the state, national, or local levels. Prior to this time, evangelical leaders debated current events, but never organized to fight for any par-ticular issue or candidate. In fact, evangelicals often criticized liberal Protestant clergy and anticommunist fundamentalist pastors for their political activism. Stud-ies in religious voting patters in the 1960s confirmed that religiously conservative people were the least likely to be involved in politics.[50] There was never a need to politically organize on an issue that placed them outside what they believed to be mainstream opinion.[51] Evangelicals also had difficulty comprehending abortion activists' calls for personal autonomy. Though *Christianity Today*'s editors supported the Equal Rights Amendment, they did not extend its equality claims to questions of reproductive rights. Evangelical leaders viewed abortion as a medical problem that required pastoral concern.[52] Initial support of liberalized abortion laws was considered a legal response to a tragic situation, never as one of rights, privacy, or reproductive control. Changing the existing abortion laws of the early 1960s was both a compassionate and legally wise decision, but it was not one that should be left to women who faced tough moral choices. For those leaders who produced the "Protestant Affirmation," a woman who sought abortion either faced a physical or mental crisis or required a compassionate and professional response to a complex set of circumstances. The concept of abortion as an individual right, protected by the state, was foreign to the worldview of most evangelicals. Moreover, they believed that permitting free access to abortion was an unnecessary intrusion of state power to promote a certain sexual agenda. By weighing in on moral subjects, the state eroded symbolic links between private morality and collective life. Evangelicals had always seen a close connection between private action and public good. Morality was never strictly an individual matter. By the early 1970s, as issues such as abortion, homosexuality, and pornography entered the public debate, voices from within evangelicalism started to call for a more concerted and organized response.[53]

Seeking Allies and Making Alliances

The "mainstream" positions staked out in the "Protestant Affirmation" found few allies among the legalization movement and gained more and more conservative critics. At a 1970 revival rally in Florida, picketers accused Billy Graham of "hedging on the abortion issue." Evangelical women scolded *Christianity Today* for its failure to effectively respond to feminists who made "mother a dirty word" and for supporting abortion and the ERA.[54] A growing number of evangelical special purpose groups appeared in reaction to permissive views on sexuality. Many of these groups reached across denominational lines for members and support. In places like Michigan and Pennsylvania, Parents Under God and Life Action Ministries battled abortion legalization efforts and sex education in public schools. In the midst of internal criticism and grassroots organizing, prominent evangelical leaders revised earlier positions on abortion.[55] Billy Graham, an early supporter of the "Protestant Affirmation," issued a statement that said he was "only beginning to come to grips with the magnitude of the problem" and planned to take a more active anti-abortion position.[56] *Christianity Today* printed several articles revisiting the question of a fetus's humanity and legal rights. These articles took issue with both the "Protestant Affirmation" and the theological rationale undergirding it.

Singled out were Bruce Waltke, Paul Jewett, and Robert Visscher, who used the Bible "to excuse indiscriminate abortions." Even if the intent of the "Protestant Affirmation" was to limit abortions, one author concluded, it nonetheless had a profound influence on how evangelicals perceived the "evils" of abortion.[57] The cultural and political ground had shifted so quickly that evangelicals began to point fingers at those who earlier pushed for liberalized abortion legislation. Even Carl Henry, the chief voice of moderate conservative evangelicalism, found it difficult to navigate in this new environment. After a series of miscommunications with the Board of Directors, Henry resigned from his editorship at *Christianity Today*, though he later claimed he was fired. He was replaced by Lindsell, a close friend and ally, but who was by temperament more theologically and politically conservative.[58] During the 1970s, new leaders and voices started to take up the issue of abortion and place it at the center of evangelical moral concern. Some of those who helped produce the "Protestant Affirmation" tried to preserve some of its relevance.[59] Most simply disappeared from the pages of evangelical publications.

The success of the legalization movement made abortion, for evangelicals, the most prominent symbol of moral disintegration and the breakdown of familial strength. By the early 1970s, under the editorship of Lindsell, *Christianity Today* began promoting a strong anti-abortion line. Over a hundred news items, editorials, and articles appeared in the years around the *Roe* decision, including a graphic, eyewitness description of an actual abortion.[60] Evangelical writers began to argue that abortion ended a human life. The medical and philosophical distinctions made by the "Protestant Affirmation" were disavowed or criticized. Lindsell himself took the lead in this effort. Despite his past support of the "Protestant Affirmation," he now argued that the most important issue was whether a fetus was to 'become a person." Innocent life, "needed protection," he wrote. To harm innocent life in an abortion was to "commit homicide."[61] No one who is truly religious, he elaborated, "could possibly tolerate abortion or institutions which indulged it, since it terminated a genuine human life." We must "stand by those," he wrote, "who understand the gravity of our position." Lindsell summoned evangelicals to "the battle of the flesh" to defeat the new sexual politics.[62] The careful, inclusive, and mainstream language of the "Protestant Affirmation" disappeared and was replaced by a more combative and overtly political tone. Evangelicals prepared for the possibility that the American state (and a large portion of its people) was in fact "hostile to religion" and unwilling to protect "innocent human life."[63]

To meet the challenges posed by "below-the-belt" issues, evangelicals needed a new political consciousness and new allies. Evangelical leaders recognized that their traditional social ethic of voluntary action and spiritual revivalism was woefully inadequate in the contemporary political environment. Evangelicals had always viewed private morality as a source of public strength. Restraint, chastity, and stable family life were private bonds that promoted the common good. But they could no longer promote "family values" without taking public stances on private matters. Abortion advocates hailed the efforts of state legislatures and the courts as a triumph of civil rights. Evangelicals, along with a growing number of religious conservatives, saw these political actions as evidence that the state would protect all choices as moral. Even though *Roe* was couched in terms of privacy and individual choice, the Court's decision sent the message that morality was too explosive to be left to individuals or tradition. In order to "protect the family" from the encroaching state, *Christianity Today* urged direct political action. "Christians need to realize that a great deal of intensive work is necessary if legislative relief . . . is to be obtained. Polemics is not enough. We need to channel more energy into seeking better jurisprudence." [64] To move past polemics, evangelical leaders sought like-minded allies. They found them, ironically, among conservative Catholics. The gulf dividing Catholics and evangelicals was large and historically antagonistic. In the cultural climate following the *Roe* decision, political allies were more important than past theological divisions.

To prepare the way for an evangelical/Catholic détente, *Christianity Today* chided its readers for their past anti-Catholicism. Its editors told readers that "evangelicals are far closer, in theology and commitment . . .[to] the church of Rome than to many liberals in the Protestant tradition." Gone were the days when evangelicals found it best "not to speak in a Roman accent" on issues of contraception and abortion or when *Christianity Today* found Catholic positions on questions of limiting human reproduction "antiquated," "intolerable," "dangerous," and "obscurantist."[65] Though most evangelical writers recognized wide chasms dividing the two largest expressions of traditional American religiosity, they nonetheless accepted many Catholic teachings concerning abortion's immorality.[66] Theological agreement, it seemed, was not as important as political agreement. Conservative social values were more crucial than supposed heterodox religious beliefs. Working against abortion brought evangelicals and Catholics together in a common political cause. For the most part, lay Catholics mobilized the early anti-abortion movement. *Christianity Today* noted that the anti-abortion movement was "mostly Catholic" and urged evangelicals to take part.[67] And they did in large numbers. Evangelical anti-abortion activists and intellectuals such as Dr. C. Everett Koop, Francis Schaefer, Harold O. J. Brown, and Robert Holbrook joined the editorial board of the journal *Human Life Review*. Southern Baptist pastor Holbrook was elected to the National Right to Life Committee (NRLC). Koop organized an ecumenical group of medical practitioners to lobby against abortion's legalization.[68] Evangelicals joined with Catholics in local NRLC chapters and in a whole series of "crisis pregnancy centers" such as Birthright (1968), National Life Center (1971), and CareNet (1974).[69] The result was an interesting politically ecumenical coalition, chartered to promote a conservative vision of sexuality and family life.

Evangelicals and Catholics cooperated in a host of grassroots and intellectual projects aimed at ending abortion's legalization. Such inclusiveness did not mean the melding of institutions. There was a shared agenda and some cross-pollination of board members and activists. At the same time, evangelicals created their own institutions, such as Baptists for Life, Presbyterians for Life, and the Christian Action Council, started by Harold O. J. Brown.[70] The strength of the early anti-abortion movement was its diversity, which seemed to cross both religious and political lines. The NRLC proudly listed a diverse coalition of members and sympathizers that included "the two Jesses (Helms and Jackson), farm wives, ghetto dwellers, peaceniks, John Birchers, Catholic bishops, Mormons, psychiatrists, Jewish rabbis, lawyers, feminists, Baptist preachers, scientists . . . Democrats and Republicans."[71] It was from this strength that early activists saw potential victory for their cause. Writing in the Catholic magazine *America,* Brown, for one, believed that ecumenical cooperation would "remind non-Catholics and non-Christians" that millions of Americans are "against permissive abortions." The size of their coalition would "make clear to lawmakers that abortion was not merely a sectarian or doctrinal issue but of fundamental importance to the whole of Western civilization." In his call to cooperative action, Brown told his Catholic audience that "[we]. . . need to come to the realization that the wall of separation is now being used to isolate the spiritual values on which America has been built from the political institutions that will shape America's future."[72] It was around such calls to organize an ecumenical and political alliance to save America from the destruction of abortion and sexual license that religious conservatives entered the public arena in the mid-1970s.

Conclusion

In the decades previous to the *Roe* decision, the politics of sex emerged from an ill-defined private sphere into the public arena.[73] Evangelicals tried to find morally permissible grounds for physicians to prescribe birth control and perform abortions and supported legislation that protected doctor's and women's decisions; however, by the late 1960s, a more aggressive sexual politics broke down the old boundaries that separated religion and politics. Activists for abortion rights, gay rights, and women's rights hoped they could build a more tolerant, inclusive, and secular society. Their agenda and tactics challenged evangelical (and Catholic) conceptions of the "good society," but also threatened their ideas about private morality and the public good. Abortion became the issue around which most evangelicals would mobilize. In the years between the "Protestant Affirmation" and the *Roe* decision a virtual consensus emerged that deeply opposed the legalization of abortion as well as any additional legal protections for homosexuality and pornography. In the 1960s, liberals argued that social welfare and civil rights programs would promote the common good and build a "Great Society." Evangelicals used the same rationale for entering the public square in the 1970s. When abortion, pornography, and homosexuality became matters of public debate and grassroots political campaigns, evangelicals organized and became active politically in order to uphold traditional morality and protect their version of the public interest.

After 1976, it was clear that a substantial coalition of religiously conservative individuals could be politically mobilized to protect their vision of the good society. For this task, Republican activists, anti-abortion and evangelical leaders, and fundamentalist Protestant clergy joined forces to create the New Religious Right

(NRR). According to historian George Marsden, the NRR revived that part of the Republican Party heritage that was built on a "militant, broadly Christian, and antisecularlist foundation." "The striking element missing," he noted, was its "anti-Catholicism."[74] On the abortion issue, evangelicals downplayed centuries of religious antagonism and made allies among Catholics. To oppose abortion's legalization, evangelical leaders found common cause and intellectual comity with conservative Catholics. They agreed that abortion was homicide (except in very rare circumstances), that the fetus had legal rights at conception, and that state power should be used to enforce these provisions. These positions have stayed firm over the decades and continue to frame contemporary discussion of the abortion issue. It was this new anti-abortion coalition that became the intellectual foundation and activist base of the New Religious Right, which would emerge full-force in the late 1970s and would find its greatest political influence when linked to the resurgent conservatism of Ronald Reagan.

Michael W. Flamm

THE POLITICS OF "LAW AND ORDER"

In retrospect, the moment signified the early rumblings of a seismic shift in the political landscape. On a chilly evening in April 1964, hundreds of white ethnics from Milwaukee's blue-collar South Side crowded into Serb Memorial Hall to hear a speech by Alabama Governor George Wallace, a candidate in the Wisconsin Democratic primary.[1] Tensions immediately flared. When rally organizer Bronko Gruber, a tavern owner and World War II veteran, attempted to introduce the candidate, a local black minister and civil rights activist yelled, "Get your dogs out!" To which Gruber hotly replied: "I'll tell you something about your dogs, padre! I live on Walnut Street and three weeks ago tonight a friend of mine was assaulted by three of your countrymen or whatever you want to call them." Cheers and whistles erupted from the audience. "They beat up old ladies 83 years old, rape our womenfolk," continued Gruber. "They mug people. They won't work. They are on relief. How long can we tolerate this?" After a near-brawl, Wallace gave his speech, interrupted by at least thirty ovations in forty minutes.[2]

The dramatic confrontation demonstrated how public anxiety over neighborhood safety could transmute into a wider critique of the civil rights movement and the liberal welfare state. Less than a week later, Wallace defied all expectations—including his own—and won over 33% of the votes cast in the primary.[3] Although it is unclear to what degree Wallace's success was the result of his invocation of the crime threat, it is clear that Wallace had tapped into a rich vein of resentment, anger, and frustration.[4] In the wake of these explosive emotions, which Arizona Senator Barry Goldwater, the Republican nominee, would also seek to exploit in 1964, "law and order" would soon emerge as the vehicle by which anxious whites transmitted their antipathy to neighborhood integration and fear of racial violence from the municipal to the presidential arena.[5] The issue would also lead many white Democrats to avoid electoral politics or switch party affiliation.[6]

As this essay will demonstrate, that process was gradual and contingent on events as well as perceptions. In 1964, "law and order" failed to derail Lyndon

Johnson's presidential campaign in part because voters perceived both Wallace and Goldwater as racial extremists. The issue also failed to gain traction because social unrest had yet to reach critical levels despite rising crime and the Harlem riot that took place in July 1964. By 1966, however, "law and order" had exposed serious cracks in the New Deal electoral coalition—most notably in New York, where white ethnics overwhelmingly rejected a civilian review board for the police department. And by 1968, amid a crescendo of riots, crime, assassination, and protests, the issue had come to dominate national politics. In that year, the conservative candidates—Republican Richard Nixon and Wallace, running as an independent—decisively outpolled the liberal candidate, Hubert Humphrey. In just four years, millions of white voters had abandoned the Democratic Party, many because they had now come to believe that it was unwilling to make personal safety a political priority.

* * *

The question of when precisely and why exactly urban white voters began to desert the Democratic Party has generated a healthy debate among scholars and commentators. Political analysts Thomas and Mary Edsall, authors of *Chain Reaction,* identify the critical moment as the 1960s and the main cause as the white reaction to the civil rights movement and Great Society programs. The Democratic Party, they and others contend, then compounded the crisis by responding to the grievances and demands of a black militant minority while ignoring the fears and desires of a white "silent majority."[7] Historian Thomas Sugrue argues, however, that urban antiliberalism predated the Johnson administration and determined the "politics of race and neighborhood" in the North in the 1940s and 1950s. In *The Origins of the Urban Crisis,* he details how opposition to racial integration dominated local elections even in Detroit, where liberal organizations like the United Auto Workers presumably held sway. Therefore, the conservative backlash of the 1960s was not, according to Sugrue, "the unique product of the white rejection of the Great Society. Instead it was the culmination of more than two decades of simmering white discontent and extensive antiliberal political organization."[8]

Neither interpretation is wholly persuasive. Sugrue has convincingly documented the existence and virulence of northern racism at the municipal level. But the disintegration of the New Deal coalition at the national level was not inevitable. Prior to the early 1960s, many urban whites in effect split their ballots. They balanced support for conservative local candidates opposed to residential integration with support for liberal national candidates committed to civil rights.[9] More important, both the Edsalls and Sugrue place too much emphasis on the role of racism and too little on the role of security. By 1968, the distance between voters and issues had narrowed as anxiety over the loss of public safety had widened.[10] The unraveling of the liberal political coalition was therefore not simply the result of a racial backlash against civil rights. It was also due to the growing sense among whites that liberal programs could not prevent social disorder, which in turn reinforced the growing popularity of "law and order."

Fearful whites received little solace from liberals, who failed to take seriously the matter of personal safety until it was too late.[11] In the face of the rise in crime (the murder rate alone almost doubled between 1963 and 1968), they initially maintained that the statistics were faulty—a response that if not incorrect was insensitive to the victims of crime as well as their friends and family, co-workers and neighbors.[12] They also tended to dismiss those who pleaded for "law and order" as racists, ignoring blacks who were victimized more often than any other group and insulting Jews who had steadfastly supported the civil rights movement. Finally, liberals insisted with some merit that the only truly effective way to fight crime was through an attack on root causes like poverty and unemployment. The argument helped to justify the War on Poverty, but soon left the Johnson administration vulnerable to conservative claims that the Great Society had worsened the epidemic of urban violence.

Above all, liberals routinely and consistently defined crime control as a local problem. Constitutionally and logistically, it was—in 1968, state and municipal governments still employed over ten times as many full-time law enforcement officers as the federal government.[13] But the definition seemed rather convenient when liberals had already classified virtually every other social ill, most notably public education, as a national imperative. "Somehow, in the minds of most Americans the breakdown of local authority became the fault of the federal government," wrote a somewhat baffled Johnson in his memoirs.[14] Implicit in the statement was his rueful acknowledgment that after four years in office, his administration had failed to convince many whites, particularly urban ethnic Democrats, that it understood their fears and frustrations.[15] The loss of "law and order" eroded popular faith in effective government, leaving liberals unable to articulate a popular position on the issue.

By contrast, conservatives spoke with a cogent and compelling voice on "law and order." In constructing a popular message with visceral appeal, they maintained that the breakdown in public order was the result of three developments aided and abetted by liberals. First, the civil rights movement had popularized the doctrine of civil disobedience, which promoted disrespect for law and authority. Second, the Supreme Court, in a series of decisions such as *Escobedo* and *Miranda,* had enhanced the rights of criminal defendants at the expense of law enforcement.[16] Finally, the Great Society trumpeted by the White House had directly or indirectly rewarded undeserving minorities for their criminal behavior during urban riots.

Conservatives also offered a positive program for the restoration of what they saw as a society of decency and security. In an inversion of their traditional stance on federalism, they maintained that the national government should assume a major role in the local fight against violence and disorder. The president should exert moral leadership from Washington, reinforcing respect for the law and promoting contempt for those who violated it. The Congress should curtail the liberal welfare state, which promoted paternalism and dependency at the expense of opportunity and responsibility. The Supreme Court should overturn recent rulings and ease excessive restraints on the police, allowing them to collect evidence and conduct interrogations as they saw fit within broad limits. And the federal courts should set a positive example by imposing harsher sentences on convicted criminals. In short, extremism in pursuit of "law and order" was no vice.

At a theoretical level, conservatives presented a dual vision of order. On the one hand, they repudiated the progressive ideal of a planned society administered by distant experts. Reasserting a conservative variant of American populism, they expressed hostility to social engineering as practiced by Supreme Court justices and Great Society bureaucrats who represented disembodied authority. Defending local institutions and individuals, conservatives praised in particular the neighborhood policeman who protected local values—political, moral, and property—and kept the civil peace despite outside interference. On the other hand, they contended that the community's right to order—to public safety as they saw it—took precedence over the individual's right to freedom. Rejecting the claim of radicals that public space was where demonstrators could assert their rights such as free speech and free assembly, conservatives maintained that it was where citizens with a legitimate stake in the community could enjoy themselves if they complied with the legitimate demands of legitimate authority.[17]

At a popular level, "law and order" resonated both as a social ideal and political slogan because it combined an understandable concern over the rising number of traditional crimes—robberies and rapes, muggings and murders—with implicit and explicit unease about civil rights, civil liberties, urban riots, antiwar protests, moral values, and drug use. Of course, street crime differed in important ways from the other causes of civil disorder, but politicians, pundits, and propagandists across the political spectrum hastened to blur this distinction. In the process, they loaded "law and order" with layers of meaning virtually impossible to disentangle and turned it into a Rorschach test of public anxiety.[18]

What ultimately gave "law and order" such potency, then, was precisely its amorphous quality, its ability to represent different concerns to different people at different moments. To be sure, the issue often rested on deliberate omissions, such as the reality that civil disobedience was often the only recourse left to demonstrators denied fundamental freedoms and confronted by officials who themselves repeatedly defied the law. But at the same time, it clarified (or simplified) a confusing image of danger and disorder. "Law and order" identified a clear cast of violent villains (protesters, rioters, and criminals), explained the causes for their actions (above all, the doctrine of civil disobedience and the paternalism of the welfare state), and implied a ready response (limited government, moral leadership, and judicial firmness).

Yet "law and order" was more than the sum of its parts. Conservatives charged that it had become the most visible sign and symbol of the perceived failure of activist government and of liberalism itself. In their view, the welfare state had squandered the hard-earned taxes of the deserving middle class on wasteful programs for the undeserving poor. It had also failed to ensure the safety and security of the citizenry—the primary duty of any government. The argument increasingly fell on receptive ears, even in supposedly liberal bastions like New York.

* * *

New York was a troubled city in 1964. During the 1950s, black migration and Puerto Rican immigration had altered considerably the complexion of New York, making boroughs like Brooklyn significantly poorer and younger, less white and more minority.[19] At the same time, a crime wave had created a near panic among whites. In the first six months of the year, murders rose 16.6%—rapes and robberies by 28 and 29%, respectively. Subway crime jumped by almost 30%. A series of spectacular incidents also provoked widespread alarm. On 21 April, a group of Jewish children were attacked by a gang of fifty black teenagers. On 10 May, the police confirmed the existence of the "Blood Brothers," a black gang in Harlem believed responsible for the murder of four whites. And over Memorial Day weekend twenty black teens vandalized and terrorized a subway train, beating and robbing passengers at random. These events, warned the conservative *National Review* on 16 July, represented more than just a deluge of delinquency: "What is happening, or is about to happen—let us face it—is race war."[20]

That same day an off-duty officer in plainclothes shot and killed a black teenager allegedly armed with a knife. The incident involved Lieutenant Thomas Gilligan, a seventeen-year veteran with a distinguished record, and James Powell, a fifteen-year-old summer-school student with a juvenile arrest record. It occurred in Yorkville, a predominantly white section of upper Manhattan, after the officer intervened in a dispute between a white superintendent and black teenagers congregated outside his building across the street from Robert Wagner Junior High School.[21] In the wake of the shooting, tensions quickly mounted. In Harlem two days later, a peaceful demonstration escalated into a violent confrontation with police. In the end, after three more nights of rioting in Manhattan and Brooklyn, one person was dead, 141 were injured (including 48 officers), and 519 were arrested.[22]

In the aftermath, most liberal leaders—black and white—placed the blame for the Harlem riot on police brutality or social conditions. But many ordinary whites depicted themselves as the victims of black criminals run amok. A woman living on Morningside Heights reported that the 125th Street subway station featured a large sign reading "Kill All Whites." She declared that she could not go to work without fear of robbery or death. Few whites tried to distinguish between street crime and civil disorder. "The situation in New York City is getting out of hand," wrote a LaSalle Street resident to Republican Governor Nelson Rockefeller. "Violence, horror, looting, rioting, stabbing, raping, purse-snatching are all around. . . . It is not safe walking in the streets and parks and riding in the elevators."[23] Similar messages poured into the White House. "We're getting floods of wires and telegrams," the president reported in a telephone conversation with FBI director J. Edgar Hoover. "Here's one. [reads aloud:] 'I'm a working girl. . . . I'm afraid to leave my house. . . . I feel the Negro revolution will reach Queens. . . . Please send troops immediately to Harlem.'"[24]

Johnson chose to reject that option, which he would later exercise during the

Detroit riot of 1967. But the White House remained in a state of alarm. "This one issue could destroy us in the campaign," concluded one analysis. "Every night of rioting costs us the support of thousands. Therefore we need to move swiftly to try to hold the line before it spreads like a contagion."[25] That advice the president would follow. In private, Johnson pleaded with the FBI to halt the riots.[26] The administration also quietly urged black leaders to cancel or postpone demonstrations until after the election and advised white liberals to withhold funds from civil rights organizations as a means of forcing compliance. In public, the president declared that the War on Poverty would constitute "a war against crime and a war against disorder"—a promise that eventually backfired.[27] But for the most part he maintained a studied silence on the critical subject of civil disorder because it was too explosive. As a result, urban whites who remained dubious about Goldwater had little choice but to support Johnson and vote for "law and order" in local races.[28]

Ultimately, the strategy of silence paid dividends. By concentrating on issues on which Goldwater was vulnerable (like Social Security and nuclear war), Johnson protected his early lead and roared to a landslide victory. His popular vote margin was 16 million (61 to 39 in percentage terms), and his electoral college margin was 486–52. The president captured 94% of the black vote, 90% of the Jewish vote, 62% of the women's vote, 20% of the registered Republican vote, and even a majority of the white vote (a feat no Democrat has managed since). He also carried every state, with the exception of Arizona and the Deep South (Mississippi, Alabama, South Carolina, Georgia, and Louisiana).[29]

In the meantime, "law and order" failed to catch fire with ethnic whites in South Philadelphia, Brooklyn, and Queens, where Italian, German, and Irish voters rejected Goldwater in greater numbers than they had Richard Nixon in 1960. The issue also failed to ignite in Polish precincts in Ohio and Chicago—and even in cities under economic and social strain like Gary and Milwaukee, where Johnson captured 82% of the vote among Bronko Gruber and his neighbors.[30] The reasons were twofold. First, Goldwater never managed to shed the label of racial extremism because of his opposition to the Civil Rights Act. Second, conditions were not yet ripe for "law and order" to take hold. But that would soon change.

By November 1966, the politics of "law and order" had erupted across the nation and had engulfed New York City, where street crime was rampant and race relations remained tense following the Harlem riot.[31] At stake was a municipal referendum with national implications. The referendum proposed to abolish the civilian review board established by newly elected Mayor John Lindsay to provide more effective oversight of the New York Police Department (NYPD) and promote better police–minority relations.[32] The image that dominated the campaign, however, came from the Patrolmen's Benevolent Association (PBA), which in opposition to the review board distributed a provocative campaign poster. Employing racial, class, and gender code to tap into widespread fears and anxieties, the poster showed a young middle-class white woman exiting nervously from the subway and emerging alone onto a dark and deserted street. "The Civilian Review

Board must be stopped!" read the accompanying text. "Her life . . . your life . . . may depend on it." The reason, it added, was that a "police officer must not hesitate. If he does . . . the security and safety of your family may be jeopardized."[33]

The message was pointed and persuasive. A WCBS-TV poll taken on 4 November showed that a clear majority of those surveyed felt that the review board would hinder police performance. Four days later, buoyed by a near-record turnout—over 2 million voters cast ballots, more than in the 1964 presidential race—the referendum passed by an almost two-to-one margin. Of the five boroughs, only Manhattan narrowly voted to retain the board.[34] In the nation's largest and arguably most progressive city, which two years earlier had given Lyndon Johnson a decisive victory and sent Robert Kennedy comfortably to the U.S. Senate, a measure identified by supporters as an extension of the civil rights cause and endorsed by every prominent liberal politician and organization had met decisive defeat.

The outcome was not unexpected.[35] But the review board referendum, contested under the spotlight of the nation's media capital, reflected in stark form the growing perception among urban whites that personal security was now a critical issue. The election also highlighted the increasing unwillingness of local Democrats to accept the racial liberalism of the national party. And the result reinforced trends from across the nation including California, where Republican newcomer Ronald Reagan handily defeated incumbent Democrat Edmund Brown in the race for governor.[36] By 1966, the politics of "law and order" had exposed serious cracks in the New Deal electoral coalition.

From the outset, white liberals in New York were divided. With Catholic voters (overwhelmingly Irish and Italian) conceded opponents of a civilian review board, the critical target became Jewish voters, for whom class, culture, and concern collided. Lower-middle-class and working-class Jews in the outer boroughs were wary of civilian review—a fact highlighted when the Bronx chapters of the American Jewish Congress voted unanimously to disregard the parent body's endorsement of the board. But even professional Jews with college degrees, higher incomes, and Manhattan addresses proved reluctant to back civilian review unless they combined an overriding commitment to civil rights with a strong sense of personal security. At Temple Rodeph Shalom in the heart of the Upper West Side, for example, congregants barraged Lindsay's press secretary with questions about why the mayor always seemed to side with lawless minorities against law-abiding taxpayers. Ultimately, despite liberal efforts to cast civilian review as a referendum on racism—"DON'T BE A YES MAN FOR BIGOTRY—VOTE NO" read thousands of posters—55% of Jews sided with their Catholic neighbors and voted against the board.[37] The scale of the Jewish defection from the liberal banner surprised observers.

The scope of the defeat was also startling. A sample of white ethnics in Brooklyn by the American Jewish Congress (AJC) revealed that class, race, and fear were significant factors. Over 80% of Catholics had voted against the review board—a level of support higher than John Kennedy had received in 1960. And over 60% of those who had backed Johnson in 1964 now took their cue from Goldwater supporters and opposed what they saw as a dangerous restraint on the NYPD. Only those in technical or professional occupations opposed the referendum—by the narrow margin of 52 to 47%—and even those with college degrees split on the issue. The survey also found that although most whites associated blacks with crime and disorder, they rejected racial stereotypes and prejudice. Thus, what was critical, concluded the survey's authors, was not racism but "a shift in the liberal perception of blacks, from victims and objects of violence and prejudice, to perpetrators of violence and social disorganization." It was then fear, above all, that united white Brooklynites, only 25% of whom stated that they were not afraid of having their homes invaded at night. The comparable figure for all Americans was 50%.[38]

The impact of "law and order" was hardly confined to New York. In California, actor-citizen Ronald Reagan shocked and surprised the political world when he upset incumbent Governor Edmund "Pat" Brown. Borrowing a page from Goldwater's playbook, Reagan skillfully exploited the white public's alarm at rising crime, disgust over the tumultuous student demonstrations at Berkeley, and fear of a repeat of the Watts riot of 1965. Combining these disparate developments into a devastating critique of the inequities and inefficiencies of the liberal welfare state, which he blamed for the disorder, Reagan won 58% of the vote. Defusing charges of extremism with his telegenic appeal, he received almost one million Democratic votes and carried all but three counties.[39]

In 1966, the Democratic Party lost forty-seven House seats, eight governorships, and three Senate seats, including twelve of thirteen senate and gubernatorial races in the ten largest states. A critical factor was the reluctance of blue-collar white voters in urban districts to go to the polls. In Chicago, the Democratic vote declined by more than 40,000 over the previous low set in 1950; in Detroit, the Democratic vote plummeted by more than 40%. The comparison, moreover, was with 1962—not 1964, when the presidential race had inflated turnout (as the New York referendum had). Similar results were reported in Cincinnati, Philadelphia, and Louisville.[40] "Roosevelt Democrats" had not yet become "Reagan Republicans" but that was scant consolation to the director of the AFL-CIO Committee on Political Education (COPE), who informed the Executive Committee that the election results had revealed the existence of "a tide that we did not see."[41]

In 1967, the tide continued to rise, carrying many Democrats out of the party. In the fall elections, following summer riots in Newark and Detroit, 80% of whites in Cleveland and 50% of whites in Boston voted Republican. In Gary, the figure was 90%—and one precinct that was 68% Democratic in 1964 was now 93% Republican.[42] In the coming year, the tide would crest, sweeping the Democrats from the White House and triggering a quarter-century of Republican dominance of the executive branch. The time had come—and conditions were certainly ripe—for the triumph of "law and order."

In 1968, political assassinations, urban riots, student demonstrations, and street crime—filmed in color and televised in homes nightly—left many Americans convinced that their society was in meltdown. First came the Tet Offensive and President Johnson's surprise announcement that he would not seek reelection. Next came the murder of Dr. King in Memphis, followed by riots and demonstrations in almost every major American city. Then came the assassination of Democratic senator and presidential candidate Robert Kennedy whose death, at the hands of a Jordanian immigrant named Sirhan Sirhan, shocked an already reeling public.

The death of Kennedy led to a intense period of hand-wringing and soul-searching. "The country does not work any more," lamented *Philadelphia Inquirer* columnist Joe McGinniss. "All that money and power have produced has been a bunch of people so filled with fear and hate that when a man tries to tell them they must do more for other men, instead of listening they shoot him in the head."[43] Across the country, the young blamed their unyielding elders; the elders blamed the disorderly young. Black militants blamed white racism; fearful whites blamed black power. "Has violence become an American way of life?" asked one newsmagazine.[44] The answer seemed painfully obvious.

In Congress, all sides sought to exploit the situation. Liberals used the tragedy to advance the cause of gun control. Conservatives used it to accelerate passage of a crime bill (the cleverly named Safe Streets Act) that, among other provisions, provided for virtually unlimited government surveillance and declared, in defiance of the Supreme Court's findings in *Mallory* and *Miranda,* that in federal cases a confession was admissible so long as the trial judge deemed it voluntary. On the day news of Kennedy's shooting reached the floor, Democratic liberals in the House, led by Judiciary Chairman Emanuel Celler of New York, were fighting to block the bill's passage. The next day Kennedy died and the House voted overwhelmingly in favor of the Safe Streets Act. "I am voting for this measure out of deference to so many expressions from constituents in my district who regard protection in our streets as their paramount anxiety today," said one Democrat.[45]

His district was not unique. Across the nation, anxious voters pressed liberal politicians to explain why the Great Society had failed to curb urban unrest and why they opposed the conservative prescription for a restoration of "law and order." Even Celler, with his seniority and popularity, was vulnerable because he represented a Brooklyn district in transition and endorsed the social programs of the Johnson administration. Many of his white backers, especially middle-class Jews, had supported the civil rights movement during the integrationist phase and continued to do so, but life on the front lines of urban decline had taken its toll. Aware intellectually that not all minorities were muggers, they wrestled emotionally with the sense that all muggers seemed either Puerto Rican or African American.

The letters to Celler reveal the depth of his constituents' anguish and the extent of the dilemma he faced. "How in God's name you would obliterate the only ray of hope existing for millions of victims of crime-ridden cities defies the imagination," declared a typical missive sent in response to Celler's public stand against the crime bill in May 1968. "Thousands of people of the Jewish faith have stood by helplessly to see their businesses destroyed, their lives in constant peril as politicians blithely court the Negro vote and ignore those who elected them to office. Why is it your sworn duty to protect robbers, muggers, and rapists?" The congressman's standard reply was that crime was a local responsibility, that federal intervention would inevitably lead to a national police force and a national police state, both of which he opposed.[46] It won Celler a deserved reputation as a civil libertarian, but also contributed to a bitter primary fight that he barely survived.[47]

The fate of the crime bill was now in the hands of a political lame duck. Ultimately, Johnson bowed to public pressure and in mid–June signed into law the Safe Streets Act with considerable reluctance. "I have decided," he said simply, "that this measure contains more good than bad and that I should sign it into law."[48] At bottom, the president probably had little choice. A diligent student of the polls and an astute politician, he knew how vociferous and virulent the cries for "law and order" were. He also knew that the presidential aspirations of Vice President Hubert Humphrey, who had received the Democratic nomination in August amid the chaos of the Chicago Convention, hung in the balance.[49]

Behind in the polls and hindered by an image of softness, Humphrey spent the fall of 1968 promising to provide Americans with "order and justice" by attacking the root causes of crime. Nixon countered with a promise to restore order without violence—and ridiculed the War on Poverty, which he claimed had exacerbated the crisis. He also vowed to provide moral leadership, trim social programs, and nominate conservative justices to the Supreme Court. The terms of debate had changed little since 1964. But the disorder of the past four years had transformed the political and cultural landscape, enhancing the appeal of the conservative platform and eroding the credibility of the liberal program. In 1968, it was above all the politics of "law and order" that doomed Humphrey's hopes.

In that pivotal election, the impact of the other great issue, Vietnam, was ambiguous for two reasons. First, although white voters generally ranked the war as the most critical issue facing the nation, they also indicated—with the exception of liberals and the young—that Vietnam was a distant, impersonal concern. By contrast, private polls commissioned by the Democratic Party indicated that "law and order" was an immediate, personal priority with virtually all Americans. The vast majority, reported Humphrey's pollster, wanted order restored without reservation or hesitation. "[It] is not a covert demand for anti-Negro action," he added. "The demand is spread through all segments of the population."[50] Second, most white voters could not distinguish between the candidates, both of whom pledged to bring the war to an end. Even in late October, survey data led the president's pollster to conclude that Vietnam was "cutting for neither Humphrey or Nixon."[51] Nor was inflation—an important political issue and economic problem by 1968—providing a significant edge to either party. By contrast, when it came to "law and order" most Americans had a clear idea where the two men stood—and by a considerable margin preferred the conservative Republican to the liberal Democrat.[52]

On the surface, Nixon narrowly won the watershed election. But the victory for conservatism was of epic proportions. In 1964, Johnson had identified himself as a liberal and received 43.1 million votes, 61% of the total. In 1968, Humphrey identified himself as a liberal and received 31.2 million votes, 43% of the total. Almost 12 million voters, including 5 million from urban areas, had either abstained or defected to Wallace or Nixon, who together claimed almost 57% of the popular vote.[53] The Republican nominee had reversed the results of 1964 in large part because a significant majority of white Americans believed that, unlike his Democratic opponent, he could and would restore authority, stability, and security, and that under his leadership the disorder of the past four years would at last come to an end.

For one white American, a father of five from North Carolina, that day could not come soon enough. Expressing the frustrations of millions, he declared:

> I'm sick of crime everywhere. I'm sick of riots. I'm sick of 'poor' people demonstrations (black, white, red, yellow, purple, green or any other color!). . . . I'm sick of the U.S. Supreme Court ruling for the good of a very small part rather than the whole of our society. . . . I'm sick of the lack of law enforcement. . . . I'm sick of Vietnam. . . . I'm sick of hippies, LSD, drugs, and all the promotion the news media give them. . . . But most of all, I'm sick of constantly being kicked in the teeth for staying home, minding my own business, working steadily, paying my bills and taxes, raising my children to be decent citizens, managing my financial affairs so I will not become a ward of the City, County, or State, and footing the bill for all the minuses mentioned herein.[54]

The rise of "law and order" had a number of important and lasting consequences. It enhanced the popular appeal of conservatism and eroded the political viability of liberalism. It helped to expose fissures within the Democratic Party and bridge divisions within the Republican Party. Above all, it enabled many white Americans to make sense of a chaotic world filled with street crime, urban riots, and campus demonstrations. The legacy of "law and order" was a political arena in which grim expectations displaced grand ambitions.

NOTES

Farber & Roche: Introduction

1. Tony Blankley, "Street-Fighting Days," *George,* July 1998, 53.
2. For more on the historiography of sixties conservatism see Jeff Roche, "Political Conservatism in the Sixties: Silent Majority or White Backlash," in David Farber and Beth Bailey, eds., *The Columbia Guide to America in the 1960s* (New York: Columbia University Press, 2001), 157–66. See also Alan Brinkley, "The Problem of American Conservatism," in *American Historical Review* 99 (April 1994): 409–29; Michael Kazin, "The Grass-Roots Right: New Histories of U.S. Conservatism in the Twentieth Century," *American Historical Review* 97 (February 1992): 136–55. See also Robert Alan Goldberg, *Barry Goldwater* (New Haven: Yale University Press, 1995); Peter Iverson, *Barry Goldwater: Native Arizonan* (Norman: University of Oklahoma Press, 1997); Mary C. Brennan, *Turning Right in the Sixties: The Conservative Capture of the GOP* (Chapel Hill: University of North Carolina Press, 1995); Rick Perlstein, *Before the Storm: Barry Goldwater and the Unmaking of the American Consensus* (New York: Hill and Wang, 2001); Matthew Dallek, *The Right Moment: Ronald Reagan's First Victory and the Decisive Turning Point in American Politics* (New York: Free Press, 2000); Dan T. Carter, *The Politics of Rage: George Wallace, The Origins of the New Conservatism, and the Transformation of American Politics* (New York: Simon and Schuster, 1995) and *From George Wallace to Newt Gingrich: Race in the Conservative Counterrevolution* (Baton Rouge: Louisiana State University Press, 1996). In addition to Carter for more on the "backlash school" see Thomas B. and Mary D. Edsall, *Chain Reaction: The Impact of Race, Rights, and Taxes on American Politics* (New York: Norton, 1991).
3. Jonathan M. Schoenwald, *A Time for Choosing: The Rise of Modern American Conservatism* (New York: Oxford Univeristy Press, 2001); Jerome Himmelstein, *To the Right: The Transformation of American Conservatism* (Berkeley: University of California Press, 1990); Godfrey Hodgson, *The World Turned Right Side Up: A History of the Conservative Ascendancy in America* (Boston: Houghton Mifflin Company, 1996).
4. For more on the Young Americans for Freedom see: John A. Andrew III, *The Other Side of the Sixties: Young Americans for Freedom and the Rise of Conservative Politics* (New Brunswick, NJ: Rutgers University Press, 1997) and Greg Schneider, *Cadres for*

Conservatism: Young Americans for Freedom and the Rise of the Contemporary Right (New York: New York University Press, 1999). For more on the shifts within the Republican Party see Kurt Schuparra, *Triumph of the Right: The Rise of the California Conservative Movement* (Armonk, NY: M.E. Sharpe, 1998) and David W. Reinhard, *The Republican Right since 1945* (Lexington, KY: University Press of Kentucky, 1983).

5. Lisa McGirr, *Suburban Warriors: The Origins of the New American Right* (Princeton: Princeton University Press, 2001).

6. Jeff Roche, "Cowboy Conservatism: High Plains Politics, 1933–1972," Ph.D. dissertation, University of New Mexico, 2001; Michelle Nickerson, "Domestic Threats: Women, Gender and Conservatism in Cold War Los Angeles, 1945–1966," Ph.D. dissertation, Yale University (forthcoming).

Farber: Democratic Subjects in the American Sixties

An earlier and less-developed version of this essay was given at the "Global Democracy: Politics and Culture Since 1968" conference held at the University of California, Berkeley, December 1998 and published in *Mid-America* 81:3 (Fall 1999): 319–32.

1. I would include the best-selling history/memoir by Todd Gitlin, *The Sixties: Years of Hope, Days of Rage* (New York: Bantam Books, 1993, revised edition); the grand narrative by Terry Anderson, *The Movement and the Sixties* (New York: Oxford, 1995); and such excellent dissertations-turned-books by such younger historians as: Doug Rossinow, *The Politics of Authenticity: Liberalism, Christianity, and the New Left in America* (New York: Columbia University Press, 1998), and Andrew E. Hunt, *The Turning: A History of Vietnam Veterans Against the War* (New York: New York University Press, 1999).

2. The richest study of national civil rights policy in the sixties era (which explores both race and gender) is by Hugh Davis Graham, *The Civil Rights Era* (New York: Oxford, 1991); an abridged version of this work useful for classroom use and a less dedicated reader is titled *Civil Rights and the Presidency* (New York: Oxford, 1992). The Supreme Court decisions are explored by J. Harvie Wilkinson III, *From Brown to Bakke: The Supreme Court and School Desegregation, 1954–1978* (New York: Oxford, 1979). From the perspective of the major civil rights organizations see Charles V. Hamilton and Dona Cooper Hamilton, *The Dual Agenda: The African American Struggle for Civil and Economic Equality* (New York: Columbia University Press, 1997). The national standard versus local organizing goals of the civil rights movement itself is richly debated in the classroom-ready, Steven F. Lawson and Charles Payne, *Debating the Civil Rights Movement, 1945–1968* (Lanham, MD: Rowman and Littlefield, 1998).

3. Dan T. Carter, *The Politics of Rage* (Baton Rouge: Louisiana University Press, 1995), 307. In this masterful biography of George Wallace, Carter argues that southern race politics played a critical role in the rebirth of conservative politics.

4. These passages appear in Stephen Lesher, *George Wallace: American Populist* (New York: Addison-Wesley, 1994), 389–90.

5. Ibid., 309–10.

6. Barry Goldwater, *The Conscience of a Conservative* (New York: Hillman Books, 1960), 38.

7. Carter, *The Politics of Rage,* 218.

8. Ibid.

9. Goldwater, *The Conscience of a Conservative,* 37.

10. No scholarly historical treatment of the prayer in the schools issue has been published; see William Martin, *With God on Our Side: The Rise of the Religious Right in America* (New York: Broadway Books, 1996).

11. For an informative discussion see Bernard Schwartz, *Super Chief: Earl Warren and his Supreme Court* (New York: New York University Press, 1983).

12. Thomas Sugrue, *The Origins of the Urban Crisis: Race and Inequality in Postwar Detroit* (Princeton: Princeton University Press, 1996), 209. The material on neighborhood associations is drawn from chapter 8. For a similar treatment of urban race issues in Chicago prior to Great Society national liberalism see Arnold Hirsch, *Making the Second Ghetto: Race and Housing in Chicago, 1940–1960* (New York: Cambridge University Press, 1983).

13. The most interesting take on Americans' relationship withe the federal government is Barry Karl, *The Uneasy State* (Chicago: University of Chicago Press, 1983).

14. The best account remains Harvard Sitkoff, *A New Deal for Blacks* (New York: Oxford, 1978).

15. Quoted in Arthur Schlesinger, *The Age of Roosevelt: The Politics of Upheaval* (Boston: Houghton Mifflin, 1960), 437–38.

16. See Alan Brinkley, *The End of Reform: New Deal Liberalism in Recession and War* (New York: Alfred Knopf, 1994).

17. See Robert Collins, "Growth Liberalism in the Sixties," *The Sixties: From Memory to History,* ed., David Farber (Chapel Hill: University of North Carolina Press, 1994), 11–44; Robert Collins, "The Emergence of Economic Growthmanship in the United States," *The State and Economic Knowledge,* eds., Mary Furner and Barry Supple (New York: Cambridge University Press, 1990).

18. See Mary Sheila McMahon, "The American State and the Vietnam War," *The Sixties,* ed. David Farber, 90–118.

19. See David Farber, *The Age of Great Dreams: America in the 1960s* (New York: Hill and Wang, 1994), 3–24, 49–66.

20. See Mary Dudziak, *Cold War Civil Rights* (Princeton: Princeton University Press, 2001).

21. Chief Justice Earl Warren, *Opinion of the Court in Brown v. Board of Education,* May 17, 1954, in Waldo E. Martin, Jr., *Brown v. Board of Education: A Brief History with Documents* (New York: Bedford/St. Martin's, 1998), 173.

22. A pithy summary is offered in Ballard Campbell, *The Growth of American Government* (Bloomington: Indiana University Press, 1995), chap. 5.

23. Farber, *The Age of Great Dreams,* 100.

24. Ibid., 202.

25. This version undergirds the best known polemic, Stokely Carmichael and Charles V. Hamilton, *Black Power: The Politics of Liberation in America* (New York: Random House, 1967). Also by Charles Hamilton, *Adam Clayton Powell, Jr.* (New York: Atheneum, 1991). The best overview of black power is William Van Deburg, *New Day in Babylon* (Chicago: University of Chicago Press, 1992).

26. See Sidney M. Milkis, *The President and the Parties: The Transformation of the American Party System Since the New Deal* (New York: Oxford, 1993).

27. "El Plan Espiritual de Aztlán," First national Chicano Youth Liberation Conference, March 1969, Denver, Colorado, http:www.brownberets.org.

28. Governor Barnett's speech is shown in the film documentary *Eyes on the Prize.*

29. Both quotes appear in Diane Ravitch, *The Great School Wars* (New York: Basic Books,

1988). Ravitch's work is a still timely analysis of the politics of public schools. The first quote appears on p. 298 and the second on p. 296.

30. The liberal ideal is evoked in Arthur M. Schlesinger, Jr., *A Thousand Days: John Kennedy in the White House* (Boston: Houghton Mifflin, 1964) and explored in Irving Bernstein, *Promises Kept: John F. Kennedy's New Frontier* (New York: Oxford, 1991).

31. The quotes are from the excellent treatment of the 1968 presidential campaign in Kathleen Jamieson, *Packaging the Presidency* (New York: Oxford, 1996), 249.

32. Ibid., 255.

33. Theodore White, *The Making of The President–1968* (New York: Pocket Books, 1970), 318.

34. Lewis L. Gould, *1968: The Election That Changed America* (Chicago: Ivan R. Dee: 1993), 103–5.

35. See Randall Kennedy, "Reflections on Black Power," *Reassessing the Sixties,* ed., Stephen Macedo (New York: Norton, 1997), 228–52.

36. Quoted in Fred Barnes, "Revenge of the Squares," *New Republic* 212:11 (13 March 1995): 29.

37. Participatory democracy is explored in James Miller, *"Democracy Is in the Streets"* (New York: Simon and Schuster, 1987).

38. For one such account see Bill Ayers, *Radical on the Run* (Boston: Beacon, 2001).

39. For an interesting attempt to relate anti-elitism to grassroots democracy see Michael Kazin, *The Populist Persuasion* (Ithaca: Cornell University Press, 1998).

Schoenwald : We Are an Action Group

Adapted from *A Time for Choosing* by Jonathan M. Schoenwald, copyright 2001 by Jonathan M. Schoenwald. Used by permission of Oxford University Press, Inc.

1. For a representative articulation of 1950s American conservative ideology, see Russell Kirk, *The Conservative Mind: From Burke to Santayana* (Chicago: Regnery, 1953), 7–8, and George H. Nash, *The Conservative Intellectual Movement in America Since 1945* (New York: Basic Books, 1976), 57–153.

2. Although the vast majority of Birchers identified with the Republican Party, thousands of conservative Democrats—especially from the South—also joined the JBS. See Fred W. Grupp, Jr., "The Political Perspectives of Birch Society Members," in Robert A. Schoenberger, ed., *The American Right Wing* (New York: Holt, Rinehart and Winston, Inc., 1969), 98–99.

3. See Jonathan M. Schoenwald, *A Time for Choosing* (New York: Oxford, 2001), 4–5.

4. See Stanley Mosk, "Report on the John Birch Society," 7 July 1961 (Sacramento: State of California Office of the Attorney General), 1. Mosk's comments enraged many on the Right.

5. Glenn A. Green to Robert Welch, 11 November 1959, T. Coleman Andrews papers, box 1, folder labeled "JBS 1," University of Oregon Special Collections.

6. Two examples of such works are Gene Grove, *Inside the John Birch Society* (Greenwich, CT: Fawcett Publications, Inc., 1961), and Richard Vahan, *The Truth About the John Birch Society* (New York: MacFadden Books, 1962).

7. The most frequently cited work is Arnold Forster and Benjamin Epstein, *Danger on the Right* (New York: Random House, 1964). Forster and Epstein's research was commissioned by the Anti-Defamation League of B'nai B'rith (ADL), a watchdog Jewish group that monitored worldwide social and political trends and their effects on Jews in

America and elsewhere. Also by Forster and Epstein, see *Report on the John Birch Society 1966* (New York: Vintage Books, 1966), and *The Radical Right: Report on the John Birch Society and Its Allies* (New York: Random House, 1966). Also published by the ADL was Harvey Schechter's *How to Listen to a John Birch Society Speaker* (New York: ADL, n.d.). After assaults by the JBS and other rightist groups like the Circuit Riders, various Christian groups published their own rebuttals to the accusations that communists had infiltrated their churches. See, for example, Lester DeKoster, *The Christian and the John Birch Society* (Grand Rapids, MI: William B. Eerdmans Publishing, 1965).

8. See figure I.1, "Sum of Column Inches in *New York Times Index* Devoted to Five Conservative or Superpatriotic Organizations, 1958–1967," in James McEvoy III, *Radicals or Conservatives?* (Chicago: Rand McNally & Company, 1971), 10.

9. Representative studies include Daniel Bell, ed., *The Radical Right* (Garden City, NY: Doubleday, 1963); the entire issue of *The Journal of Social Issues* 19, no. 2 (April, 1963), which examined the "problem" of political extremism; Fred W. Grupp, Jr., "The Political Perspectives of Birch Society Members," 83–118; and Barbara J. Stone, "The John Birch Society: A Profile," *Journal of Politics* 36 (February 1974): 184–87.

10. See, for example, "The Question of Robert Welch," *National Review*, 13 February 1962, 83–88; William F. Buckley, Jr., "Goldwater and the John Birch Society," *National Review*, 19 November 1963, 430; Hans Engh, "The John Birch Society," *The Nation*, 11 March 1961, 209–11; and Cushing Strout, "Fantasy on the Right," *The New Republic*, 1 May 1961, 13–15.

11. These scholars include Matthew Dallek, *The Right Moment* (New York: Free Press, 2000); Lisa McGirr, *Suburban Warriors* (Princeton: Princeton University Press, 2001); Rick Perlstein, *Before the Storm* (New York: Hill and Wang, 2001); and Schoenwald, *A Time for Choosing*.

12. On Welch's life before the John Birch Society, see "Salesman of the Right," *New York Times*, 1 April 1961, 5; "The Ultras," *Time*, 8 December 1961, 22–25; Rick Perlstein, *Before the Storm*, 110–16; Lisa McGirr, *Suburban Warriors*, 75–77; Matthew Dallek, *The Right Moment*, 104–5; and Schoenwald, *A Time for Choosing*, 64–76. See also Robert Alan Goldberg, *Barry Goldwater* (New Haven: Yale University Press, 1995), 136–38; and Godfrey Hodgson, *The World Turned Right Side Up* (Boston: Houghton Mifflin, 1996), 61.

13. "The Scoreboard," *American Opinion* (July–August, 1958): 22.

14. For a more detailed discussion of the different categories of conservatism, see Paul Gottfried, *The Conservative Movement: Revised Edition* (New York: Twayne Publishers, 1993), 5–18; Nash, *The Conservative Intellectual Movement in America Since 1945*, 172–82; Charles W. Dunn and J. David Woodward, *The Conservative Tradition in America* (Lanham, MD: Rowman and Littlefield, 1996), 48–61; and Schoenwald, *A Time for Choosing*, 8, 17–22.

15. The best description of Welch's ideology is by Welch himself in either *The Politician* (Belmont, MA: Self-published, 1963) or *The Blue Book* (Belmont, MA: Self-published, 1959), which is a verbatim transcript of the first meeting Welch held in creating the John Birch Society. Welch's philosophy is also accessible through issues of *One Man's Opinion*, which he published during the 1950s (known as *American Opinion* after the birth of the JBS), and *The John Birch Society Bulletin*, the society's official newsletter.

16. Welch, *The Politician*, 278.

17. G. Edward Griffin, *The Life and Words of Robert Welch* (Thousand Oaks, CA: American Media, 1975), 244–45.

18. J. W. Clise to B. E. Hutchinson, 19 February 1959, James Clise Papers, box 1, University of Oregon Special Collections.

19. By 1961 *The Blue Book* had gone through seven printings.

20. Robert Welch, *The Blue Book* (Belmont, MA: Western Islands Publishers, 1961), 124.

21. See transcript of "Meet the Press," 21 May 1961, Lawrence Spivak papers, box 158, folder "TV Transcripts: Welch, Robert, 5/21/61," Manuscript Division, Library of Congress.

22. Among the dozens of articles on the controversy surrounding *The Politician*, see "The Americanists," *Time*, 10 March 1961, 21–22; John D. Morris, "Inquiry Is Sought on Birch Society," *New York Times*, 31 March 1961, 10; "Birch Group Head Disclaims Charge," *New York Times*, 1 April 1961, 5; "Birch Group Head Asks U.S. Inquiry," *New York Times*, 2 April 1961, 63; "Storm Over Birchers," *Time*, 7 April 1961, 18–19; "The John Birch Society," *Congressional Record—Senate*, 12 April 1961 (Washington, D.C.: U.S. Government Printing Office, 1961), 5607–12; "Hatemongers," *Congressional Record—House*, 24 April 1961, 6627–30; and "The John Birch Society," *Congressional Record—House*, 27 March 1961, 4930–31.

23. William F. Buckley to Robert Welch, 16 December 1958, box 6, folder "Welch, Robert," William F. Buckley, Jr., Papers, Yale University Library.

24. A. C. Wedemeyer to Robert Welch, 6 February 1959, Howard Kershner Papers, box 19, University of Oregon Special Collections.

25. Arnold Forster and Benjamin Epstein, *Danger on the Right* (New York: Random House, 1964), 39.

26. Lawrence Swanson, "MMM Summary, Week of November 2, 1964," box 7, folder "64," John Birch Society Records, Brown University Library; name expurgated to MMM Department, n.d., box 6, folder "Tim Welch," John Birch Society Records, Brown University Library.

27. See Fred W. Grupp, Jr., "The Political Perspectives of Birch Society Members," 83–118.

28. Robert Welch to Robert C. Hill, 28 May 1963, in Robert C. Hill Papers, box 111, folder 111–83, Hoover Institution Archives, Stanford, California.

29. Enrollment estimates varied widely. Since the society kept its membership lists secret, analysts could only speculate about the number of dues-paying members. Liberal investigators Forster and Epstein reckoned the society had between 20,000 and 50,000 in 1964, although they also noted that others had guessed between 50,000 and 100,000. See *Danger on the Right*, 11. The Kennedy administration calculated somewhere between 20,000 and 100,000 in 1963. See Myer Feldman, "Memorandum for the President. Subject: Right-Wing Groups," 15 August 1963, Papers of John F. Kennedy, Presidential Papers, President's Office Files, box 106, folder "Right Wing Movements, Part 1," John F. Kennedy Library.

30. [Name expurgated] to Lawrence Spivak, n.d., Lawrence Spivak Papers, box 11, folder "Viewer Mail Program Response—Robert Welch 5/21/61," Manuscript Division, Library of Congress.

31. See Fred W. Grupp, Jr., "The Political Perspectives of Birch Society Members," 86–102. Welch, however, contended that at least half of all members and staff were Catholic. See Robert Welch to Neil McCarthy, 22 April 1961, Granville Knight Papers, box 3, University of Oregon Special Collections.

32. Benjamin Epstein and Arnold Forster, *Danger on the Right* (New York: Random House, 1964), 16.

33. On women in conservative politics, see Andrea Dworkin, *Right-Wing Women* (Lon-

don: The Women's Press, 1983); Rebecca Klatch, *Women of the New Right* (Philadelphia: Temple University Press, 1987); and Lisa McGirr, *Suburban Warriors*, 87.

34. Alan Stang, "War on Women," *American Opinion* (December, 1969): 46.

35. Quote from McGirr, *Suburban Warriors*, 87.

36. Jeff Roche, "Cowboy Conservatism: High Plains Politics, 1933–1972," Ph.D. dissertation, University of New Mexico, 2001, 151–52.

37. Robert Welch to T. Coleman Andrews, 7 January 1959, T. Coleman Andrews Papers, box 1, folder 2, University of Oregon Special Collections.

38. Robert Welch, "A Letter to the South on Segregation," *One Man's Opinion* (September 1956): 34.

39. Robert Welch, "The Americus Story," John Birch Society *Bulletin* (February 1970): 11.

40. Welch even brought his views on civil rights to the campus of Howard University, where he called the United States "insane," citing, among other examples, "Negro rioting sparked by Communist agitation." *Facts on File* 25, no. 1310, 2–8 December 1965, 450.

41. "Thunder on the Far Right," *Newsweek*, 4 December 1961, 19.

42. Hilaire du Berrier, "Asia: The Year of the Cock," *American Opinion* (July–August 1969): 89–90.

43. Wallis W. Wood, "The Betrayed," *American Opinion* (January, 1969): 4.

44. Ibid., 90.

45. Other national projects the JBS pursued included exposing the New Left using Truth About Civil Turmoil (TACT), organizing to lower taxes and thus shrink the federal government (Tax Reform Immediately), and joining in the fights against police civilian review boards (under the auspices of Support Your Local Police) and the Equal Rights Amendment.

46. John Birch Society, "Leaders' Manual," n.d., John Birch Society Records, box 41, Brown University Library, 16.

47. See California Teachers Association, "The Pattern of Attack on Public Education in California by the John Birch Society and Similar Groups," 27 March 1961, in Granville Knight Papers, box 23, University of Oregon Special Collections. The JBS also tried to make similar inroads into the Parent-Teacher Association.

48. W. E. Dunham to Robert Welch, 17 August 1964, John Birch Society Records, box 40, Brown University Library.

49. For presentations see "A Presentation Meeting," n.d., box 4, folder "Presentations," John Birch Society Records, Brown University Library; for questions see "Suggested Questions for Discussion," Bryton Barron Papers, box 10, University of Oregon Special Collections.

50. John Birch Society, "Leaders' Manual," n.d., box 41, John Birch Society Records, Brown University Library, 4.

51. [Name expurgated] to J. Edgar Hoover, 5 June 1965, FBI file no. 62–104401 sec. 40, Federal Bureau of Investigation, Washington, D.C.

52. For more on the FBI and the JBS, see Schoenwald, 93–96. Although it was not supposed to operate domestically, the CIA also kept a small file on the society.

53. Harold W. Chase and Allen H. Lerman, eds., *Kennedy and the Press* (New York: Thomas Y. Crowell Co., 1965), 68.

54. Myer Feldman, "Memorandum for the President. Subject: Right-Wing Groups," John F. Kennedy Presidential Papers, President's Office Files, box 106, folder "Right Wing Movements, Part I," John F. Kennedy Library.

55. Robert Welch, "About Barry Goldwater," 10 July 1963, box 3, folder "Barry Goldwater," John Birch Society Records, Brown University Library.

56. At the founding meeting of the JBS in 1958, Welch had told the attendees, "I'd love to see [Goldwater] President of the United States, and maybe some day we shall." But Welch still thought that even though Goldwater was thoroughly conservative, he could not get the job done by himself. Furthermore, because Goldwater was a politician, he "will inevitably think and move in terms of *political* warfare." See Welch, *The Blue Book,* 96.

57. Goldwater, Buckley, Kirk, and others had met as early as 1962 to try to solve the JBS problem. See Robert Alan Goldberg, *Barry Goldwater* (New Haven: Yale University Press, 1995), 159.

58. For more detailed discussions of the role of the John Birch Society in the 1964 election and in the Republican Party in general, see Goldberg, 202–4, 219; McGirr, 111–46; Perlstein, 177–516; and Schoenwald, 124–61.

59. Goldwater with Casserly, *Goldwater,* 185.

60. George Bush, "The Republican Party and the Conservative Movement," *National Review,* 1 December 1964, 1053.

61. Raymond M. Lahr, "30-37-33: That's the Shape—and Dilemma—of the GOP," *Louisville Courier-Journal,* 28 February 1965, 1. On the role of the JBS in Reagan's 1966 campaign, see Dallek, 103–19, 121–27, 230–31; McGirr, 206–8; Schoenwald, 208–14; and Kurt Schuparra, *Triumph of the Right* (Armonk, NY: M. E. Sharpe, 1998), 125, 130–32, 135–36.

62. James Miller, *"Democracy Is in the Streets": From Port Huron to the Siege of Chicago* (New York: Simon and Schuster, 1985), 255.

Schlatter : "Extremism in the Defense of Liberty"

1. I capitalize Communist when the term is in reference to pre-1970s America. I do not capitalize anticommunism because it is a less specific term, and is actually still in use at the beginning of the twenty-first century among Right-leaning residents of this country.

2. "Minutemen Founder, Aide Nabbed on Road Near TorC" (TorC is the shortened spelling of Truth or Consequences), *Albuquerque Journal,* 14 July 1969, A1, A5, and "Area Residents Unaware of Minutemens' [sic] Identity," A1, A10; "Minutemen Leader, Aide Jailed in New Mexico," *Denver Post,* 14 July 1969, B17; "Minutemen Chief Captured by F.B.I.," *New York Times,* 14 July 1969, 25. The men were arrested on 12 July.

3. I used the *Times* because of its inclusion of church and political officials in the arguments about the extremist right. Also, it proved the easiest way for me to track the activities of the Minutemen. The *Times* followed the group and its leader throughout the 1960s, providing a broad context without having to use localized news sources. Some examples of the widespread disavowal of the radical right are: "Rightists Scored by Hebrew Union," 17 November 1961, 20; "Interfaith Head [head of the National Conference of Christians and Jews] Hits Extremists," 4 December 1961, 22; "Catholics Assail Right Extremists," 2 March 1962, 1, 26; "Teachers Urged to Fight Back If Attacked by Rightist Groups" [Denver, National Education Association meetings], 6 July 1962; "Democrats Rally on Rightist Issue," 21 January 1962, 41; "U.S. Official [Harlan Cleveland, Assistant Secretary of State for International Organizational Affairs, speech at the Astor Hotel for National Roosevelt Day] Sees Extremist Peril," 2 February 1962, 17.

4. "Donegan Warns on Birch Society," *New York Times,* 10 May 1961, 39.

5. "Goldberg Chides 'Silent' Churches," *New York Times,* 16 November 1961, 22.

6. "Senator Scores Group Calling Eisenhower a Red," *New York Times,* 9 March 1961, 12.

7. "Senator Attacks Welch," *New York Times,* 13 April 1961, 29.
8. "Javits Urges Inquiry," *New York Times,* 9 April 1961, 48. The senator called for a congressional inquiry into the activities of the JBS. This was one of several articles that appeared in the *Times* that year that deal with Javits and his misgivings about the extreme right. See also "Javits Hits Birchers," 13 December 1961, 46.
9. "Lehman Attacks Right-Wing Trend," *New York Times,* 13 December 1961, 46. I'm uncertain about the "report" to which Lehman referred, but the numbers he cited are inflated. The extremist right has never garnered such support in this country's history; the only comparable instance is the strength of the Ku Klux Klan during the 1920s. See, for example, David Chalmers, *Hooded Americanism: The First Century of the Ku Klux Klan, 1865-1965* (Garden City, NY: Doubleday, 1965) and Nancy MacLean, *Behind the Mask of Chivalry: The Making of the Second Ku Klux Klan* (New York: Oxford, 1994).
10. "Kennedy Asserts Far-Right Groups Provoke Disunity," *New York Times,* 19 November 1961, 1.
11. "Bailey Expects a Fight," *New York Times,* 1 January 1926, 21.
12. "Bailey Says G.O.P. Splits, With Radical Right Forming," *New York Times,* 8 July 1962, 18. Though Mr. Bailey undoubtedly would have liked to see a Republican split, the opposition party did not do so but its ranks were full of argument about the place of the extremist right (if any) in the party. This debate would prove one of the most contentious issues of the 1964 Republican convention. See *Time,* 24 July 1964, 17.
13. "Right-wing Groups Multiplying . . . Appeals In Southern California," *New York Times,* 29 October 1961, 43.
14. Homer Bigart, "Election Returns Are a Blow to the Right Wing," *New York Times,* 8 November 1962, 19.
15. Jerome L. Himmelstein, *To the Right: The Transformation of American Conservatism* (Berkeley: University of California Press, 1990), 66.
16. Ibid.; David W. Reinhard, *The Republican Right Since 1945* (Lexington: University of Kentucky Press, 1983), 153.
17. Himmelstein, *To the Right,* 66-67; Arnold Forster and Benjamin R. Epstein, *Danger on the Right* (New York: Random House, 1964), 212.
18. For a brief discussion about anticommunism and its influence among conservatives, see Maurice Isserman and Michael Kazin, *America Divided: The Civil War of the 1960s* (New York and Oxford: Oxford, 2000), 208-9. For a superb overview of the intellectual roots of conservatism during the 1960s, see George Nash, *The Conservative Intellectual Movement in America Since 1945* (New York: Basic Books, 1976).
19. Robert DePugh, "Political Platform for the Patriotic Party," *Blueprint for Victory* (Norborne, MO: n.p., 1966). DePugh was active throughout the 1960s in a variety of political pursuits, including the (failed) organization of a new party. This platform outlines his basic beliefs and was repeated in a variety of formats, including Minutemen literature. The platform can also be found in *Extremism in America: A Reader,* ed. Lyman Tower Sargent (New York: New York University Press, 1995). For an overview of conservative positions, see McGirr, *Suburban Warriors,* introduction especially; Nash, *The Conservative Intellectual Movement in America Since 1945;* Joshua Freeman, "Putting Conservatism Back into the 1960s," *Radical History Review* 44 (1989): 94-99; and Raymond E. Wolfinger, Barbara Kaye Wolfinger, Kenneth Prewitt, and Sheilah Rosenhack, "America's Radical Right: Politics and Ideology," in *The American Right Wing: Readings in Political Behavior,* ed. Robert A. Shoenberger (New York: Holt, Rinehart and Winston, 1969).

20. DePugh was actually very effective at his brand of "leaderless resistance." He would claim in a 1961 interview that he himself didn't even know how many Minutemen there actually were; dues were not required (though appreciated) so he had little contact with independent Minuteman cells. The only stipulation he did have was that the primary coordinator of individual cells provide a name and address for correspondence. DePugh said that the name a coordinator gave could be an alias. Gladwin Hill, "Minutemen Guerrilla Unit Found To Be Small and Loosely Knit," *New York Times,* 12 November 1961, 1, 76.

21. In the fall of 1992, just days after the standoff at Ruby Ridge, Idaho, in which white separatist Randy Weaver's wife and son were shot and killed by FBI sharpshooters, a Colorado Far Right pastor organized a gathering of Extreme Right leaders, writers, and ministers. The Estes Park, Colorado, conference he organized, which included some 160 attendees, convened to discuss the government actions at Ruby Ridge and to develop a network and plan to combat what they perceived as increasing government hostility to American citizens. One report in particular emerged from the gathering. Former Texas Klansman and then-Aryan Nations member Louis Beam had penned a work called "Leaderless Resistance" at least ten years prior to Ruby Ridge. Beam advocated legal, aboveground groups but also smaller, underground units that could engage in illegal activities that could not be traced back to the parent organization. All units would operate independently of each other and would never report to a central headquarters or single leader. Beam's essay was already circulating among a variety of right-wing groups by 1992. By 1994, Beam's leaderless resistance—probably derived from the strategies DePugh and other groups like his had advocated—had become a model for the modern American militia movement. Stern, *A Force Upon the Plain,* 35–36; Dees and Corcoran, *Gathering Storm,* 35. I found a copy of part of Louis Beam's "Leaderless Resistance" essay in an issue of the *Inter-Klan Newsletter and Survival Alert (INKSA)*, a newsletter that circulated among Extreme Rightist groups during the 1980s. Issue number 2 (1983), folder 1, Aryan Nations, Wilcox Collection, Kenneth Spencer Research Library, University of Kansas, Lawrence, Kansas, 17–19.

22. In all the materials that I found in archival repositories regarding the Minutemen and Robert DePugh, I was struck by the virulence of his anticommunism but also by the fact that his platform and information flyers spent more time attacking the federal government and suggesting ways to implement improvement (usually through elected and appointed committees) than spouting gratuitous racism like his Klan and ANP counterparts. In fact, during the 1960s at least, he didn't seem to use racist slurs. When he did mention "the Negro problem" in reference to the civil rights movement, he did not use slurs nor did he mention or advocate violence against African Americans. He merely addressed the "problem" as a result of communism that would be resolved somehow once the problems with the federal government were solved according to his organizational (and very bureaucratic) strategy.

23. Robert Welch, *The Blue Book of the John Birch Society,* fourth printing (Boston: Western Islands, 1961), 101.

24. Robert DePugh (presumably), information flyer about the Minutemen, ca. 1961, Minuteman files, ephemeral materials, Wilcox Collection, Kenneth Spencer Research Library, University of Kansas, Lawrence, Kansas (hereafter cited as Minuteman files).

25. Alan Westin, " The John Birch Society," in *The Radical Right,* ed. Daniel Bell (New York: Anchor Books, 1961), 244–46.

26. *New York Times,* 1 April 1961, 1; and 7 April 1961, 15; John A. Andrew III, *The Other Side*

of the Sixties (New Brunswick: Rutgers University Press, 1997), 152. Regarding other media articles about the JBS and the right in relation to these incidents, see "Wide-Swinging Bitter-Enders of the Right," *Newsweek* 57 (10 April 1961): 38; "Subversion of the Right" and "Why They Crucify," *The Christian Century* 78 (12 April 1961): 379–80, 443–44; Alan C. Elms, "The Conservative Ripple," *The Nation* 192 (27 May 1961): 458–60; Eugene V. Schneider, "The Radical Right," *The Nation* 193 (30 September 1961): 199–203; William S. White, "The New Irresponsibles," *Harper's* 223 (November 1961): 104–8 and "Thunder on the Far Right," *Newsweek* 58 (4 December 1961): 18–30. The Minutemen can also be found in the *New York Times,* 22 October 1961 and 11 October 1961.

27. J. Harry Jones, Jr., *The Minutemen* (Garden City, NY: Doubleday and Company, Inc., 1968), 22–23.
28. "Minutemen's Soft-Sell Leader: Robert B. DePugh," *New York Times,* 12 November 1961, 76.
29. Ibid. DePugh also claimed to hold a Bachelor of Science degree from Washburn University in Topeka, Kansas. When questioned about it, he claimed that he did not hold the degree and that he didn't try to make it seem otherwise (p. 31).
30. Jones, Jr., *The Minutemen,* 27–28.
31. Ibid., 29–31.
32. "Chief Minuteman Upsets His Town," *New York Times,* 13 November 1961, 23.
33. Robert DePugh (probably), "A Short History of the Minutemen," Minutemen Files, circa 1962, 1.
34. Ibid. DePugh also provided this information to the *New York Times;* Hill, "Minutemen Guerrilla Unit Found To Be Small and Loosely Knit," 76.
35. Robert DePugh (probably), "Facts About the United States Minutemen," Minuteman files, 1. In this particular literature, the founding date of the modern Minutemen is listed as 19 April 1951. DePugh may have been thinking about organizing a group that early, and he did network, but all the evidence I've seen lists 1960 as the official debut year of the named organization. DePugh may have tacked on an extra ten years to give added weight and legitimacy to his project.
   On a different note, One of the enduring historical ironies and coincidences with regard to the American Extremist Right is the date 19 April. The Battle of Lexington, fought by squads of Minutemen and community militias, occurred on 19 April 1775. DePugh cites the date in "Facts About the United States Minutemen" and claims that his Minutemen were chartered on 19 April 1951, in honor of that battle. Many 1990s militia and Patriot groups also cite the bravery of the eighteenth-century Minutemen during that battle as they fought for the enduring American "values" of liberty and freedom against a tyrannical (then-British) government. In a pure coincidence, on 19 April 1993, the Branch Davidian compound outside Waco, Texas, burned to the ground during a government standoff. Some eighty Davidians, among them children, died in the fire. On the morning of the two-year anniversary of Waco, Timothy McVeigh bombed the Alfred P. Murrah government building in Oklahoma City as retaliation for Waco. 168 people—including children—died as a result of the explosion and subsequent structural collapse. See Mark S. Hamm, *Apocalypse in Oklahoma: Waco and Ruby Ridge Revenged* (Boston: Northeastern University Press, 1997). Regarding the Minuteman historical precedent among 1990s militia groups, see Neil A. Hamilton, *Militias in America: A Reference Handbook* (Santa Barbara, CA: ABC-CLIO, Inc., 1996).

36. Robert DePugh (probably), "Facts About the United States Minutemen," 1; Hill, "Minutemen Guerrilla Unit Found To Be Small and Loosely Knit," 76.

37. Hill, "Minutemen Guerrilla Unit Found To Be Small and Loosely Knit." Hill doesn't provide details about which local papers, but I suspect they included papers in Missouri and Kansas, DePugh's home territory, and southern California, where Minuteman groups got some media attention.

38. Ibid.

39. "Police Seize Arms of '61 'Minutemen,'" *New York Times*, 22 October 1961, 32. This is one of two instances that I came across mention of a woman associated with the Minutemen. I could find no further information about this incident and I suspect that the woman and the boy were family of one of the arrested men.

40. Article from *Kansas City Star*, a magazine included in the Sunday edition of the paper. This clipping was in the Minutemen files of the Kenneth Spencer Research Library and had been stamped 19 February 1978. If there was an article title, it did not appear on the clipping.

41. "Houses of Critics of Right bombed," *New York Times*, 3 February 1962, 17. The two critics were religious officials; one was a pastor of St. Matthew's Lutheran Church of North Hollywood and the other was a pastor of Emerson Unitarian Church of Canoga Park. I could not determine whether these were Minutemen-instigated bombings, but given later activities of the group, it certainly is a possibility.

42. Robert DePugh (probably), "Warning to Patriots!" *On Target*, 1 April 1963, Minutemen files, 1–2.

43. Robert DePugh (probably), "Warning to Patriots!" *On Target*, 1 April 1964, Minutemen files, 1–2; "How Communists Promote Racial Violence," *On Target*, 1 June 1964, Minutemen files, 11; "Anti-United Nations Month," *On Target*, 1 October 1964, Minutemen files, 1.

44. "'Crusade' On Reds Is Brought East," *New York Times*, 10 May 1961, 39.

45. Janson, "Minutemen Plan Active but Clandestine Drive for Goldwater." Despite this response, race was not an issue that seemed to weigh prevalently in DePugh's mind. Most of the literature for the group that I have seen is not specifically racist, though references to "Negroes" as Communist pawns exist. In the other media appearances I've come across, DePugh did not express racist sentiment though he may have done so in private.

46. Ibid.

47. "Tax Agents Seize Midwest Arsenal," *New York Times*, 20 May 1964, 57.

48. Jones, Jr., *The Minutemen*, 45–48.

49. "Minutemen Aide Is Freed on Bond," *New York Times*, 11 July 1965, 44; "Minuteman Chief Held in Felony," *New York Times*, 17 August 1965, 36.

50. "Minutemen Form A Political Party," *New York Times* 4 July 1966, 16. The *Times* would report after DePugh's 1969 arrest that the JBS had once denounced the Minutemen and DePugh as "too extreme." I could not find this original declaration. See Donald Janson, "DePugh Says He Eluded F.B.I. With Hippie Disguise," *New York Times*, 18 July 1969, 11.

51. "New Rightist Party Counsels 'Leaders' To Enlist Others," *New York Times*, 5 July, 1966, 13. I haven't been able to determine whether these events took place.

52. "Leader of the Minutemen Scores U.S. Agents' Tactics," *New York Times*, 26 August 1966, 13.

53. "20 Right-Wingers Arrested in State In Weapons Plot," *New York Times*, 31 October, 1966, 1, 40.

54. "Lefkowitz Urges Law to Curb Activities of Minutemen in State," *New York Times*, 26 October 1967, 34. I could not locate a copy of this report, though it reportedly circulated to New York Governor Nelson Rockefeller, New York state county district attorneys and law enforcement personnel, the governors of fourteen unnamed states, and the Secretary of Defense. Two years earlier, calls to ban the Minutemen and other extremists echoed from California and an Ohio senator. The latter urged the Department of Justice to take action against the Minutemen, whom he described as a "'band of psychotics'" in a Senate speech. California State Attorney General Thomas Lynch urged his state to ban paramilitary organizations like the Minutemen, the American Nazi Party, the National States Right Party, and the Black Muslims (Right and Left). See "Senator Young Asks for Curb on Minutemen," 5 February 1965, 15; "California Urged to Ban Extremism," 13 April 1965, 15, both in *New York Times*.

55. "Resignation Spurs Minuteman Study," *New York Times*, 15 January 1967, 38. Edward Gerber was assistant district attorney in Onondaga County.

56. "19 Minutemen Here Linked To De Pugh [sic; I found both spellings in newspapers. J. Harry Jones uses DePugh.]," *New York Times*, 8 November 1966, 46. I don't know whether or not he did go to New York to testify. I could find no record of it.

57. "Minuteman Leader Guilty in Arms Case," *New York Times*, 15 November 1966, 1, 35; "Ex-Minuteman Says He Refused To Train 'Nuts' To Be Assassins," 9 November 1966, 77; "U.N. Plot Traced by Ex-Minuteman," 10 November 1966, 14, both in *New York Times*.

58. Donald Janson, "Minutemen's Leader Is Sentenced to Four Years," *New York Times*, 18 January 1967, 20.

59. "DePugh Quitting Minutemen Post," *New York Times*, 24 January 1967, 38.

60. "Wallace Is Choice of Patriotic Party," *New York Times*, 5 July 1967, 22.

61. Jones, Jr., *The Minutemen*, 54–55.

62 "Minutemen Founder Cited in Theft Plot," *New York Times*, 5 March 1968, 19.

63. "DePugh Says He Eluded F.B.I. with Hippie Disguise."

64. Rachel Davis Dubois, director of Friends Center Workshop, Letter to Editor titled "Superpatriots With Guns," 1 June 1968, 26; "Minutemen Leaflets Fired," 19 November 1968, 93; "Crude Mortar Erupts Near the White House," 23 November 1968, 46, all in *New York Times*.

65. "Bursting Bombs Scatter Hate Leaflets in 3 Cities," *New York Times*, 24 February 1969, 35.

66. "Minutemen Chief Captured by F.B.I.," *New York Times*, 14 July 1969, 25.

67. Donald Janson, "Fugitive Minutemen Never Aroused Suspicion in New Mexico," *New York Times*, 20 July 1969, 47.

68. Martin Waldron, "Militants Stockpile Illegal Guns Across the U.S.," *New York Times*, 28 December 1969, 42.

69. Ibid., 68.

70. Ibid.; William A. Rusher, *The Rise of the Right* (New York: Morrow, 1984), 119–24, 189–90.

71. Anti-Defamation League of B'nai B'rith, *Extremism on the Right: A Handbook* (New York: Anti-Defamation League of B'nai B'rith, 1995). See "Robert DePugh."

Nickerson: Moral Mothers and Goldwater Girls

1. Milton Auerbach, *Report on the Gledhill Elementary School P.T.A. Meeting* (Los Angeles: Community Relations Committee, [November 14, 1961]). The Community Relations

Committee was a Los Angeles Jewish organization, affiliated with the Jewish Community Federation, that monitored anti-Semitic and right-wing activity in southern California. Their collection, located in the Urban Archives at California State University, Northridge, will hereafter be referred to as CRC.

2. Local studies of women's activism suggest that community and family interests have long been the basis of women's political organizing. Sylvie Murray's dissertation, "Suburban Citizens: Domesticity and Community Politics in Queens, New York, 1945–1960" (Ph.D. diss., Yale University, 1994) shows that the postwar emphasis on domesticity not only failed to keep women in the home, but inspired them to enter politics in the form of "homeowners', tenants', and parents' associations." Mary Pardo's *Mexican American Women Activists: Identity and Resistance in Two Los Angeles Communities* (Philadelphia: Temple University Press, 1998) documents the organized efforts of two groups of Mexican-American mothers to battle crime, toxic waste, and lead poisoning in their neighborhoods in the 1980s and 1990s. Pardo is attentive to the gendered division of labor that patterned men's and women's activism in localized contexts. In "Female Consciousness and Collective Action: The Case of Barcelona, 1910–1918," *Signs* 7 (Spring, 1982): 545–66, Temma Kaplan used "female consciousness" to explain the motivation behind women's collective action during a nineteen-teens strike in a Barcelona working class community. In addition to "female consciousness," Nancy Cott's essay, "What's in a Name? The Limits of 'Social Feminism'; or, Expanding the Vocabulary of Women's History," *Journal of American History* 76:3 (December 1989): 809–29 suggests that "communal consciousness" might be another mind-set that prompts women's political activism, but one that implies solidarity with men and women. Cott argues that instead of using "feminism" to describe all forms of women's political consciousness, distinctions should be made between categories of awareness, even though "as motives of action, the three [female, communal and feminist] may inhabit the same mind simultaneously."

3. Virginia Knowles, interview by author, tape recording, South Pasadena, California, 21 February 2001.

4. Kurt Schuparra, "Freedom Versus Tyranny," chap. 2 in *Triumph of the Right: The Rise of the California Conservative Movement, 1945–1966* (Armonk, NY: M.E. Sharpe, Inc, 1998), 28.

5. Ibid.

6. Barry Goldwater, *Conscience of a Conservative* (1960, reprint New York: MacFadden Books, 1961), 2–3.

7. Robert Welch, *The Blue Book of the John Birch Society* (Appleton, WI: Western Islands Publishers, 1992), xvii.

8. Fred Schwarz, *Christian Anti-Communist Crusade: Condensed Statement of Receipts and Disbursements for the Year Ended December 31, 1960*, n.d. Alternative, Underground and Extremist Collection, UCLA Special Collections.

9. Ibid.

10. Schuparra, *Triumph of the Right,* 57. The California Right, as a vital component of the American Right, has become the focus of recent histories. Kurt Schuparra's *Triumph of the Right,* Matthew Dallek's *The Right Moment: Ronald Reagan's First Victory and the Decisive Turning Point in American Politics* (New York: Free Press, 2000) and Lisa McGirr's *Suburban Warriors: The Origins of the New American Right* (Princeton: Princeton University Press, 2001) together examine the grassroots and formal political mechanisms through which conservatives came to power in California. McGirr's work focuses on how men and women in Orange County built a homegrown movement.

11. Most studies of women and conservatism in postwar America focus on the "New Right" movement of the late 1970s and 1980s. Journalist Andrea Dworkin's *Right-Wing Women* (New York: Coward-McCann Inc., 1983) argues that the American Right is a movement controlled by men, "but built largely on the fear and ignorance of women" who obey their orders. Other researchers have taken conservative women's political ideology more seriously than Dworkin. Kristin Luker's *Abortion and the Politics of Motherhood* (Berkeley: University of California Press, 1984) as well Jane DeHart's and John Matthews *Sex, Gender, and the Politics of ERA* (New York: Oxford, 1990) pay attention to the worldviews that drove women into the anti-abortion and anti-ERA movements respectively. Sociologist Rebecca Klatch's *Women of the New Right* (Philadelphia: Temple University Press, 1987) examines the distinctions between the two ideologies that, she contends, shaped women's activism in the New Right: "social" and "laissez-faire" conservatism. However, Klatch does not acknowledge women's activism in the earlier part of the Cold War era. She argues in "The Two Worlds of Women of the New Right," *Women, Politics and Change*, eds. Louise A. Tilly and Patricia Gurin (New York: Russell Sage Foundation, 1990), that one of things "new" about the "New Right" is "the visible presence of women."

12. Betty Friedan, *The Feminine Mystique* (1963, reprint New York: Norton, 1974).

13. Elaine Tyler May, *Homeward Bound* (New York: Basic Books, 1988), 12–14.

14. Although white supremacy did not drive California conservatism the way it did southern conservatism, civil rights opponents in both places used anticommunist rhetoric to attack race politics as a threat to social order. For accounts of how southern upholders of segregation relied on anticommunist rhetoric, see Numan Bartley's *The Rise of Massive Resistance: Race and Politics in the South During the 1950's* (Baton Rouge: Louisiana State University Press, 1969) and Jeff Roche's *Restructured Resistance: The Sibley Commission and the Politics of Desegregation in Georgia* (Athens: University of Georgia Press, 1998).

15. Cecil Kenyon, "President's Corner," *The Federation*, 20 May 1958.

16. McGirr, *Suburban Warriors*, 74 and 84; and Patricia Cullinane (formerly Gilbert), interview by author, tape recording, Pasadena, California, 16 February 2001.

17. Schuparra, *Triumph of the Right*, 81–82; and the Devin-Adair Company, *No Red Ribbons*, book catalogue featuring Rafferty's *Suffer Little Children*, n.d. CRC.

18. Schuparra, *Triumph of the Right*, 81–82.

19. Cullinane, interview.

20. Ibid.

21. Ibid.

22. Ibid.; and "Education Policy up to Whole State," *Los Angeles Herald Examiner*, 29 February 1963, A-2, CRC.

23. Cullinane, interview.

24. Ibid.

25. Ibid.

26. Gilbert, interview.

27. John Stormer, *None Dare Call It Treason* (Florissant, MO: Liberty Bell Press, 1964), 106–9.

28. Ibid., 105.

29. McGirr, *Suburban Warriors*, 75.

30. Ibid., 203.

31. "PTA Critic Faces Court," *The Valley Times Today*, 7 February 1963, CRC.

32. Glen Ingles, "Civic Groups Hear Crusader's Charges," *The Tarzana Herald Tribune,* 26 February 1962, CRC.

33. Ibid.

34. Jack Langguth, "Rightists Hold Secret Coordinating Sessions," *Valley News Today,* 10 May 1962, CRC.

35. *Report on the Emily Philips Meeting* (Los Angeles: Community Relations Committee, [March 18, 1962]), CRC.

36. Langguth.

37. *Report on Emily Philips Meeting,* CRC.

38. Ingles.

39. Ibid.

40. "Crusader Against 'Sex Testing' Wins Acquittal," *Los Angeles Times,* 16 March 1963, CRC.

41. "Emily Philip Sheds Grateful Tears Over 'Not Guilty' Verdict," *The Valley News & Green Sheet,* 17 March 1963, CRC.

42. "Young GOP Unit to Hear Talk on Communist Peril," *The Van Nuys News* 8 April 1963, CRC.

43. *Report on Meeting Held at Encino Community Center, Sponsored by the San Fernando Valley for Goldwater for President Club* (Los Angeles: Community Relations Committee [March 7, 1963]), CRC.

44. Beverly Hills Republican Club, *Beverly Hills Bulletin* (Beverly Hills: January, 1963), 5, CRC.

45. "Mrs. Miller Served FBI, Hoover Says," *Los Angeles Times,* 23 May 1965, CRC.

46. *Report on Meeting Held at Encino Community Center,* CRC.

47. Dee Dickson, "Help Wanted to Spread Knowledge," *Los Angeles Times,* 26 September 1962; and "Parents Open Statewide Drive on CTA Policies," *Los Angeles Herald Examiner,* 23 April 1963, CRC.

48. *Project Prayer: Constitutional Amendment Action* (Los Angeles: Anti-Defamation League [January 20, 1964]); and "School Prayer Court Victory Hopes Sounded," *Citizen-News,* 12 March 1966, CRC.

49. "GOP Women Hear Attacks on Books, Television, Movies," *Valley News and Green Sheet,* 22 April 1965, CRC.

50. Parents in Protest, *To the People of California* (flyer, Sierra Madre, CA: 1966), CRC; H.V. Witty, "Freedom at Any Price," *Industrial Post,* 5 May 1966, CRC; and Dick Turpin, "New History Textbook Gets Severe Criticism," *Los Angeles Times,* 11 May 1966, CRC.

51. May, 4–11 and 146.

52. "Women for America Sponsor Quiz," *The Valley News,* 14 May 1964, CRC.

53. Ibid., and "New Library for Valley," *The News,* 30 October 1964, CRC.

54. "Facts" stood for Fundamental Issues, Americanism, Constitutional Government, Truth, Spiritual Values. Frances Bartlett, "Editorial Policy," *FACTS,* November–December 1957, Knox Mellon Collection, UCLA Special Collections.

55. Paul Neipp, *Let's Take the Offensive!* (Nashville: Parthenon Press, 1962), 7.

56. Paul Neipp, *For Women Only* (leaflet) October, 1961, CRC. Neipp's supporters distributed his leaflets in public places. The Community Relations Community obtained a copy of the leaflet from a correspondent who received one at a restaurant in Hermosa Beach.

57. Catherine Rymph, "Fashioning a Republican Club Woman Style of Politics," in chap. 2

in "Forward and Right: The Shaping of Republican Women's Activism, 1920–1967," Ph.D. dissertation, University of Iowa, 1998, 311–12; and Rick Perlstein, *Before the Storm: Barry Goldwater and the Unmaking of the American Consensus* (New York: Hill and Wang, 2001), 494–95.

58. Rymph; and "Form Unit of Mothers for Moral America," *Valley News,* 30 October 1964, CRC.

59. Rymph, 102–7.

60. California Federation of Republican Women, *17th Biennial Convention Program,* Fresno, California, Fresno Convention Center, 1971, California Federation of Republican Women Office, Sacramento, California.

61. *Notes on American Public Relations Forum Meeting* (Los Angeles: Community Relations Committee [May 2, 1952]), CRC.

62. Priscilla Buckley, "Siberia U.S.A.: The Rocky Road of H.R. 6376," *National Review* (July 25, 1956): 10.

63. For more on how conservatives took over the Republican Party in the 1960s, see May C. Brennan, *Turning Right in the Sixties: The Conservative Capture of the GOP* (Chapel Hill: University of North Carolina Press, 2001).

64. Jane Crosby, interview by author, tape recording, San Juan Capistrano, California, 26 February 2001.

65. Network of Patriotic Letter-Writers, "How to Write Effective Letters," n.d. Knox Mellon Collection, UCLA Special Collections.

66. Ibid.

67. Group Research, Inc., *Group Research Report* 5:2 (June 15, 1966), 3, CRC; and Network of Patriotic Letter-Writers, *Newsletter* (n.d., ca. 1962), box 20, Knox Mellon Collection, UCLA Special Collections.

68. Letter from Gertrude Bale, Network of Patriotic Letter-Writers to Della Root, Pasadena, California, 18 November 1959, Knox Mellon Collection, UCLA Special Collections.

69. May, 26.

70. Ibid., 26–27.

71. Carrol Mills, "More 'Inspiring' Book Urged for 8th Grade," *The Press,* 29 June 1967, B-2; and letter from Marie Koenig to author, 17 August 2001, Pasadena, California.

72. Ibid., 28.

73. Sylvie Murray, "As Mothers or Experts," chap. 6 in "Suburban Citizens: Domesticity and Community Politics in Queens, New York, 1945–1960," Ph.D. dissertation, Yale University, 1994, 262–336.

74. Dee Dickson, "Americanism Center Sets Up Shop," *Los Angeles Herald Express,* 18 December 1961, CRC.

75. Ibid., and Jane Crosby, interview.

76. "Americanism Center to Hold Open House," *Valley Times,* 12 March 1964, CRC.

77. Mrs. Sam Woolington, "Dear Fellow Americans," letter to prospective Americanism Center contributors, 1965, CRC. Although most of the Americanism Centers had already closed by 1970, the John Birch Society opened American Opinion bookstores to take their place. Some of these shops still operate around Los Angeles.

78. Florence Ranuzzi, interview by author, tape recording, Tehachapi, California, 11 February 2001.

79. Ibid.

80. Mary Cunningham, interview by author, tape recording, Tehachapi, California, 12 February 2001.

81. Ibid.

82. Florence Ranuzzi, interview; and "Former Screen Siren Wars on Income Tax," *Los Angeles Times,* 23 September 1962, CRC.

83. *Standard Daily Journal* (South Pasadena, CA: Main Street Americanism Center [January 20 and February 8, 1965]).

84. Ibid., February 12 and 15, 1962.

85. Patty Newman and Joyce Wenger, *Pass the Poverty Please!* (Whittier, CA: Constructive Action, Inc, 1966), 5 and back cover.

86. Christian Anti-Communist Crusade, *A New and Effective Anti-Communist Weapon: Janet Greene Sings Fascist Threat and Commie Lies,* n.d. Freedom Center, California State University, Fullerton.

87. Ibid.

Brennan: Winning the War / Losing the Battle

1. The term "Eastern Establishment" is used in this book as conservatives used it: to refer to a group of Republicans who accepted New Deal–style reforms and an internationalist foreign policy. For a discussion of the composition of the liberal faction, see, among others, Robert Griffith, "Dwight D. Eisenhower and the Corporate Commonwealth," *American Historical Review* 87 (February 1982): 87–122; Thomas Ferguson and Joel Rogers, *Right Turn: The Decline of the Democrats and the Future of American Politics* (New York: Hill & Wang, 1986), 53; and Nicol C. Rae, *The Decline and Fall of the Liberal Republicans* (New York: Oxford, 1989), 10–46.

2. See George H. Nash, *Conservative Intellectual Tradition* (New York: Basic Books, 1976), 36–84, for a full discussion of the traditionalist school. As an example of traditionalist writings, see Russell Kirk, *The Conservative Mind* (Chicago: University of Chicago Press, 1953), 7–8. For a discussion of classical liberalism, see Nash, *The Conservative Intellectual Tradition,* 3–35.

3. Lisa McGirr, *Suburban Warriors: The Origins of the New American Right* (Princeton: Princeton University Press, 2001), 20–53; and Kirkpatrick Sale, *Power Shift: The Rise of the Southern Rim and its Challenges to the Eastern Establishment* (New York: Vintage, 1976), 5–15.

4. Richard Whalen, "'McCarthyism' Revisited," *Human Events,* 11 February 1959, 2. The quickest way to grasp the breadth and number of these grassroots movements is to look at the finding aid for the "Social Documents Collection" at the University of Iowa Library [SDC]. Another indication of the number and variety of right-wing organizations can be found in Group Research, Inc., "The Finances of the Right Wing: A Study of the Size and Sources of Income of 30 Selected Operations," 1 September 1964, Special Report #16, "Finances of RightWing," box 88, Papers of Marvin Liebman Associates, Hoover Institution on War, Revolution and Peace, Stanford University, Palo Alto, California [hereafter MLA].

5. Robert Welch, *The New Americanism* (Boston: Western Islands, 1966), 115–52.

6. See Miles, *Odyssey of the American Right,* 47–123, for a discussion of postwar conservative foreign policy. See also information on the anti-Krushchev rally sponsored by Crusade for America and *National Review* in "Forum, NR (1959)," box 7, General Correspondence, William F. Buckley, Jr. Papers, Yale University Library, New Haven, Connecticut [hereafter WFB Papers]. Burnham, *Struggle for the World,* 1. For a discussion of the way

the movement brought various conservatives together, see Nash, *Conservative Intellectual Tradition*, 84–131.

7. Nash, *Conservative Intellectual Tradition*, 131–53; John Judis, *William F. Buckley, Jr.* (New York: Simon and Schuster, 1988); and David W. Reinhard, *The Republican Right* (Lexington: University of Kentucky Press, 1983), 171–72. For youth organization, see Edward Cain, *They'd Rather Be Right* (New York: Macmillan, 1963), 156–77; "History of the Young Republicans," booklet, [1972?], box 7, Republican National Committee Library, RNC Library, NARA, DC; and M. Stanton Evans, *Revolt on the Campus* (Chicago: Henry Regnery, 1961), 34–5; John A. Andrew III, *The Other Side of the Sixties: Young Americans for Freedom and the Rise of Conservative Politics* (New Brunswick, NJ: Rutgers University Press, 1997); and Greg Schneider, *Cadres for Conservatism: Young Americans for Freedom* (New York: New York University Press, 1999).

8. Charles C. Alexander, *Holding the Line* (Bloomington: Indiana University Press), 160, 242, 256–61; Arthur Larson, *A Republican Looks at His Party* (New York: Harper & Row, 1956), 1–19; also see chaps. 4, 11, 22 in Dwight D. Eisenhower, *Waging Peace* (New York: Doubleday, 1965); and chaps. 14–16, 20–21 in Stephen Ambrose, *Eisenhower* (New York: Simon and Schuster, 1984).

9. Richard Nixon, statement in Fresno, California, 4 November 1960, "RN's Copies [#1]," box 2, series 45, Richard Nixon Vice Presidential Papers, NARA, Laguna Niguel, California [hereafter RNVP Papers]. For civil rights views, see Herbert Parmet, *Richard Nixon and His America* (Boston: Little, Brown, 1990), 268–69, 383–84; Tom Wicker, *One of Us* (New York: Random House, 1991), 226, 238; James Hagerty, interview #1, 2 March 1967, OH91, 38, Columbia Oral History Project, Oral History Collection, Columbia University, New York [hereafter COHP]; and Richard M. Nixon, *RN* (New York: Grosset and Dunlap, 1978), 185–93, 203–14.

10. Barry Goldwater, *With No Apologies* (New York: William Morrow, 1979), 62. There are several scholarly biographies of Goldwater, including Robert Goldberg, *Barry Goldwater* (New Haven: Yale University Press, 1995) and Rick Perlstein, *Before the Storm* (New York: Hill and Wang, 2001).

11. Goldberg, *Goldwater*, 110–11.

12. Barry Goldwater, *Conscience of a Conservative* (Shepherdsville, KY: Victory, 1960), 18, 21, 97–134.

13. Frank S. Meyer, "A Man of Principle," *National Review*, 23 April 1960, 269–70. For Goldwater's impact on youth, see Reinhard, *The Republican Right*, 172–73.

14. All information on these groups can be found in the box 3H497, Goldwater Collection, Center for American History, University of Texas, Austin, Texas [hereafter GCCAH]. For Nixon's move to the Left, see Stephen Ambrose, *Nixon: The Education of a Politician, 1913–1962* (New York: Simon and Schuster, 1987), 551; Nixon, *Six Crises*, 314; and [Chuck Lichenstein], Memorandum on the Joint Nixon–Rockefeller Statement of July 23, 1960, 15 September 1960, "1960 Election Chapter," box 1, series 258, RNVP Papers.

15. Russell Baker, "Goldwater Hits Platform Accord," *New York Times*, 24 July 1960; Goldwater, *With No Apologies*, 109–17; and Barry Goldwater, Speech Withdrawing Name from Nomination, 27 July 1960, reprinted in *New York Times*, 28 July 1960.

16. Theodore White, *The Making of the President, 1960* (New York: Atheneum, 1961), 359; Sale, *Power Shift*, 109–10.

17. V. O. Key, *Southern Politics in State and Nation* (New York: Alfred A. Knopf, 1949) is the standard work on early twentieth-century southern politics. See also Earl Black and

Merle Black, *Politics and Society in the South* (Cambridge: Harvard University Press, 1987), 3–72; James C. Cobb, *Industrialization and Southern Society, 1877–1984* (Lexington: University Press of Kentucky, 1984), 99–120; Gavin Wright, *Old South, New South* (New York: Basic Books, 1986), 239–74; Pete Daniel, "Going Among Strangers: Southern Reactions to World War II," *Journal of American History* 77 (December 1990): 886–911; and Sale, *Power Shift*, 17–53.

18. Daniel, "Going Among Strangers," 910; Black and Black, *Politics and Society*, 236; and Phillips, *Emerging Republican Majority*, 203.

19. Mary C. Brennan, *Turning Right in the Sixties* (Chapel Hill: University of North Carolina Press, 1995), 43. A more historical analysis of the continuation of southern conservative values can be found in Cobb, *Industrialization and Southern Society, 1877–1984*, 151, 154–56.

20. There are numerous biographies of Kennedy and books dealing with his administration. Among others, see Herbert Parmet, *Jack* (New York: Dial Press, 1989); *JFK* (New York: Dial Press, 1983); David Burner and Thomas R. West, *The Torch Is Passed* (New York: Atheneum, 1984); and Arthur M. Schlesinger, Jr., *A Thousand Days* (Boston: Houghton Mifflin, 1965); Theodore Sorenson, *Kennedy* (New York: Harper & Row, 1965).

21. Rae, *The Decline and Fall of the Liberal Republicans*, 49–53; and Brennan, *Turning Right*, 46.

22. For background on the civil rights movement in the South, see, among others, David J. Garrow, *Bearing the Cross* (New York: Random House, 1986); and Taylor Branch, *Parting the Waters* (New York: Simon and Schuster, 1988). For Kennedy's views on the issues, see Parmet, *JFK*, 249–76; Burner and West, *The Torch Is Passed*, 161–63; and Matusow, *Unraveling*, 60. For conservative views of the movement, see Goldwater, *Conscience of a Conservative*, 31–37; Robert Parker, "Bobby in the Black Belt," *National Review*, 20 May 1961, 309; Robert Lewis Taylor, "On the Palm Beach Frontier," *National Review*, 10 April 1962, 241–42; Jackie Robinson, "The GOP: For White Men Only," *Saturday Evening Post*, 10–17 August 1963, 10–12; Brauer, *Second Reconstruction*, 298–99, 301–3; Cobb, *Industrialization and Southern Society*, 153–54.

23. Parmet, *JFK*, 131–56; Schlesinger, *A Thousand Days*, 745–47; Editorial, "The Vietnam Booby Trap," *The Nation*, 10 March 1962, 205; Editorial, "Vietnam: Fact and Fiction," *The Nation*, 2 March 1963, 169; and John Stormer, *None Dare Call It Treason* (Florissant, MO: Liberty Bell Press, 1964), 54–92. Each issue of *National Review* during the years 1961–64 contains at least one article expressing concern over the political intentions and actions of the emerging nations of the world.

24. Alice Widenor, "Middle Class Against Welfare State," *ACA Newsletter*, 24 August 1964, A2, Reel 1, SDC; Mildred Willis Harris, letter to editor, *National Review*, 11 March 1961, 160; Tom Anderson, "For Once Conservatives Have a Choice," *The American Way*, 14 January 1964, A54, Reel 8, SDC. See Rieder, "The Rise of the Silent Majority," in Steve Fraser and Gary Gerstle, eds, *The Rise and Fall of the New Deal Order* (Princeton: Princeton University Press, 1989), 243–68 for a general discussion of the public's discontent.

25. For further information see the material in "Goldwater Presidential Campaign, 1964 Draft Goldwater Endeavor—1962–63," box 4, Denison Kitchel Papers, Hoover Institution on War, Revolution and Peace, Stanford University, Stanford, California [hereafter HIWRP]. For a detailed chronology of the actions of his group, see F. Clifton White, *Suite 3505* (New Rochelle, NY: Arlington House, 1967). See also F. Clifton White Papers, Division of Rare and Manuscript Collections, Cornell University Library, Ithaca, NY [hereafter FCW Papers].

26. F. Clifton White, "1962 Report," "Chicago—December 1962," box 20 [White to Chicago group], "Confidential Memo," 24 August 1962, "Group Mailings"; F. Clifton White to Barry Goldwater, 31 January 1963, "Goldwater Correspondence," box 18, FCW Papers; White, *Suite 3505*, 48–50; Robert Chapman to F. Clifton White, 27 December 1961, "South Carolina," box 20; "Budget Figures," 27 November 1962, "Chapter X—'Secret Meeting,'" box 9; and [White to Chicago group], "Confidential Memo," 24 August 1962, "Group Mailings," box 18, FCW Papers.

27. Goldwater, *Goldwater*, 121–22; Barry Goldwater, interview by Ed Edwin, 15 June 1967, OH21, transcript, 28–29, COHP; Barry Goldwater, *Why Not Victory?* (New York: McGraw-Hill, 1962). Books concerning Goldwater included three biographies and a 'history' with him as the hero appeared: Jack Bell, *Mr. Conservative: Barry Goldwater* (Garden City, NY: Doubleday, 1962); Stephen Shadegg, *Barry Goldwater: Freedom Is His Flight Plan* (New York: Fleet, 1962); Edwin McDowell, *Barry Goldwater: Portrait of an Arizonan* (Chicago: Henry Regnery, 1964); and Phyllis Schlafly, *A Choice Not an Echo* (Alton, IL: Pere Marquette Press, 1964).

28. For evidence of Goldwater's early knowledge of and participation in the White group, see among others William Rusher to Barry Goldwater, 9 November 1961, "Steering Committee Reports," box 9, FCW Papers; Barry Goldwater to F. Clifton White, 12 June 1963, "Goldwater Correspondence," box 18, FCW Papers. In his latest memoir, Goldwater denies any and all knowledge of what transpired with White's group. Goldwater, *Goldwater*, 134. For attempts to convince Goldwater to run, see William Rusher to Barry Goldwater, 23 January 1963, "Goldwater Correspondence," box 18, FCW Papers; F. Clifton White to Barry Goldwater, 7 June 1963, "Goldwater Presidential Campaign Correspondence General—1963," box 4, Kitchel Papers, HIWRP; Frank Meyer to Barry Goldwater, 11 February 1963, "Goldwater Correspondence"; and F. Clifton White to Barry Goldwater, 31 January 1963, "Goldwater Correspondence," box 18, FCW Papers. For Goldwater's ambivalence on the race, see Barry Goldwater to Kenneth Kellar, 4 December 1962, "Kellar, Kenneth C. 1962-1979," box 2, Kitchel Papers, HIWRP; Barry Goldwater to Dean Burch, 14 January 1963, "Burch, Dean Correspondence," box 20, GPASU; Barry Goldwater to F. Clifton White, 12 June 1963, "Goldwater Presidential Campaign Correspondence General—1963," box 4, Kitchel Papers, HIWRP; Goldwater, *With No Apologies*, 157–58; Barry Goldwater, notes to diary, 25 June 1976, box 3, Alpha File, GPASU.

29. White, *Suite 3505*, 115–26; Shadegg, *What Happened to Goldwater?*, 57–62. For the complete story on the NDGC, see White, *Suite 3505*, 127–44. See also National Draft-Goldwater Committee, Constitution, 8 April 1963, "Constitution," box 5, FCW Papers; Ione F. Harrington and Judy G. Fernald to "Conference Chairman," 18 April 1963, "Women—(Nat'l Committee—Women's Federation)," box 20; "Republican Governor's Meeting—Denver," [13 September 1963], "Governor's Conference Biographies," box 5, FCW Papers; Report on Goldwater Hospitality Room at Missouri Republican Lincoln Day, 8–9 February [1963], "Draft Goldwater Endeavor—1962–63," box 4, Kitchel papers, HIWRP; and "Conventions," box 5, FCW Papers.

30. Brennan, *Turning Right*, 69.

31. White, *Suite 3505*, 199–213, 264.

32. Goldwater, *With No Apologies*, 160–61; Goldwater, *Goldwater*, 149, 154; [Stephen Shadegg], "Notes Dictated on B Side of Record #20," envelope "Dean Burch 12/64," GCCAH; F. Clifton White to "JH and DK," 18 December 1963, Memo—Status

Report, "JH"; NDGC, Minutes of Steering Committee Meeting, 11 December 1963, "Steering Committee Reports," box 9, FCW Papers; Goldwater interview, 72–73.

33. For information on Romney's candidacy, see Theodore White, *The Making of the President, 1964* (New York: Atheneum, 1965), 155–61; and Parmet, *Nixon,* 479–81. For information on the Rockefeller campaign, see Michael Kramer and Sam Roberts, *"I Never Wanted to Be Vice-President"* (New York: Basic Books, 1976), 242–47, 266–86; White, *1964,* 64–136. For a discussion of Nixon's efforts in 1964, see Richard Nixon, "Recent Statements . . . in response to questions concerning the 1964 Campaign, Jan 1964," "1964 Statements," box 1, series 127; "1964 Letters Urging Nixon to Run for Presidency," box 1, series 129, RNPP Papers; "Ronald Sullivan, "Nixon Will Expand His Political Staff," *New York Times,* 13 March 1964; See the correspondence between Fred Seaton and RoseMary Woods, "Nixon 1964 Campaign—Memos of Conversations," box 8, Seaton Papers, Post-Eisenhower Administration Series, DDE. White, *1964,* 147–48; and Parmet, *Nixon,* 480.

34. For Eisenhower's efforts to encourage Scranton, see Dwight Eisenhower, 23 May, 5, 6, 11, 12, 16, 17, and 29 June 1964, Calls and appointments 1964 (3), Appointment Book Series, Post-presidential Papers, DDEL. For Scranton letter, see News Release, Draft Scranton National Campaign Committee, 5 June 1964, "A15–38," box A15, General Correspondence and Constituent Case File, Gerald R. Ford Library, Ann Arbor, Michigan [hereafter GCCCF, GRF].

35. Brennan, *Turning Right,* 82–103; Goldberg, *Goldwater,* 210–33.

36. Brennan, *Turning Right,* 99.

37. Goldwater interview, 13–14; White, *Suite 3505,* 415; F. Clifton White, interview by author, tape recording, Ashland, Ohio, 21 October 1987; and Herbert E. Alexander, *Financing the 1964 Election* (Princeton, NJ: Citizens' Research Foundation, 1966), 11, 73–75; and Republican National Committee, Transcript of Proceedings of Executive Session of Meeting, 22 January 1965, box 8, Republican National Committee Papers, Jo Good Files, NARA, Washington, D.C. [hereafter RNC-JGF].

38. For Eisenhower's efforts, see among others Dwight Eisenhower, 31 July 1964, Calls and Appointments 1964 (4); Dwight Eisenhower, 21 October 1964, Calls and Appointments 1964(7), box 2, Appointment Book Series [hereafter ABS], Dwight D. Eisenhower Presidential Library, Abilene, Kansas [hereafter DDE]; and Dwight Eisenhower, Address at Percy Dinner, 24 September 1964, "Illinois—Oct 7 and 29," box 4, series 127, RNPP Papers. For Nixon's efforts, see Nixon, *RN,* 263; Office of Richard Nixon, news release, 29 September 1964, "1964 Campaign re: Schedules," box 1; Loie Grace Gaunt to Vera Ash, 19 December 1964, "1964 Campaign re: Schedules," box 1, series 127. For the Romney and Rockefeller contributions, see Gwen Barnett to Ione Harrington, 8 October 1964, "Idaho," box 2, FCW Papers; David Halberstam, "Keating Stumps with Rockefeller," *New York Times,* 9 October 1964; George Romney, statement, 12 August 1964, "Michigan—Oct. 16, 1964," box 4, series 127, RNPP Papers; and Arthur Summerfield to Richard Nixon, 7 February 1968, Album IX—"Richard Nixon (1)," box 2, Summerfield Papers, DDE. See also Myer Feldman to Bill Moyers, 10 September 1964, "EX PL2 9/6/64—9/14/64," EX PL2, box 84, White House Central Files, Lyndon Baines Johnson Library, Austin, Texas [hereafter WHCF, LBJ].

39. Rusher, *The Making of the New Majority Party,* 47–48.

40. Brennan, *Turning Right,* 84–85; Barry Goldwater, "What Are the Issues on Which Voters Should Decide the 1964 Election?," "On Business and the Economy," statement for publication, "Mag., Newspapers and Other Articles by BG," box 20, 1964 Presidential

Campaign Papers, GPASU. See also, Goldwater, *The Conscience of a Conservative*, chap.
7. Barry Goldwater, "A Free and Prosperous American Agriculture," "To Promote the
General Welfare," and "How Do You Feel About Federal Aid to Depressed Areas?,"
statements for publication, box 20, 1964 Presidential Campaign Papers, Goldwater
Papers, Arizona State University, Tempe, Arizona [hereafter GPASU].

41. Brennan, *Turning Right*, 85; Goldwater, "What Are the Issues . . . ?"; Barry Goldwater,
"Captive Nations Form Statement," and "Defense Policy," statements for publication,
"Mag., Newspaper, and Other Articles by BG," box 20, 1964 Presidential Campaign
Papers, GPASU.

42. For information on the movie, "Choice," see "Choice," 2nd draft of script, 1 October
1964, "Choice," box 6, FCW Papers; Shadegg, *What Happened to Goldwater?*, 244–45;
and White, *Suite 3505*, 414–15.

43. Taylor Branch, *Pillar of Fire: America in the King Years 1963–1965* (New York: Simon
and Schuster, 1998); Stokely Carmichael and Charles V. Hamilton, *Black Power* (New
York: Vintage Books, 1967); Matusow, *Unraveling*, 345–75; Dan T. Carter, "The Politics
of Anger," in *From George Wallace to Newt Gingrich: Race in the Conservative Counterrevolution, 1963–1994* (Baton Rouge: Louisiana University Press, 1996), 1–23; and E. J.
Dionne, *Why Americans Hate Politics* (New York: Simon and Schuster, 1992), 81–96.

44. George C. Herring, *America's Longest War*, 2nd ed. (New York: Alfred A. Knopf,
1986), 170.

45. Barry Goldwater to "Bob and Harry" [1978?], unmarked folder and box, GPASU. See
also Dean Burch to Karl Hess, 10 August 1965, "Burch, Dean," box 1, Kitchel papers,
HIWRP; "The Week," *National Review*, 29 June 1965, 534; Goldwater, *With No Apologies*, 207; Barry Goldwater, Notes to Diary, 28 August 1972; and Barry Goldwater,
Notes to Diary, 25 June 1976, box 3, Alpha File, GPASU.

46. Richard A. Viguerie to Users of Conservative Mailing List, 10 February 1966, "Richard
A. Viguerie and Co.," box 35, MLA, HIWRP. By that time, the list had 300,000 names
on it. For examples of uses of list, see John Wayne to "My Fellow American," n.d.,
"American Economic Foundation," box 7, MLA, HIWRP; Richard Viguerie to Marvin Liebman, 16 December 1965, "Richard A. Vigueire and Co.," box 35; and Marvin
Liebman to Admiral Ben Moreell, 15 February 1965, "Americans for Constitutional Action," box 7, MLA, HIWRP.

47. William Rusher to William F. Buckley, Jr., 3 March 1965, "Interoffice Memos Jan 1965–
June 1965," box 35, General Correspondence, WFB Papers; and Robert F. Ellsworth to
Bob Wilson, 18 May 1965, A4, box A29, GCCCF, GRF; Frank Meyer to "All Concerned,"
23 May 1966, "Interoffice Memos May–December 1966," box 39; and William F.
Buckley, Jr. to Barry Goldwater, 18 June 1965, "Goldwater, Barry," box 35, WFB Papers.

48. Brennan, *Turning Right*, p. 113; "Talk About Demonstrations!," *National Review*, 11 January 1966, 12; Letters to LBJ from YAF members, "Young, Alfreda," box 26, Name
File, WHCF, LBJ Library; Ron Docksai, "New York State Y. A. F. Liberates SDS Office
for Election Day," 6 November 1968, "Young Americans for Freedom—Misc.," box 37;
and "World Youth Crusade for Freedom, Inc.: A Report and Prospectus," box 107; for
more information, see pertinent folders in box 36, MLA, HIWRP.

49. Donald E. Lukens, interview by author, tape recording, 6 February 1988, Hamilton,
Ohio; and Garry Wills, *Nixon Agonistes* (Boston: Houghton Mifflin, 1970), 246–57.

50. Nixon, *RN*, 263. For examples of Reagan's early support see, among others, William F.
Buckley, Jr. to Ronald Reagan, 11 November 1964, "Reagan, Ronald," box 32, General
Correspondence, WFB Papers; Wills, *Reagan's America*, 287–88, 290–91; Drew Pearson,

"An Actor Is Groomed to be President," *The Washington Post,* 19 September 1966; Ronald Reagan to Leonard Finder, 7 July 1966, "Reagan, Ronald," box 24, Finder Papers, DDE; Farley Clinton, "Ronald Reagan: A Light in the West," *National Review,* 28 June 1966, 613–15; Bill Boyarsky, "Reagan—The Favorite Son," *The Houston Post,* 1 October 1967; George Gallup, "Reagan's Appeal Not Limited to State," 16 November 1966, *Gallup Poll;* White, *1968,* 35; and John Wayne to "My Fellow American," n.d., "American Economic Foundation," box 7, MLA, HIWRP.

51. Brennan, *Turning Right,* 128; Fred Seaton to Walter Williams, 8 November 1967, "Nixon for President Committee 1967," box 9, Seaton Papers, Post-Eisenhower Administration Series, DDE; and Wicker, *One of Us,* 342–44.

52. Herring, *America's Longest War,* 184–94; and Matusow, *Unraveling,* 391.

53. Ibid., 331–35, 396; Todd Gitlin, *The Sixties* (New York: Bantam, 1987), 306–9; James Simon Kunen, *The Strawberry Statement* (New York: Avon, 1968), 39, 43; Kim McQuaid, *The Anxious Years* (New York: Basic Books, 1989), 160; and Peter N. Carroll, *It Seemed Like Nothing Happened* (New Brunswick, NJ: Rutgers University Press, 1982), 56–61.

54. Thomas Byrne Edsall and Mary D. Edsall, *Chain Reaction* (New York: W. W. Norton, 1991), 71–2.

55. Barry Goldwater, statement, 7 March 1968, "Republican Party—National(60)," box A90; and Oscar DeJong to Gerald Ford, 23 March 1968, A10, box A89, GCCCF, GRFL.

56. Phillips, *The Emerging Republican Majority,* 25–42. For a somewhat milder version of the same theory, see Richard Scammon and Ben J. Wattenberg, *The Real Majority* (New York: Coward, McCann, and Geoghehan, 1970), 35–44.

Roche: Cowboy Conservatism

1. Barry M. Goldwater with Jack Casserly, *Goldwater* (New York: Doubleday, 1988), 388.

2. Although historians of modern American conservatism have almost all recognized the "western" appeal of Barry Goldwater, Ronald Reagan, or George W. Bush, few have explored this phenomenon in detail. Perhaps the best treatment of the western aspect of modern conservative politics is Lisa McGirr, *Suburban Warriors: The Origins of the New American Right* (Princeton: Princeton University Press, 2001). See also Mary Brennan, *Turning Right in the Sixties: The Conservative Capture of the GOP* (Chapel Hill: University of North Carolina Press, 1995); Robert Alan Goldberg, *Barry Goldwater* (New Haven: Yale University Press, 1995); Kurt Schuparra, *Triumph of the Right: The Rise of the California Conservative Movement* (Armonk, NY: M. E. Sharpe, 1998); Matthew Dallek, *The Right Moment: Ronald Reagan's First Victory and the Decisive Turning Point in American Politics* (New York: Hill and Wang, 2000); Rick Perlstein, *Before the Storm: Barry Goldwater and the Unmaking of the American Consensus* (New York: Oxford University Press, 2001); Jonathan M. Schoenwald, *A Time for Choosing: The Rise of Modern American Conservatism* (New York, 2001).

3. See, for example, Doug Rossinow, *The Politics of Authenticity: Liberalism, Christianity, and the New Left in America* (New York: Columbia University Press, 1998); Beth Bailey, *Sex in the Heartland* (Cambridge, MA: Harvard University Press, 1999); Jeff Roche, "Cowboy Conservatism: Politics on the High Plains, 1932–1972," Ph.D. dissertation, University of New Mexico, 2001.

4. *Texas Observer,* 13 May 1961.

5. *Texas Observer,* 19 January 1962, 22 September 1961, 13 October 1961, 8 December 1961, 2 March 1962; Amarillo *Globe,* 26 February 1962.

6. Amarillo *Globe,* 26 February 1962.

7. *Texas Observer,* 2 March 1962; Amarillo *Globe,* 26 February 1962.

8. For more on the John Birch Society, see *The Blue Book of the John Birch Society* (Belmont, MA: Western Islands, 1959); Seymour Lipset and Earl Raab, *The Politics of Unreason: Right Wing Extremism in America, 1790–1970* (New York: Harper and Row, 1970); Arnold Forster and Benjamin Epstein, *Danger on the Right* (New York: Random House, 1964); Richard Hofstadter, *The Paranoid Style in American Politics and Other Essays* (New York: Knopf, 1965), 70–72; Sara Diamond, *Roads to Dominion: Right-Wing Movements and Political Power in the United States* (New York: Guilford Press 1995), 52–58.

9. Ben Ezzell, *The Editor's Ass and Other Tales from 50 Years behind the Desk of Editor* (Canadian, TX: The Canadian Record, 1986), 32–37; *The Canadian Record,* 9 March 1961. Panhandle editor Ben Ezzell attended the meeting and then exposed what he saw. His expose of the JBS that appeared in the *Canadian Record* soon spread to newspapers across the country; he was one of the first reporters to reveal the potential power of the organization. For more on the continued influence of the JBS in the Panhandle see Carroll Wilson, "The Blue Book of Birchers," *Accent West* 10 (July 1981).

10. Not all Amarilloans respected Jerry Lee and his efforts. Throughout June 1961, he was the victim of several practical jokes. Every few days or so, a driver would deliver a rental truck, or a typewriter, or a mechanic, or a wheelchair to his home. Lee had ordered none of these items. The *Amarillo News* claimed his fierce campaigns against communism drew the ire of those less understanding of the communist menace. *Amarillo Globe,* 6 June 1961. For more on Jerry Lee see *Saturday Evening Post,* 26 March 1955; Bob Embree, "The Evening Tour," *Amarillo Globe-News* Archive, Clipping File, Jerry Lee. The JBS spread across most of Texas during this same time. It was particularly strong in Dallas and Houston.

11. *State Line Tribune,* 13 July 1962.

12. Walker was asked to resign from the air force when he forced his men to read JBS literature. He also gained national recognition when he was among the rioters in Oxford, Mississippi, when that institution, under federal court order, desegregated its campus. He made several visits to the Texas Panhandle during the 1960s.

13. Buck Ramsey, "Is Amarillo Ready for Self-Government?," 8 December 1967; *The Texas Observer,* 2 November 1962.

14. Panhandle Texans, like other Americans were learning more about the JBS in 1962; national media outlets had begun to examine the group more closely and Robert Welch's pronouncements about the supposed communist leanings of prominent Americans (including Dwight Eisenhower) brought the organization negative publicity. Conservatives like William F. Buckley, Barry Goldwater, and others condemned Welch even while coveting the huge following of the JBS. By 1962, the JBS had been discredited throughout the nation and membership dropped off. Diamond, *Roads to Dominion,* 55–58. "Panhandle Birchers Poured It On and Lost," *Texas Observer,* 6 November 1962. See also Amarillo *Daily News* and *Globe,* November 1962.

15. Richard Brooks interview with author, 17 July 2000.

16. Ibid.

17. In 1960, Texas Republicans launched a bid to unseat Senator Lyndon Johnson. Johnson,

also the Democratic nominee for vice president, had convinced the Texas legislature to pass a special law that enabled him to run for both offices. The Republican nominee, former college professor and conservative John Tower, ran an invigorated campaign. He captured a surprising 41% of the votes in the general election. He won 46% of the Panhandle vote. The next spring, Tower narrowly won a special election to fill Johnson's then-vacant Senate seat. He was the first Texas Republican elected to the Senate since Reconstruction. He dominated the election in the Panhandle. See Mike Kingston, Sam Attlesey, and Mary G. Crawford. *The Texas Almanac's Political History of Texas* (Austin: Eakin Press, 1992); Paul Casdorph, *A History of the Republican Party in Texas, 1862–1965* (Austin: Pemberton Press, 1965), 220–24; Roger M. Olien, *From Token to Triumph: The Texas Republicans Since 1920* (Dallas: Southern Methodist University Press, 1982), 6–14.

18. As Goldwater himself once argued, Texas was the best place to examine the "grass roots" of Republican organizing in 1964. Goldwater and Casserly, *Goldwater*, 210.

19. For more on Barry Goldwater as a "westerner" see Peter Iverson, *Barry Goldwater: Native Arizonan* (Norman: University of Oklahoma Press, 1997). See also Michael Paul Rogin and John L. Shover, *Political Change in California* (Westport, CT: Greenwood Press, 1970), for a scathing critique of California conservatives' preference for "Ronald Reagan, the man who plays cowboys" to "the actual cowboy, Barry Goldwater," 200–1. For more on the regional shift of political power and the resultant conservatism in the South and West see Kevin Phillips's classic *The Emerging Republican Majority* (Garden City, NY: Anchor Books, 1970).

20. Brooks interview. Barry M. Goldwater, *Conscience of a Conservative* (Sheperdsville, KY: Victor Publishing, 1960), 13.

21. Goldwater, *Conscience of a Conservative,* See also Goldberg, *Barry Goldwater*, 138–41; Goldwater and Casserly, *Goldwater*, 119–22; Richard Brooks interview.

22. For more on the emergence of the term "conservative" among Texans, see John R. Knaggs, *Two-Party Texas: The John Tower Era, 1961–1984* (Austin: Eakin Press, 1986), 58–60. Belden's Texas Poll, October 1964, Belden's Texas Poll, June 1968, Roper Center, Storrs, Connecticut; Walter L. Shelly, "Political Profiles of the Nixon, Humphrey, and Wallace Voters in the Texas Panhandle, 1968: A Study in Voting Behavior," Ph.D. dissertation, Texas Tech University, 1972, 49–56.

23. Interestingly, when the Department of Defense closed the Amarillo Air Base in 1966, local conservatives claimed (and still claim) that the act was retribution by Johnson for the Panhandle's support of Goldwater. See A. G. Mojtabai, *Blessed Assurance: At Home with the Bomb in Amarillo, Texas* (Albuquerque: University of New Mexico Press, 1986), 38–45.

24. George Mahon Constituent Ballots, 1966, George Mahon Papers, SWC (Mahon Papers) Steve Dunlap to editor, *Amarillo Globe-Times*, 6 October 1972; Earl to Grady Hazelwood, 19 February 1969, Grady Hazelwood Papers, Panhandle-Plains Historical Museum, Canyon, Texas (PPHM) (Hazelwood Papers); Manuel DeBusk quoted in Jane Gilmore and Kline A. Nall, *Evolution of a University: Texas Tech's First Fifty Years* (Austin: Madrona Press, 1975), 178; Darrell Munsell interview with author, 6 July 2000; MCH to Hazelwood, 19 March 1969; Hazelwood to MCH 21 March 1969, Hazelwood Papers.

25. Marshall Formby speech before Muleshoe Rotary Club, 9 October 1973, Formby Papers, SWC.

26. BWA to Hazelwood, 18 March 1966, Preston Smith Papers, Box 703, SWC; Mrs. REW

to Hazelwood, 29 March 1966; ES to Hazelwood, 17 March 1966; JFG to Hazelwood, 16 March 1966, Hazelwood Papers, Drawer 19. To protect the privacy of those who wrote to Hazelwood I have included only their initials.

27. "New Mood: a Harder Line of College Disturbances," *U.S. News and World Report* 66 (24 February 1969): 30; Hazelwood to JFM, 4 March 1969, Hazelwood papers.

28. John Rhinehart, interview with author, 20 May 2000; Lou Rizzuto, interview with author, 29 June 2000; Edgar Sneed, interview with author, 18 July 2000; Frederick Rathjen, interview with author, 29 June 2000.

29. Rhinehart interview; Rizzuto interview; *The Prairie* (WT's campus newspaper), 16 December 1968; *Amarillo Globe-Times,* 4 October 1968; Carol Drerup, "History Prof Says Campus Activism Is Dead," *The Prairie,* 10 November 1978.

30. Ibid.

31. Paige Carruth interview with author, 3 July 2000; Darrell Munsell interview; Frederick Rathjen interview.

32. Duane Thomas and Paul Zimmerman, *Duane Thomas and the Fall of America's Team* (New York: Warner Books, 1988), 29–42; Eugene "Mercury" Morris and Steve Fiffer, *Against the Grain* (New York: McGraw-Hill, 1988), 32–51; John Rhinehart, interview, 21 May 2000; Frederick Rathjen, interview with author, 29 June 2000; Carruth interview; Carroll Wilson, interview with author, 11 July 2000; Louis Rizzuto interview with author, 29 June 2000; Franklin Thomas, interview with author, 16 July 2000; Darrell Munsell, interview with author.

33. *The Prairie,* 5 March 1969; Franklin Thomas, interview with author, 16 July 2000.

34. *The Prairie,* 23 April 1969; Thomas interview.

35. Marshall Formby, oral history interview, 19 September 1975 (Formby Papers).

36. Potter County Democratic Executive Committee, Press Release, 30 July 1968, Hazelwood Papers, Drawer 23.

37. PFS to Grady Hazelwood, 8 August 1968; Mrs. Wayne Maddox to the Editor, Amarillo *Daily News,* 3 August 1968.

38. LHB to Grady Hazelwood, 25 July 1968; RSW to Grady Hazelwood, 4 February 1969; FW to Grady Hazelwood 14 October 1968; LP and KH (of the Hutchinson County Teenage Republicans) to Grady Hazelwood, 30 August 1968; MM to Grady Hazelwood 6 August 1968; OBH to Grady Hazelwood, 7 August 1968, all in Hazelwood Scrapbook, Hazelwood Papers.

39. RW to Grady Hazelwood, 1 August 1968, in Hazelwood Scrapbook. For a striking example of how historians can use constituent mail to explore questions about political culture see David Thelen, *Becoming Citizens in the Age of Television: How Americans Challenged the Media and Seized Political Initiative During the Iran-Contra Debate* (Chicago: University of Chicago Press, 1996); Brooks interview.

40. *Amarillo News,* 9 August 1968.

41. Shelly, "Political Profiles." For a concise synopsis of Shelly's findings see *Amarillo Globe,* 8 September 1969.

42. Shelly, "Political Profiles," 18–20, 27; Ghassan Arnaoot, Sam Keeley, and Patrick Kelso, *Economic Analysis of the Texas Panhandle,* Panhandle Regional Planning Commission, 1971; Terry G. Jordan, John L. Bean, Jr., and William M. Holmes, *Texas: A Geography* (Boulder and London: Westview Press, 1984), 60–65, 91.

43. Panhandle supporters of the Alabama governor's campaign differed in important ways from other Wallace constituencies. They were, like other Wallace voters, predominantly male (65%). Unlike Wallace voters elsewhere, who were on the average in the

youngest categories, 79% of Panhandle Wallace voters were over thirty-five years old. Moreover, they were from the middle or upper classes and decidedly conservative in *both* their social and economic beliefs. This population of Wallace voters reveals a political culture in a state of flux. These were not voters, as others have argued, who were so young as to not have an allegiance to a political party nor were they immediately exposed to desegregation after the *Brown* decree. For over thirty years, social scientists have been trying to unlock the secret to Wallace's national appeal. Most have tended to focus on either the Alabama governor's southern support or his support outside the South; a basic ideological split occurs at the South's borders. Southern Wallace voters, found primarily in regions with high concentrations of African Americans, were mostly concerned with stemming the advances of the civil rights movement. "Black Belt" voters had consistently been devoted to racial politics since before the Civil War. Wallace was the latest incarnation of a political trend that stretched back more than a century. The best historiographic examination of Wallace's appeal is William B. Hixson, Jr., *Search for the American Right Wing: An Analysis of the Social Science Record, 1955–1987* (Princeton: Princeton University Press, 1992), 113–74. For Wallace's southern support, see 115–37. See also Lipset and Raab, *The Politics of Unreason*, 338–427; Philip Crass, *The Wallace Factor* (New York: Mason Charter, 1976) 135–50; Gerald C. Wright, "Contextual Models of Electoral Behavior: The Southern Wallace Vote" *American Political Science Review*, 71 (June): 497–508; Robert A. Schoenberger and David R. Segal, "The Ecology of Dissent: The Southern Wallace Vote in 1968" *Midwest Journal of Political Science* 15 (August 1971): 583–86. For Wallace voters in Texas see Robert D. Wrinkle and Charles Elliot, "Wallace Party Activists in Texas" *Social Science Quarterly* 52 (June 1971): 197–203.

44. Belden Texas Poll. November 1972. Roper Center. Bob Price quoted in Ezzell, *The Editor's Ass*, 29. Price later denied having made the statement.

45. Darrell Munsell interview; Peter Petersen interview; Carroll Wilson, *Canyon in the Sixties*, 51.

46. John Matthews, interview with author, 25 July 2000.

47. Drerup, "History Prof"; Munsell interview; Rathjen interview; Petersen interview.

48. Munsell interview; Rathjen interview.

49. Carruth interview; Belden's Texas Poll, October 1969, Roper Center.

50. Munsell interview; Petersen interview; Matthews interview.

51. Buck Ramsey, "Letter from Amarillo" *Texas Observer*, 17 April 1970; Ramsey interview; Ezzell, *The Editor's Ass*, 101–2; Wilson, *Canyon in the Sixties*, 55, 58.

52. Buck Ramsey, "Letter from Amarillo." The practice of giving prisoners "haircuts" was not limited to Amarillo. *Amarillo Globe-Times*, 19 October 1972

53. Dale E. Pontius and Theodore J. Taylor, "The *Catalyst* Wins Its Suit," *Texas Observer*, 4 September 1970. See also *The Catalyst*, newspaper collection SWC.

54. *Amarillo Globe-Times*, 7 October 1972.

55. Belden Texas Poll, November 1972. Roper Center. Early September revealed that most Texans believed that McGovern was pitching his campaign to "youths and minorities." *Amarillo Globe-Times*, 5 October 1972.

56. *Amarillo Globe-Times*, 8 November 1972.

57. For more on the emergence of conservatism in the 1970s, see Bruce Schulman, *The Seventies: The Great Shift in American Culture, Society, and Politics* (New York: The Free Press, 2001), 193–252.

Schuparra : "A Great White Light"

1. Ronald Reagan, *A Time for Choosing: The Speeches of Ronald Reagan 1961–1982* (Chicago: Regnery, 1983), 61. On the shift in the use and meaning of the word "freedom," see Daniel Rodgers, *Contested Truths: Keywords in American Politics Since Independence* (New York: Basic Books, 1987), 217–23.

2. Of the many biographies and other studies of Reagan, the best perspectives on Reagan in the 1960s include Bill Boyarsky, *The Rise of Ronald Reagan* (New York: Random House, 1968); David Broder and Stephen Hess, *The Republican Establishment: The Present and Future of the GOP* (New York: Harper and Row, 1967); Lou Cannon, *Ronnie and Jesse: A Political Odyssey* (Garden City, NY: Doubleday, 1969), and *Reagan* (New York: G.P. Putnam's Sons, 1982); Matthew Dallek, *The Right Moment: Ronald Reagan's First Victory and the Decisive Turning Point in American Politics* (New York: The Free Press, 2000); Kurt Schuparra, *Triumph of the Right: The Rise of the California Conservative Movement 1945–66* (Armonk, NY: M. E. Sharpe, 1998); and Garry Wills, *Reagan's America* (New York: Penguin Books, 1988).

3. Michael Schaller, *Reckoning with Reagan: America and its President in the 1980s* (New York: Oxford, 1992), 6.

4. On Humphrey and Gahagan Douglass, see Jonathan M. Schoenwald, *A Time for Choosing: The Rise of Modern American Conservatism* (New York: Oxford, 2001), 300; ". . . too liberal" in Lou Cannon, *President Reagan: The Role of a Lifetime* (New York: Simon and Schuster, 1991), 286; and Reagan quoted in Matthew Dallek, *The Right Moment,* 38.

5. Joseph Roddy, "Ronnie to the Rescue," *Look,* 1 November 1966, 53.

6. Ronald Reagan and Richard Hubler, *Where's the Rest of Me? The Autobiography of Ronald Reagan* (New York: Karz-Segil Publishers, 1965), 139, 141, 162. On Reagan's relationship with GE, see Wills, *Reagan's America,* 332–43.

7. The extremist label stuck almost exclusively to the Republican Right, particularly after the anticommunist inquisition led by Republican senator Joseph McCarthy in the early 1950s. In the decade following the McCarthy hearings, journalists and academics alike identified an aberrant angst in the behavior and worldview of ardent right wingers, emphasizing a rather monolithic conservative mindset as opposed to a spectrum of conservative perspectives—from extreme to relatively moderate. In 1962, sociologist Daniel Bell warned that the anxiety of entrenched conservatives manifested in the emergence of the "radical right," and that the ideas and behavior of these individuals threatened the centrist pluralism and "'fragile consensus' that underlies the American political system." The preeminent historian Richard Hofstadter joined with Bell in this critique. Identifying a certain "paranoid style" as a chief characteristic of Barry Goldwater's backers, Hofstadter claimed that while not clinically paranoid, the exponents of the paranoid style saw a "'vast' or 'gigantic' conspiracy as *the motive force* in history." Despite their often-perspicacious analyses and observations on conservatism within this paradigm of social pathology, Bell and Hofstader, along with other notable critics, significantly overstated their arguments. The groundbreaking essays that fostered the right-wing "anxiety" thesis (commonly referred to as the "status anxiety" thesis) are Hofstadter's "The Pseudo Conservative Revolt," and Seymour Martin Lipset's "The Sources of the 'Radical Right,'" in Daniel Bell, ed., *The New American Right* (New York: Criterion Books, 1955). The book was reissued in 1963 in an "expanded and updated" form, with the new and clearly pejorative title *The Radical Right: The New American Right* (Garden City,

NY: Doubleday). Bell quoted (above) in his essay "The Dispossessed," 2; and Hofstadter in *The Paranoid Style in American Politics and Other Essays* (Reprint, Chicago: University of Chicago Press, 1979, originally 1965), 1, 29.

8. Cannon, *Ronnie and Jesse: A Political Odyssey* (Garden City, NY: Doubleday, 1969), 75; and Reagan, *A Time for Choosing*, 56–57.

9. Fan magazine quoted in Stephen Vaughn, *Ronald Reagan in Hollywood* (New York: Cambridge University Press), 37.

10. "Biography of Ronald Reagan: A Truly Qualified Citizen Politician," California Republican Assembly (CRA) Collection, box 2, University of California, Los Angeles, Special Collections Library.

11. *TV Guide* comment cited in Michael P. Rogin, *Ronald Reagan, the Movie: and Other Episodes of Political Demonology* (Berkeley: University of California Press, 1987), 33.

12. Reagan and Hubler, *Where's the Rest of Me?*, 267.

13. Ibid., 205.

14. The best description of this tendency is in Wills, *Reagan's America*, 396–405. For another perspective, see Rogin, *Ronald Reagan, the Movie*, 1–43.

15. Wills, *Reagan's America*, 111.

16. Boyarsky, *The Rise of Ronald Reagan*, 104.

17. Reagan, "On Becoming Governor," University of California Oral History (Berkeley, 1979), 3.

18. Reagan, "A Moment of Truth," *Vital Speeches of the Day*, 1 September 1965, 686.

19. Reagan, "On Becoming Governor," 5–6.

20. Quotes from the *Los Angeles Times*, 5 January 1966.

21. "Biography of Ronald Reagan," CRA Collection; and Schuparra, *Triumph of the Right*, 113–14.

22. All quotes from Boyarsky, *The Rise of Ronald Reagan*, 148–49. Christopher tried in vain to make more of an issue of this matter but failed to prod Reagan into continuing this contentious dialogue. See Christopher to Reagan, 4 May 1966, Thomas Kuchel Papers, box 477, University of California, Berkeley, Bancroft Library (UCBBL).

23. Reagan and Hubler, *Where's the Rest of Me?*, 8; on his participation in anti-discrimination productions, see Vaughan, *Ronald Reagan in Hollywood*, 171–81; and Reagan quoted (at rally) in Edmund Morris, *Dutch: A Memoir of Ronald Reagan* (New York: Random House, 1999), 228.

24. Reagan quoted in Robert Scheer, "The Reagan Question," *Playboy*, August 1980.

25. Roddy, "Ronnie to the Rescue," 54; and Reagan quoted in the *Los Angeles Times*, 2 June 1966.

26. Christopher quoted in the *Los Angeles Times*, 3 June 1966.

27. See John Judis, *William F. Buckley, Jr.: Patron Saint of the Conservatives* (New York: Simon and Schuster, 1988), 146–47; and George Nash, *The Conservative Intellectual Movement in America Since 1945* (New York: Basic Books, 1976), 148–53.

28. William F. Buckley, "How Is Ronald Reagan Doing? *National Review*, 11 January 1966, 17.

29. For an overview of Brown's political career, see Dallek, *The Right Moment*, 1–24.

30. Totten J. Anderson and Eugene C. Lee, "The 1966 Election in California," *Western Political Quarterly* 20 (June 1967): 538; and "transparent hack" in Fred Dutton, "Democratic Campaigns and Controversies," University of California Oral History (Berkeley, 1977–78), 142.

31. See Byron W. Rumford, "Legislator for Fair Employment, Fair Housing, and Public

Health," University of California Oral History (Berkeley, 1970–71), 119–33; and the *New York Times*, 10 May 1964. See also Martin Scheisl, "The Struggle for Equality: Racial Reform and Party Politics in California, 1950–1966," *California Politics & Policy* (California State University, Los Angeles: Pat Brown Institute, 1997), 55–68.

32. See the *New York Times*, 7 September 1964; and "The Committee for Home Protection" literature, William Knowland Papers, box 158, UCBBL.

33. Quoted in the *Los Angeles Times*, 11 May 1966.

34. Reagan quoted in the *Los Angeles Times*, 13 September 1966; and in McGirr, *Suburban Warriors*, 205.

35. For an overview of the Watts riot and its political implications, see Dallek, *The Right Moment*, 128–49. (On Reagan and Watts, see pp. 186–89.) A backlash, fueled by rising civil unrest, affected white perceptions of black America. A nationwide Harris Poll taken shortly before the 1966 elections showed that the number of whites who believed that blacks had "tried to move too fast" grew from 34% in 1964 to 85%. Poll cited in the *Los Angeles Times*, 6 November 1966. Brown quoted in ibid., 29 October 1966; and Reagan quoted in ibid., 31 October 1966.

36. Quoted in Editors, "Golly Gee, California is a Strange State," *Ramparts*, October 1966, 15. (Reagan commented on this moment in his inaugural address.)

37. Reagan quoted in *The Register* (Santa Ana, California), 21 October 1966; and in Cannon, *Ronnie and Jesse*, 83.

38. Socially conservative union sentiment, R. E. Lawson to Pat Brown, 28 October 1966, Pat Brown Papers, box 921, UCBBL; and Longshoremen's plea, Paul Perlin to Pat Brown, 1 August 1966, ibid., box 922. California poll of union households cited in *The San Francisco Chronicle*, 12 October 1966.

39. William Becker to Hale Champion et al., 12 August 1966, Pat Brown Papers, box 921. See also William Becker, "Working for Civil Rights," University of California Oral History (Berkeley, 1979) 57–59. President Nixon later faced a similar accusation. In a devious tactical twist, he supported a policy of "preferential treatment" for minorities in employment practices and a strong affirmative action agenda with the goal of increasing tension between blacks and predominantly white labor unions members. See Schuparra, *Triumph of the Right*, 146.

40. McGirr, *Suburban Warriors*, 199.

41. Ibid., 201, 328. For further analysis of how Republicans attempted to capitalize on the growing disillusionment of conservative Democrats on racial issues, see Edward G. Carmines and James A. Stinson, *Issue Evolution: Race and the Transformation of American Politics* (Princeton: Princeton University Press, 1989); Thomas Byrne Edsall and Mary D. Edsall, *Chain Reaction: The Impact of Race, Rights and Taxes on American Politics* (New York: W. W. Norton, 1992); and Jonathan Reider, "The Rise of the Silent Majority," in Steve Fraser and Gary Gerstle, eds., *The Rise and Fall of the New Deal Order, 1930–1980* (Princeton: Princeton University Press, 1989), 243–68.

42. Quoted in Jessica Mitford, "The Rest of Ronald Reagan," *Ramparts*, November 1965, 65.

43. Quoted in Ben Bagdikian, "In the Hearts of the Right, Goldwater Lives," the *New York Times Magazine*, 18 July 1965, 41.

44. Dallek, *The Right Moment*, 215.

45. Reagan to Murphy, August 19, 1966, Reagan Papers, Hoover Institute on War, Revolution and Peace (HIWRP), Stanford University box 23; and "citizen advisor" in Vernon Cristina, "A Northern Californian Views Conservative Policies and Politics," University of California Oral History (Berkeley, 1983), 20.

46. Reagan to Goldwater, 11 June 1966, Reagan Papers, box 23.

47. Robert Dallek, *Ronald Reagan: The Politics of Symbolism* (Cambridge: Harvard University Press, 1984), 34.

48. Kiwanis Club remark is from a Leon Panetta memorandum to his boss, Senator Tom Kuchel, 22 June 1966, Thomas Kuchel Papers, box 477, UCBBL. Dan Carter, *The Politics of Rage: George Wallace, the Origins of the New Conservatism, and the Transformation of American Politics* (New York: Simon and Schuster, 1995), 313–14.

49. Reagan, *A Time for Choosing*, 66–67.

50. Jackson K. Putnam, *Modern California Politics* (3rd ed. Sparks, NV: MTL, 1990), 60–61; and Boyarsky, *The Rise of Ronald Reagan*, 189–91.

51. Rumford quoted in *New York Times*, 8 August 1967; and Reagan, "On Becoming Governor," 15. Bagley's recollections are from an interview with the author, 29 October 1997, Sacramento, California.

52. *New York Times*, 27 September 1967.

53. Reagan quoted in Matthew Dallek, *The Right Moment*, 198. As with civil rights, white America's changing perception of welfare fueled the nascent collapse of the liberal New Deal coalition in the latter half of the 1960s. As Jonathan Reider has noted, "No longer did [liberalism] suggest a vision of transcendent justice or the support of vulnerable working people. Liberalism meant taking the side of blacks, no matter what"; see Reider, "The Rise of the Silent Majority," 258.

54. Reagan quoted in F. Clifton White and William J. Gill, *Why Reagan Won: The Conservative Movement 1964–1981* (Chicago: Regnery Gateway, 1981), 95–96.

55. On the "welfare queen," see Cannon, *President Reagan*, 319; Reagan quoted in "Reagan Talks of the Issues and his Plans," *U.S. News & World Report*, 25 March 1968, 57.

56. Ibid., 57.

57. W. J. Rorabaugh, *Berkeley at War: The 1960s* (New York: Oxford, 1989), 83–84; and the *Los Angeles Times*, 27 October 1968.

58. Poll on public disapproval of campus demonstrations cited in ibid. For Berkeley and San Francisco State University disturbances and Reagan's reaction, see Boyarsky notes on "Higher Education," Bill Boyarsky Papers, box 2, HIRWP. Also see Rorabaugh, *Berkeley at War*, 85, 159–64. A member of both the national and state YAF advisory boards, Reagan privately worried that the factious state chapter "had gone off the deep end." On Reagan and the YAF, see Gregory L. Schneider, *Cadres for Conservatism: Young Americans for Freedom and the Rise of the Contemporary Right* (New York: New York University Press, 1999), 137–38.

59. The song Baez sang, "Drug Store Truck Drivin' Man," was written by Roger McGuinn and Gram Parsons of the Byrds. Baez changed a few of the lyrics to make her rendition more relevant to Reagan.

60. Boyarsky notes on "Higher Education," Boyarsky Papers, box 2.

61. Reagan quoted in *CRA News*, May 1970, CRA Collection, box 10, folder 7; and "academy" speech, 11 April 1969, Boyarsky Papers, box 2.

62. On the mixed success of Berkeley radicals in the battle over People's Park, and on the dismay of radicals and liberals over Reagan's popularity, see Todd Gitlin, *The Sixties: Years of Hope, Days of Rage* (Toronto: Bantam Books, 1987), 353–61, 434 (quote). Rorabaugh, *Berkeley at War*, 166.

63. Cannon, *Reagan*, 171–72; and Reagan quoted in *New York Times*, 27 September 1970.

64. Reagan campaign literature, CRA Collection, box 4, folder 6.

65. Reagan and Nixon quoted in Cannon, *Reagan*, 175.

66. This assertion draws upon an interpretation in Rogin, *Ronald Reagan, the Movie*, 32.
67. Reagan, *A Time for Choosing*, 171–72, 219.

Critchlow: Conservatism Reconsidered

1. Quoted in Clinton Rossiter, *Conservatism in America: The Thankless Persuasion* (New York: Knopf, 1962), 195–96.
2. Quoted in ibid., 196.
3. See Richard Hofstadter, *The Paranoid Style in American Politics and Other Essays* (New York: Vintage Books, 1967) and his *Anti-Intellectualism in American Life* (New York: Knopf, 1963).
4. Lionel Trilling, *The Liberal Imagination* (New York: Viking Press, 1950), ix.
5. In 1983, Leo Ribuffo offered an important reassessment, based on a detailed reading of archival sources, of the grassroots Old Religious Right. Leo Ribuffo, *The Old Christian Right: The Protestant Far Right from the Great Depression to the Cold War* (Philadelphia: Temple University Press, 1983).
   By the 1980s and 1990s, historians were recasting religious fundamentalists and followers of the Ku Klux Klan in the 1920s and Father Charles Coughlin in the 1930s as representing a "republican" tradition. For the KKK in the 1920s, see Richard K. Tucker, *The Dragon and the Cross: The Rise and Fall of the Ku Klux Klan in Middle America* (Hamden, CT.: Archon Books, 1991); Leonard Moore, *Citizen Klansmen: The Ku Klux Klan in Indiana, 1921–1925* (Chapel Hill: University of North Carolina Press, 1991); and Nancy MacLean, *Behind the Mask of Chivalry: The Making of the Second Ku Klux Klan* (New York: Oxford University Press, 1994). On the Coughlin movement, see Alan Brinkley, *Huey Long, Father Coughlin, and the Great Depression* (New York: Vintage Books, 1983).
   The populist roots of the Right drew the attention of historians Michael Kazin and Alan Brinkley who explored in the early 1990s, with some controversy, the meaning of the grassroots Right in American politics. Michael Kazin, "The Grass-Roots Right: New Histories of U.S. Conservatism," *American Historical Review*, 97 (February 1992): 136–55; and Alan Brinkley, "The Problem of American Conservatism," *American Historical Review* (April 1994): 409–29), with responses, 430–52.
   More recently, a new generation of historians produced a proliferation of dissertations, articles, and books that allowed for a new construction of political history in modern America that incorporates modern conservatism. See, for example, John Andrew, *The Other Side of the Sixties: Young Americans for Freedom and the Rise of Conservative Politics* (New Brunswick, NJ: Rutgers University Press, 1997); and Gregory L. Schneider, *Cadres for Conservatism* (New York: New York University Press, 1999). Grassroots conservatism is explored in Lisa McGirr, *Suburban Warriors: The Origins of the New American Right* (Princeton, NJ: Princeton University Press, 2000); Rick Perlstein, *Before the Storm: Barry Goldwater and the Unmaking of the American Consensus* (New York: Hill and Wang, 2001); Robert Alan Goldberg, *Barry Goldwater* (New Haven: Yale University Press, 1995); and Mary C. Brennan, *Turning Right in the Sixties: The Conservative Capture of the GOP* (Chapel Hill: University of North Carolina Press, 1995).
6. A more graphic lesson of communist diversionary tactics came in the form of a forty-two-page colored comic book, "Is this Tomorrow, America Under Communism," published by the Catechetical Guild Education Society in 1947. In this futuristic tale about a communist seizure of power in the United States, an early frame shows a heavy-mustached

communist leader telling his followers, "We have done an exceptional job of making different classes and religions hate one another." The following frame shows a communist
whispering to a dull-looking worker at a union meeting, "And the first thing you know,
they'll having us working with a Jew and Nobody's gonna make me." "Is this Tomorrow,
American Under Communism," Catechical Educational Guild Society (1947).

7. Phyllis Schlafly, Notes of Speech, Robert Welch, 14–15 August 1959, Notes from Phyllis
Schlafly Office Subject Files Pre-1972 (12 pages); Robert Welch, *The Blue Book of the
John Birch Society* (Boston: Western Islands, 1961), 19–20. The relative insignificance of
the race issue within the John Birch Society is apparent in Gerald Schomp, *Birchism
Was My Business* (New York: Macmillan, 1970). For a counterperspective, see Milton
A. Waldor, *Peddlers of Fear, The John Birch Society* ((Newark, NJ: Lynnross Publication
Company, 1966). Dan T. Carter, *The Politics of Rage: George Wallace, the Origins of the
New Conservatism, and the Transformation of American Politics* (Baton Rouge: Louisiana
State University Press, 1995) argues that the race issue is central to understanding the
origins of the New Right in America, even though few New Right leaders were asso-
ciated with the Wallace campaign.

8. McGirr, *Suburban Warriors,* 10.

    On conservative intellectuals, see Ted V. McAllister, *Revolt Against Modernity* (Law-
rence: University Press of Kansas, 1996), which discusses the influence of Leo Strauss
and Eric Voeglin on conservative intellectuals, but their influence remained limited to a
small circle of academics. Other historians of American conservatives also place a heavy
emphasis of the role of intellectuals in shaping the conservative movement. See, for example, George Nash, *The Conservative Intellectual Movement in America Since 1945*
(New York: Basic Books, 1979); J. David Hoeveler, Jr. *Watch on the Right* (Madison:
University of Wisconsin Press, 1991).

9. The author would like to acknowledge William A. Rusher for pointing out this symbiotic relationship between "popularizers" and "intellectuals" in his reading of an early
draft of this essay.

10. McGirr, *Suburban Warriors,* 9–10.

11. This point is evident in David W. Reinhard, *The Republican Right Since 1945* (Lexing-
ton: University of Press of Kentucky, 1983) and James T. Patterson, *Mr. Republican: A
Biography of Robert Taft* (Boston: Houghton Mifflin, 1972). Anticommunism and
McCarthyism are placed within a long-term historical context by David Oshinsky, *A
Conspiracy So Immense: The World of Joe McCarthy* (New York: Free Press, 1983) and
Richard Fried, *Men Against McCarthy* (New York: Columbia University Press, 1976).
A broad perspective of anticommunism is offered by M. J. Heale, *American Anti-
Communism: Combating the Enemy Within, 1930–1970* (Baltimore: Johns Hopkins
University Press, 1990).

12. Rebecca Klatch, *Women of the New Right* (Philadelphia: Temple University Press, 1987);
Sara Diamond, *Road to Dominion: Right-Wing Movements and Political Power in the
United States* (New York: Guilford Press, 1995); and Elinor Burkett, *The Right Women:
A Journey Through the Hearts of Conservative America* (New York: Scribner, 1998).

13. There is a rich and extensive literature on female reformers in the nineteenth and early
twentieth centuries. For the purpose of this essay, especially useful are Jane Dehart,
"Gender on the Right: Meanings behind the Existential Scream," *Gender and History,* 3
(Autumn 1991); Zillah R. Eisenstein, "The Sexual Politics of the New Right," *Feminist
Theory,* 7 (Spring 1982); Kathleen M. Blee, *Women of the Klan: Racism and Gender in the
1920s* (Berkeley: University of California Press, 1991); and Leonard J. Moore, *Citizen*

Klansmen: The Ku Klux Klan in Indiana, 1921–1928 (Chapel Hill: University of North Carolina Press, 1991). Of particular value for understanding the role of women in public life in the nineteenth century are Mary P. Ryan, *Cradle of the Middle Class: The Family in Oneida County, New York, 1790–1865* (Cambridge: Cambridge University Press, 1981); Ryan, "The Power of Female Networks: A Case Study of Female Moral Reform in Antebellum America," *Feminist Studies* 5 (1979); Barbara Leslie Epstein, *The Politics of Domesticity: Women, Evangelism, and Temperance in Nineteenth Century America* (Middletown, CT: Wesleyan University Press, 1981); Ruth Bordin, *Women and Temperance: The Quest for Power and Liberty, 1873–1900* (Philadelphia: Temple University Press, 1981); Lori Ginzberg, "'Moral Suasion is Moral Balderdash': Women, Politics, and Social Activism in the 1850s," *Journal of American History,* 73 (1986); Karen Blair, *The Clubwoman as Feminist: True Womanhood Redefined, 1868–1914* (Urbana: University of Illinois Press, 1980); Kathyrn Kish Sklar, "Hull House in the 1890s: A Community of Women Reformers," *Signs* 10 (1985); Paula Baker, "Domestication of Politics: Women and American Political Society, 1780–1920," *American Historical Review* 89 (1984); Ellen Carol DuBois, *Feminism and Suffrage: The Emergence of an Independent Women's Movement in America, 1848–1869* (Ithaca, NY: Cornell University Press, 1978); and Susan Lebsock, "Women and American Politics, 1880–1920," in Louise Tilly and Patricia Gurin, eds., *Women, Politics, and Change in Twentieth-Century America* (New York: Russell Sage Foundation, 1992).

14. Odile Stewart traced her ancestry to early colonial French settlers in the Mississippi Valley, the Jean Baptiste Pratte family. She was also related to the Dodge family (her maiden name), who were related to General Henry Dodge. He later became the first senator from Wisconsin, while his son Augustus later became a congressman from Iowa. Thus the father sat in the Senate, while his son served in the House. Odile Dodge's father served as an assistant district attorney in St. Louis and made an unsuccessful election bid for district attorney. See "Additional Manuscript Containing the Roger Heriot Branch," and Notation and Clipping, "Funeral Service Tomorrow for E. D. Dodge Lawyer," "Scrapbook, 13–15 years," Phyllis Schlafly Home Papers, St. Louis Missouri.

15. See "Scrapbook, 13–15 years," Phyllis Schlafly Home Papers, St. Louis, Missouri; also quoted in Carol Felsenthal, *The Sweetheart of the Silent Majority: The Biography of Phyllis Schlafly* (New York: Doubleday, 1981).

16. "Student Memories" Scrapbook, Phyllis Schlafly Home Papers.

17. Her poem, "When I Saw Her," published in the college's literary magazine, expressed this piety: "When I saw her that day/In the first lush of Dawn/ Nothing could I say/ When I saw her that day/Like all cowards I pray/With dreams that are gone/Since I saw her that day/In the flush of dawn." Phyllis Stewart, "When I Saw," *The Maryville Magazine,* May 1942, 64. Phyllis wrote in her diary that "though I will be sorry to lose the girls and all the lovely traditions." The "nuns gave me the cold shoulder when I went to graduation on June 5" Entry 1 June 1941, Notebook, Began June 6th Ended October 3, 1944," Phyllis Schlafly Home Papers.

18. The rigors of her job at the St. Louis ordnance plant are captured in her diary entries in "Notebook, Began June 6," Phyllis Schlafly Home Papers.

19. See, for example, her term paper, Phyllis Bruce Stewart, "The Controversy Concerning the Division of Economic Research of the National Labor Relations Board, 1940," paper for Public Administration, 25 April 1945, Eagle Forum Papers, Pre-1949, Eagle Forum, St. Louis, MO.

20. Phyllis Schlafly to John T. Salmon, 8 September 1966, NFRW Republican Clubman Folder, NFRW Draw, Eagle Forum Office File, St. Louis, MO.

21. James Daniel to Phyllis Schlafly, 3 November 1945, Scrapbook Washington, D.C., Phyllis Schlafly Home Papers.

     She had written in one of her term papers at Radcliffe, "Better Public Personnel," that "a problem which threatens to take on vast proportions in the near future is veteran's preference. Few people realize what a potent force this is." She worried that this preferential standard would subvert the necessity of "a staff of alert, well-trained, independent, purposeful public officials to perform the increasing number of tasks imposed on government." Phyllis Bruce Stewart, "Better Public Personnel," 20 November 1944, Public Administration, Eagle Forum Office Files, Pre-1949, Eagle Forum.

22. American Enterprise Association, "A Statement of Purposes: Extracts from an Address" by Lewis H. Brown, 1 June 1945.

23. For speeches, see Phyllis Stewart, "The Trust Company: Its Development and Function," "Women's Financial Problems," "Wives and Wills," "The Marital Deduction," "Minor Beneficiaries," ""Living Trusts," and "Estate Planning," in Eagle Forum Office File, Pre-1949, Eagle Forum.

24. Speeches written for Bakewell included, "Veteran Housing," "America at the Crossroads," "The Housing Confusion," "A Year of Confusion," "Labor and Labels," "A Square Deal for Veterans," "The Issue of the PAC," "Communist Infiltration," "Republican Labor Policy," "Crisis Government," "The Local Machine," "Beer and the New Deal," "Military Justice," and "Tolerance and Liberalism" in Phyllis Eagle Forum Office Files, Pre-1949, Eagle Forum.

25. "Citizens Council Urges Bond Issue as Step to Big Housing Projects," *St. Louis Post Dispatch,* 17 October 1948, 1; and Clipping, "Phyllis Schlafly Makes Front Page of *Post,*" *St. Louis Junior League,* November 1949, 1.

26. Schlafly's children included John, a lawyer in Alton, born 1950; Dr. Bruce Stewart, surgeon, St. Louis, born 1955; Roger Sherwood, mathematician, Scotts Valley, CA, born 1956; Liza Forshaw, lawyer, born 1958; Andrew Layton, lawyer, born 1961; Anne Valle, businesswoman, St. Louis, born 1964.

27. Phyllis Schlafly, "I Wanted to Nurse My Baby, But . . ." Speech in Phyllis Schlafly Annual Correspondence, 1959, Phyllis Schlafly Home Papers.

28. Phyllis Schlafly, "Practical Hints on Feeding Your Family More Healthful Food," Phyllis Schlafly Annual Correspondence, 1959, Phyllis Schlafly Home Papers.

29. Phyllis Schlafly, "The Big Things are Done by Little People," box 1960–61, Schlafly Annual Correspondence, Phyllis Schlafly Home Papers.

30. Dr. Fred Schwarz, *Beating the Unbeatable Foe* (Washington, D.C.: Regnery Pub., 1996).

31. Leading authors and speakers included Herbert Philbrick, W. Cleon Skousen, Louis Budenz, Anthony Bouscaren, Robert Morris, Clarence Manion, Rosalie Gordon, and John T. Flynn.

32. A useful summary of anticommunism in these years is found in M. J. Heale, *American Anticommunism: Combating the Enemy Within, 1830–1970* (Baltimore: Johns Hopkins University Press, 1990), 145–91.

33. Associated Industries of Missouri Newsletter, "The Manifesto," 20 December 1955.

34. American Coalition of Patriotic Societies, "Fight for Survival" (New York, 1962).

35. For example, see Freedom Bookshelf, "What Can I Do (Just One Person)," (Lombard, IL, 1963) and Phyllis Schlafly, "Reading List for Americans" (Alton, IL: Mrs. Phyllis Schlafly, 1957).

36. This genre of memoir literature intensified a view that communist regimes could never be trusted. As a result, grassroots anticommunists opposed trade deals, cultural exchanges, and arms treaties with the Soviet Union. This literature needs further exploration by scholars.

    For example, see W. G. Krivitsky, *I Was Stalin's Agent* (London: London Right Book Club, 1939); Victor Kravchenko's moving account of life in Soviet factories and torture under the N.K.V.D, *I Chose Freedom* (New York: C. Scribner's Sons, 1946); Alexander Barmine's heroic account of Soviet life in the Ukraine before the German invasion, *One Who Survived; The Life Story of a Russian under the Soviets* introduction by Max Eastman (New York: G.P. Putnam's Sons, 1946); Jerzy Glikksman's memoir of a Polish communist in the Soviet Union during the Second World War, *Tell the West* (New York: Gresham Press, 1946); Helena Sikorska's *Dark Side of the Moon* with a preface by T. S. Eliot (New York: Scribner, 1946); Elinor Lipper's powerfully written, *Eleven Years in Soviet Prison Camps* (Chicago: H. Regnery, 1951); John H. Noble's tale of an American arrested and sent to a Soviet labor camp, *I Was a Slave in Russia* (New York: Devin-Adair, 1960); Unto Parvilahti's story of a Finn sent to the gulag, *Beria's Gardens: A Slave Laborer's Experiences in the Soviet Union* (New York: Dutton, 1960); Richard Wurmbrand, a Lutheran minister, describes religious oppression in Rumania in his *In God's Underground* (Greenwich, CT: Fawcett, 1968); Walter J. Ciszek, S.J., *With God in Russia: My 23 Years as a Priest in Soviet Prisons* (New York: McGraw-Hill, 1964); and Bela Szasz reveals life in Hungarian prison, *Volunteers for the Gallows* (New York: Norton, 1971). In addition, a comparable memoir literature developed out of Communist China. An account of China in the first years of the revolution is found in Robert Loh, *Escape from Red China* (New York: Coward-McCann, 1962); inspiring accounts of religious faith are found in Harold Rigney, S.V.D., *Four Years in a Red Hell* (Chicago: H. Regnery, 1956); and Robert W. Greene, *Calvary in China* (New York: Putnam, 1953).

37. Council members originally included the spiritual director of the foundation, C. Stephen Dunker, a former Chinese missionary; Fr. John A. Houle, assistant director of the American Jesuits in China; Fr. Harold W. Rigney, S.V.D., once imprisoned by the Chinese communists and then working in a leper colony in the Philippines; Fr. John Kelley who ran a Catholic boys school in Chile; Fr. Vincent Loeffler who worked among black parishioners in Panama; Bishop Rembert Kowalski, who had spent seventeen years in a Chinese prison. Joining the board in the next two years were Rev. Robert Crawford, who had been imprisoned for five years in China, Rev. Warren DiCharry a missionary in China under communist rule before he was expelled, and Rev. Ismael Teste, an exiled Cuban priest.

38. Phyllis Schlafly to Vincent P. Ring, 4 July 1960, Schlafly Annual Correspondence, box 1959–60, Phyllis Schlafly Home Papers.

39. Cardinal Mindszenty Foundation, "The Cardinal Mindszenty Foundation Invites You to Combat Communism with Knowledge and Facts," Brochure (1957).

40. Cardinal Mindszenty Foundation, "We Invite You to Join a Cardinal Mindszenty Speakers Club" (1960).

41. Duncan Stewart, "America's Freedom Fighters," *Priest Magazine,* August 1961, 1–5.

42. Speech, Phyllis Schlafly, "What Can One Individual Do for Freedom?" (1960), Schlafly Annual Correspondence, box 1960, Phyllis Schlafly Home Papers.

43. Speech, Phyllis Schlafly, "Report of the President of the Legislative Chairman of the Tenth Biennial Convention of the IFRW" (1960), Schlafly Annual Correspondence, box 1960, Phyllis Schlafly Home Papers.

44. Phyllis Schlafly, "Women in Politics" (draft manuscript), Annual Correspondence, box 1960–61, Phyllis Schlafly Home Papers.

45. Phyllis Schlafly, "Report of the National Vice President of the NFRW," NFWR Minutes, 29 May 1965, NFRW Files, Eagle Forum Office Files, Eagle Forum.

46. Clipping, "GOP Faction Lists Endorsements," *East St. Louis Journal,* 26 March 1952; "Opponent Can Have Machine Backing—Mrs. Schlafly," *Alton Telegraph,* 27 March 1952; "Primary Race Quickens 4 Days Voting," *Alton Telegraph,* 3 April 1952, in 1952 Scrapbook, Phyllis Schlafly Home Papers.

47. Clipping, "Young Alton Housewife in District Race for GOP Nomination to Congress," *East St. Louis Journal,* 22 February 1952, in 1952 Scrapbook.

48. Clipping, "Mrs. Schlafly Delivers Keynote for GOP Convention in Springfield," *East St. Louis Citizen,* 27 June 1952.
    The *Illinois National Journal* offered the opinion that "Mrs. Schlafly did not rely on her beauty to hold her audience captive through every word of her prepared speech." See, Clipping, "The Grape Vine," *Illinois National Journal,* June 1952; Clipping, Campaign Scrapbook, Phyllis Schlafly Home Papers.

49. For Goldwater's response to Manion's Committee of One Hundred, see Frank Brophy to Clarence Manion, 1 June 1959, Clarence Manion Papers, box 69, Clarence Manion Papers, Chicago Historical Society.

50. For details of this proposed third party, see J. Bracken Lee to Clarence Manion, 23 July 1959, box 70; Clarence Manion to Dan Hanson, 21 September 1959, box 70; Hub Russell to Chief Justice M. T. Phelps, 21 September, box 70; Clarence Manion to Chief Justice M. T. Phelps, 21 September 1959; and Clarence Manion to Hon. William Bryan Dorr, 22 October 1959, box 70, Clarence Manion papers.

51. Rick Perlstein in his biography of Goldwater claims that Manion sought to enlist Arkansas Orville Faubus as the candidate best able to lead this new third party. A closer reading of the Manion papers, however, shows that Manion, while considering Faubus as a possible candidate, thought Hollings would make a more viable candidate. Manion expressed concern that Faubus had been damaged by his role in Little Rock school integration. Also, Manion approached General Robert Wood to see if he was interested in being a presidential candidate for this new party. On Faubus as a potential candidate, see Perlstein, *Before the Storm,* 14–15. For another perspective, see the following: the initial discussion of a Faubus candidacy is found in Jim Johnson to Clarence Manion, 24 March 1959, box 69; on Manion's doubts about Faubus, Manion to A. G. Heinsohn, Jr., 23 November 1959, box 70; on Hollins as the leading candidate, see Clarence Manion to Honorable William Jennings Bryan Dorn, 22 October 1959, and William Jennings Bryan Dorn to Manion, 28 October 1959, box 70 in Clarence Manion Papers, Chicago Historical Society.

52. Manion to Mrs. J. F. Schlafly (4 May 1964), and Fred Schlafly to Clarence Manion, 31 March 1964, Manion Paper, box 79.

53. Kurt Schuparra, *Triumph of the Right: The Rise of the California Conservative Movement, 1945–1966* (Armonk, NY: M. E. Sharpe, 1998). Also, for this campaign, see Theodore White, *The Making of the President, 1964* (New York: Atheneum Publishers, 1965); F. Clifton White, *Suite 3505: The Story of the Draft Goldwater Movement* (New Rochelle, NY: Arlington House, 1967); McGirr, *Suburban Warriors,* 11–147; Goldberg, *Barry Goldwater;* Brennan, *Turning Right in the 1960s;* William Rusher, *The Rise of the Right* (New York: W. Morrow, 1985), especially 129–61: Barry Goldwater, *With No Apologies: The Personal and Political Memoirs of United States Senator Barry M. Goldwater* (New

York: Morrow, 1979); and Barry Goldwater with Jack Casserly, *Goldwater* (New York: Doubleday, 1988).

54. Stephen Shadegg, *What Happened to Goldwater?* (New York: Holt, Rinehart and Winston, 1965), 266, quoted also in Schuparra, *Triumph of the Right*, 95–96.

55. Pamphlet, William Rusher, *The Plot to Steal the GOP* (1967).

56. Clipping, David Broder, "Who Runs the Republican Party," *Washington Post*, 9 May 1967, in NFRW Files, Eagle Forum Office Files.

57. Bliss's charges of "extremism" in the GOP were specifically directed toward members of the John Birch Society, but many saw the attack as aimed at the right wing of the party in general. Ray Bliss, "Statement of Extremism by Republican National chairman Ray C. Bliss" (November 5, 1965), in NFRW Files, Eagle Forum Office Files.

58. Clipping, Richard Dudman, "Mrs. Schlafly Shunted from a Top GOP Job," *St. Louis Post-Dispatch*, 23 September 1965, NFRW Files, Eagle Office Files.

59. Clipping, "Prediction of Floor Fight for Head of GOP Women," *Chicago Tribune*, 26 January 1967, NFRW Files, Eagle Forum Files.

60. Lucille Young, "The Other Side" (undated mimeograph, 1967), NFRW Files, Eagle Forum Office Files.

61. Clipping, "Adversity Will Make Governor Reagan Stronger, Daughter Predicts," *San Diego Union*, 15 March 1967; and Press Release, "Schlafly Announces Candidacy," 5 April 1967, NFRW Files, Eagle Office Files.

62. Charges that Schlafly was a member of the Minuteman were repeated in a letter, Pauline (?) to Schlafly, 6 June 1967, NFRW Convention Files, Eagle Forum Office Files. Schlafly denied charges of being a member of the John Birch Society, although Robert Welch, the founder of the society, had called Schlafly, "one of our most loyal members." Schlafly associated with many Birchers, including a number of JBS Council members, but her biographer Carol Felsenthal, a Chicago reporter, "after trying to get the goods on her" concluded that there was no evidence that Schlafly belonged to the JBS. It is worth noting that *American Opinion*, the JBS magazine, strongly criticized Schlafly for her views on warning of an external Soviet missile threat, contrary to its opinion that the Soviet threat was only "internal" infiltration of agents into the government. Charges of Schlafly's being a member of the JBS would be raised again during the ERA fight. See Fesenthal, *The Sweetheart of the Silent Majority*, xviii–ix, 185–86.

63. Clipping, "Moderate-Conservative GOP Women Prepare for a Showdown," *The Grand Rapids Press*, 1 May 1966; for divisions in the California NFRW, see Grace Thackery to Barry Goldwater, copy of letter in NFRW Files, Eagle Forum Office Files. NFRW Files, Eagle Forum Office Files.

64. Mrs. Audrey R. Peak to Robert Greenway, 22 April 1967, NFRW Files. Robert Greenway, the publisher of the *DeKalb Daily Chronicle* (Illinois), surveyed party officials as to their positions in the NFRW fight. These responses were sent by Greenway to Schlafly. See NFRW files, Eagle Forum.

65. Clipping, Angela Bryce Column, *Arizona Eagle*, 25 May 1967, NFRW Files, Eagle Forum Office Files.

66. Clipping, "Senator Murphy Aids O'Donnell," *Rockford Morning Start*, 12 May 1967, NFRW Files, Eagle Forum Office Files.

67. For a detailed summary of these charges, see Phyllis Schlafly, *Safe Not Sorry* (Alton, IL: Pere Marquette Press, 1968). For her concession speech, Phyllis Schlafly, "Note on Defeat" (1967), NFRW Files, Eagle Forum Office Files. The NFRW Files provide a detailed record of this fight.

68. Phyllis Schlafly, "The Future of Republicans Liberals' Raid on the GOP," *Human Events* (May 11, 1968), copy in 1968 Folder, Eagle Forum Office Files.
69. Phyllis Schlafly, "Phyllis's Confidential Notes on the Republican National Convention, Miami Beach, Florida, August 1968," Schlafly Kingmaker Folder, Eagle Forum Office Files.
70. This attempt at forming a third party is discussed by Rusher in his *The Rise of the Right*, 286–89. A more detailed record of these efforts are found in the William A. Rusher Papers, Library of Congress, Washington, D.C.
71. The ERAmerica papers in the Library of Congress offer a detailed and rich record of the strategy, tactics, and changing perceptions of the proponents of the Equal Rights Amendment. The view that women's groups had failed to connect with "homemakers" is found in Bownnie Cowan to Jane Wells (National Coordinator ERAmerica), 19 March 1976, ERAmerica, box 1, Library of Congress, Washington, D.C.

    A full account of Schlafly's organizing effort is found in her ERA Files, contained in twenty four-drawer office cabinets in the Eagle Forum Office Files.

    There is an extensive literature on the ERA fight. Especially good discussion of the ERA debate is David E. Kyvig, *Explicit and Authentic Acts: Amending the U.S. Constitution, 1776–1995* (Lawrence: University Press of Kansas, 1996); also see, Janet K. Boles, *The Politics of the Equal Rights Amendment: Conflict and the Decision Process* (New York: Longman, 1979); Jane J. Mansbridge, *Why We Lost the ERA* (Chicago: University of Chicago Press, 1986).
72. See Michael Kazin, *The Populist Persuasion* (New York: Basic Books, 1995), especially his discussion of "Race First," 225–29.
73. For example, historian Dan Carter makes racism the causal factor in the rise of "new conservatism" in *The Politics of Rage*. Michael Kazin offers a similar explanation of the origins of the Right in Ibid.
74. Moreover, her politics were not anti-modernist, if by this term we mean opposition to technological advancement. Indeed, she upheld technology as a key to social and political advancement. In the 1990s, along with Ralph Nader, she warned about the invasion of privacy by new federal banking and health regulations made possible by new computer technology.
75. Rebecca Klatch downplays such differences in *Women of the Right* and *Generation Divided*.

Flipse: Below-the-Belt Politics

1. Phone Interview with Harold Lindsell, 3 August 1997. Additional background information gained from phone interview with *Christianity Today* Associate Director David Kucharsky, 5 May 1997.
2. Harold Lindsell, "Abortion and the Court," *Christianity Today* (CT) 17 (16 February 1973): 32–33.
3. *Christianity Today* was the major voice of traditional, conservative evangelicalism. The magazine was read by clergy, professors, and other evangelical opinion leaders. The twice-monthly publication was first published in 1956 in Washington, D.C. It was started by Billy Graham and Carl F. H. Henry who served as the magazine's first editor-in-chief. Lindsell was associate editor from 1964 to 1967 when he was elevated to the

editorship. During Lindsell's editorship, *Christianity Today* became the pole around which religious and political conservatives rallied.

4. This same point was made by George Marsden, "Religion, Politics, and the Search for an American Consensus," in Mark Noll, ed., *Religion and American Politics* (Oxford: Oxford University Press, 1990), 388. An excellent discussion of the nineteenth-century evangelical politics found in Daniel Walker Howe, *The Political Culture of the American Whigs* (Chicago: University of Chicago Press, 1979).

5. The story of religious-political realignment is told in Jose Casanova, *Public Religions in the Modern World* (Chicago: University of Chicago Press, 1994). There are many other titles detailing this transformation. The best bibliographies can be found in Robert Liebman and Robert Wuthnow, eds., *The New Christian Right: Mobilization and Legitimation* (Hawthorne, NY: Aldine Publishing, 1983), 239–50; David Bromley and Anson Shupe, eds., *New Christian Politics* (Macon, GA: Mercer University Press, 1984), 269–84; Steve Bruce, *The Rise and Fall of the Christian Right* (Oxford: Oxford University Press, 1988), 195–207.

6. I will not discuss fundamentalist Protestantism of the type that formed the backbone of the Moral Majority in the 1980s. Fundamentalist politics is largely a post-*Roe* phenomenon. Though fundamentalists and evangelicals had somewhat strained relations since the late 1940s, they are close religious cousins, and eventually form the core of conservative Protestant political action of the late 1970s. Considering my interest in tracking the growth of a new Christian political consciousness provoked by changing notions of sex and family, it is interesting to note that after the *Roe v. Wade* decision of 1973, the positions and proscriptions of many evangelical and fundamentalist leaders coincided. The distinctions between them are important but too complicated to detail. A concise look at American fundamentalism from the turn of the twentieth century to the present can be found in Nancy T. Ammerman, "North American Protestant Fundamentalism," in Martin Marty and R. Scott Appleby, eds, *Fundamentalism Observed* (Chicago: University of Chicago Press, 1991).

7. The move to the political Right by evangelicals is told by Robert Booth Fowler, *A New Engagement: Evangelical Political Thought, 1966–1976* (Grand Rapids, MI: Eerdmans, 1982); Gary Wills, *Under God: Religion and American Politics* (New York: Touchstone Press, 1990); James Skillen, *The Scattered Voice: Christians at Odds in the Public Square* (Grand Rapids, MI: Zondervan Publishing, 1990); and Robert Wuthnow, *The Restructuring of American Religion: Society and Faith Since World War II* (Princeton, NJ: Princeton University Press, 1988).

8. George Gallup, Jr., *Religion in America, 1977–78* (Princeton: Princeton Religion Research Center, 1978), 42, 27, 19. In the survey, 34% of American adults, or 50 million people, revealed that they too were "born again." See also the article by Kenneth Woodward, "Born Again: The Year of the Evangelicals," *Newsweek,* 25 October 1976, 68–78, as an example of early journalistic attempts to describe evangelicalism.

9. The story of Protestant religious conservatives' move to the fringes of American life told in George Marsden, *Fundamentalism and American Culture: The Shaping of Twentieth-Century Evangelicalism, 1870–1925* (Oxford: Oxford University Press, 1980). See also Joel Carpenter, *Revive Us Again: The Reawakening of American Fundamentalism* (Oxford: Oxford University Press, 1997).

10. George Marsden, *Reforming Fundamentalism: Fuller Seminary and the New Evangelicalism* (Grand Rapids, MI: Eerdmans, 1987), 1–11, has a great description of the issues and

personalities that gave rise to the "new evangelicalism." Robert Wuthnow, *The Restructuring of American Religion*, 173–85, describes well the process by which the new evangelicalism became a national movement.

11. For more extensive definition of evangelicalism and fundamentalism, see George Marsden, "The Evangelical Denomination" in *Evangelicalism and Modern America*, ed. Marsden (Grand Rapids, MI: Eerdmans, 1984). Marsden is the preeminent interpreter of American fundamentalism and evangelicalism. It is on his definitions and categories that I draw most heavily. For two other studies that view evangelicalism within a context of belief and cultural boundaries, see both Lyman Kellstedt, "The Meaning and Measurement of Evangelicalism Problems and Prospects," in *Religion and Political Behavior in the United States*, ed. Ted Jelen (New York: Praeger, 1989), 3–21, and Randall Balmer, *Mine Eyes Have Seen the Glory: A Journey Into the Evangelical Subculture* (Oxford: Oxford University Press, 1989).

12. Joel Carpenter, "From Fundamentalism to the New Evangelical Coalition," in George Marsden, ed., *Evangelicalism and Modern America*, 15. Also see Joel Carpenter, "The Fundamentalist Leaven and the Rise of an Evangelical United Front," in Leonard Sweet, ed., *The Evangelical Tradition in America* (Macon, GA: Mercer University Press, 1984), 257–58.

13. Lowell Streiker and Gerald Strober, *Religion and the New Majority: Billy Graham, Middle America, and the Politics of the 1970s* (New York: Association Press, 1972), 139–40. A similar point made in Martin Marty, "The Revival of Evangelicalism and Southern Religion," in David Harrell, ed. *Varieties of Southern Evangelicalism* (Macon, GA: Mercer University Press, 1981), 7–22.

14. Joel Carpenter, "Fundamentalist Institutions and the Rise of Evangelical Protestantism, 1929–1942," *Church History* 49 (March 1980): 62–75. See also Wuthnow, *The Restructuring of American Religion*, 175–76.

15. Robert Booth Fowler, *A New Engagement: Evangelical Political Thought, 1966–1976* (Grand Rapids, MI: Eerdmans, 1982), 23–30.

16. Carl F. Henry, "Evangelicals in the Social Struggle," *Christianity Today* (CT) 10 (8 October 1965): 4. See also "The Church in Politics," *CT* 10 (13 May 1966): 835; and "War and Peace in Vietnam," *CT* 11 (17 February 1967): 509.

17. Carl F. Henry, *Aspects of Christian Social Ethics* (Grand Rapids, MI: Eerdmans, 1964), 4, 81.

18. Marsden, *Reforming Fundamentalism*, 81.

19. Henry, *The Uneasy Conscience of Modern Fundamentalism*, 17, 78.

20. For more information on these groups, see Leo Ribuffo, *The Old Christian Right: The Protestant Far Right from the Great Depression to the Cold War* (Philadelphia: Temple University Press, 1983).

21. Wuthnow, *Restructuring of American Religion*, 190.

22. Henry, "The Vigor of the New Evangelicalism," *Christian Life* (April, 1948): 32. The emphasis is in the original. See also Marsden, *Understanding Fundamentalism and Evangelicalism*, 102–3.

23. George Marsden, "Evangelicals and Scientific Culture: An Overview," in Michael J. Lacey, ed., *Religion & Twentieth Century American Intellectual Life* (Washington, D.C: Cambridge University Press/Woodrow Wilson Center, 1989), 45–47. See also Wuthnow, *Restructuring of American Religion*, 185. Wuthnow calls the educational and organization structure of evangelicalism of the late 1950s "an impressive array of nationally organized special purpose groups and some of the fastest growing denominations in the country."

24. Carl F. Henry, "Foreword," Walter Spitzer and Carlyle Saylor, eds., *Birth Control and the Christian: A Protestant Symposium on The Control of Human Reproduction* (Wheaton, IL: Tyndale House & Coverdale House, 1969), vii–viii.

25. "Exploding Populations and Birth Control," *CT* 4 (1 February 1960): 366–67; Richard Fagley, "Birth Control," *CT* 4 (28 March 1960): 553; "News," *CT* 7 (21 December 1962): 297; Harold W. Hermann, "Medical Indications for Contraception," in *Birth Control and the Christian*, 154–55. See also the debate held in a special issue of *Eternity*, an evangelical news magazine. Irene Soehren, "The Battle Over Birth Control," *Eternity* 17 (September 1966), 12ff.

26. Paul Rees, "Review of Current Religious Thought," *CT* 5 (10 April 1961): 616. See Donald Critchlow's, *Intended Consequences: Birth Control, Abortion, and the Federal Government in Modern America* (Oxford: Oxford University Press, 1999), 3–5. Most Protestant denominations approved of federal aid to promote family planning. See also parallel positions on birth control from non-evangelical denominations—*Social Pronouncements of the Augustana Lutheran Church and Its Conferences, 1937–56* (Minneapolis: Augustana Publishing, 1956), 23–24; United Presbyterian Church in the USA, *Responsible Marriage and Parenthood*, 174th General Assembly (Philadelphia: Westminster Press, 1962); Board of Social Ministry, Lutheran Church of America, *Ethics of Conception and Contraception* (St. Louis: Concordia, 1960); Richard Fagley, ed., *The Population Explosion and Christian Responsibility* (Oxford: Oxford University Press, 1960); Alastair Heron ed., *Towards a Quaker View of Sex* (Philadelphia: Friends Home Service Committee, 1963); and William Hulme, "A Theological Approach to Birth Control," *Pastoral Psychology* (April, 1960).

27. Paul Rees, "Birth Control: Which Methods Are Moral?" *CT* 11 (17 February 1967): 523–24.

28. See Dwight Harvey Small, *Christian: Celebrate Your Sexuality* (Old Tappan, NJ: Revell, 1971); Tim and Beverly LaHaye, *The Act of Marriage* (Wheaton, IL: Tyndale House, 1974); Marabel Morgan, *The Total Women* (Old Tappan, NJ: Revell, 1973). It must be said that Morgan's advice was controversial when it first came out.

29. Robert Booth Fowler, *A New Engagement: Evangelical Political Thought*, 192–93.

30. Harold Lindsell, "Editorial: The Debilitating Revolt," *CT* 11 (21 July 1967): 24–25. See also Orville Waters, "Contraceptives and the Single Person," *CT* 12 (8 November 1968): 16–17; L. Nelson Bell, "Poison in the Cup," *CT* 14 (11 September 1970): 38–39; Irene Soehren, *Eternity* 17 (September 1966): 12; Dr. Merville Vincent, "Birth Control and the Purpose of Marriage," *Eternity* (March 1969): 21.

31. Donald Bastian, "Sex in a Theological Perspective," *CT* 12 (19 July 1968): 8.

32. First quote from Harold B. Kuhn, "Current Religious Thought," *CT* 8 (17 July 1964): 982. Second quote from "Evangelical Scholars Endorse Birth Control," *CT* 12 (27 September 1968): 1265. Billy Graham blurb supporting "family planning" and birth control to stop the "population explosion" given in response to Pope Paul VI's *Humanae Vitae* (1968). One of the major arguments used by evangelicals to commend the use and distribution of birth control was their concern that world population growth would outstrip food, medical, and development aid that a plethora of evangelical missionary organizations were distributing. For an example of this argument, see Paul Rees, "Review of Current Religious Thought," 616; and "Birth Control: Which Methods Are Moral?" *CT* 11 (17 February 1967): 523–24.

33. Henry, "Foreword," in *Birth Control and the Christian*, vii–viii.

34. Evangelical luminaries attending the conference included William Kiesewetter, chief surgeon of the Pittsburgh Children's Hospital; V. Elving Anderson, Professor of

Genetics at the University of Minnesota; Tom Clark, former Supreme Court Associate Justice; and Thomas Lambert, former Nuremberg trial prosecutor and head of the American Trial Lawyers Association. For a complete list of the conference attendees and presenters, see *Birth Control and the Christian: A Protestant Symposium on the Control of Human Reproduction*, xi.

35. See Kristen Luker, *Abortion and the Politics of Motherhood* (Berkeley: University of California Press, 1985), 66–77. The ALI Model Law was written in response to the much publicized case of Sheri Finkbine, an Arizona television personality who had ingested Thalidomide, a sedative later proven to cause severe birth defects. Finkbine sought an abortion, but the public outcry forced her hospital to cancel the procedure. She went to Sweden to have an abortion on a severely deformed fetus. Her case, along with the rubella scare of 1964, are given as the main antecedent to abortion reform.

36. See Christopher Reilly, MD, "Threatened Health of Mother as an Indication for Therapeutic Abortion," in *Birth Control and the Christian*, 188; Harold W. Hermann, MD, "Medical Indications for Contraception," in *Birth Control and the Christian*, 153; Kenneth Kantzer, "The Origins of the Soul Related to the Abortion Question," in *Birth Control and the Christian*, 551ff; Paul Jewett, "The Relationship of the Soul to the Fetus," in *Birth Control and the Christian*, 53.

37. All these quotes are taken from "A Protestant Affirmation on the Control of Human Reproduction," *CT* 12 (8 November. 1968): 18–19.

38. Ibid.

39. "A Protestant Affirmation," 18–19.

40. Paul Jewett, "The Relation of the Soul to the Fetus," *CT* 12 (8 November 1968): 22–24. A longer version, "The Relationship of the Soul to the Fetus," is in *Birth Control and the Christian*, 66.

41. Bruce Waltke, "The Old Testament and Birth Control, *CT* (8 November 1968): 3–4. The biblical passage he comments on is Exodus 21:22–24.

42. Robert Meye, "The New Testament and Birth Control," *CT* 13 (8 November 1968): 106–8.

43. See Bruce Waltke, "Eutychus and His Kin," *CT* 13 (3 January 1969). Waltke claims that the "weight of scholarly opinion" agrees with his position. William Freeland, "Inter-Faith Debate on Easing Abortion Laws," *CT* 11 (28 April 1967): 779.

44. Robert Visscher, "Therapeutic Abortion: Blessing or Murder?," *CT* 12 (27 September 1968): 1238–40. See also "Birth Control: Which Methods Are Moral?," 524. The following paragraph depends on these two articles.

45. Nancy Hardesty, "When Does Life Begin?," *Eternity* (February 1971). Lloyd Kalland, "Fetal Life," *Eternity* (February 1971). Billy Graham quoted in *CT* 14 (17 July 1970): 31. See also Richard Quebeaux, *The Young Evangelicals: A Revolution of Orthodoxy* (New York: Harper and Row, 1974).

46. Henry, phone interview with author, 10 February 1996.

47. Luker, *The Politics of Motherhood*, 110ff.

48. Leslie J. Reagan, "Crossing the Borders for Abortions: Mexican Clinics and the Creation of a Feminist Health Agency in the 1960s," *Feminist Studies*, 26 (Summer 2000): 323.

49. See Faye Ginsburg, *Contested Lives: The Abortion Debate in an American Community* (Berkeley, University of California Press, 1989), 23–61. The above section depends on Ginsburg's description of the success of the abortion legalization movement.

50. Alan Winter, "Political Activity Among the Clergy," *Review of Religious Research* 14: 178–79.

51. Similar point made by Wuthnow, *Restructuring of American Religion*, 198–99.
52. See, for example, the arguments put forward by Robert Meye, "New Testament Texts Bearing on the Problem of the Control of Human Reproduction," in *Birth Control and the Christian*, 32, 43–46. Meye, a biblical scholar, surveyed New Testament and early church writings and found little additional guidance. Evangelicals concerned with the question of abortion, wrote Meye, should rely on such pragmatic and professional counsel as "scientific testing," "Christian doctors," "compassion," and "the freedom of conscience." Such advice would not permit "unrestricted abortions," but would allow them in certain cases. Meye admitted that he supported "a liberal abortion policy" because "there was no final verdict possible." He wanted the decision to be left to mothers and their doctors even if they are "called to go against the religious norms of [the] immediate society." He counsels "restraint" in the use of abortion, but warns that "anyone who permits abortion for some reasons has opened the door to abortion for any reason." See also similar versions of the same argument put forward by Christopher Reilly, MD, "Threatened Health of Mother as an Indication for Therapeutic Abortion," in *Birth Control and the Christian*, 188; Harold W. Hermann, MD, "Medical Indications for Contraception," in *Birth Control and the Christian*, 153.
53. This last point also made by Wuthnow, *Restructuring of American Religion*, 201.
54. "News: Picketers at Graham Meeting," *CT* 14 (17 July 1970): 31. Quote taken from Mary Bouma, "Liberated Mothers," *CT* 15 (7 May 1971): 4–6. See also the works of Elizabeth Elliot, *Let Me Be a Women* (Wheaton: Tyndale, 1976) and Edith Schaeffer, *What Is a Family?* (Old Tappan: Revell, 1975.) Both were frequent contributors to *Christianity Today*. Schaeffer had a monthly column. For *Christianity Today*'s initial support of the ERA, see "Editorial: That Women's Rights Amendment," *CT* 14 (6 November 1970): 34.
55. Wuthnow, *Restructuring American Religion*, 190–91.
56. *National Right to Life Newsletter*, 10 (October 1975): 4.
57. Jack Coltrell, "Abortion and the Mosaic Law," *CT* 17 (16 March 1973): 66–69. See also Harold Kuhn, "Now-Generation Churchmen and the Unborn," *CT* 14 (1971), 434; Lindsell, "A License to Live," *CT* 18 (26 July 1974): 32–33.
58. Carl F. Henry, *Confessions of a Theologian: An Autobiography* (Waco, TX: Word Publishing, 1986), 281. See also the discussion in Marsden, *Reforming Fundamentalism*, 260.
59. Letha Scanzoni and Nancy Hardesty, *All We're Meant to Be—A Biblical Approach to Women's Liberation* (Waco, TX: Word Publishing, 1976); Wesley Pippert, *Faith at the Top* (Chicago: Cook Publishing, 1973), 75; Clifford Bajema, *Abortion and the Meaning of Personhood* (Grand Rapids, MI: Baker Book House, 1974), chap. 8; John Scanzoni, "A Sociological Perspective on Abortion and Sterilization," in *Birth Control and the Christian*, chap. 16.
60. Examples include "Editorial: A Case for Sexual Restraint," *CT* 13 (27 February 1970): 31–32; "Editorial: The Sophists Guide to Sex," *CT* (12 April 1974): 31; "Editorial: A License to Live," *CT* 16 (26 July 1974): 32–33; Richard Selzer, "What I Saw at the Abortion," *CT* 20 (16 January 1976): 11–12.
61. "Editorial: The War on the Womb," *CT* 14 (5 June 1970): 824–25. This was the first editorial that stated the new evangelical position on abortion.
62. Harold Lindsell, *The World, The Flesh, the Devil* (Grand Rapids, MI: Canon Press, 1973), 97–101, 123.
63. See Harold Lindsell, "Editorial: Abortion and the Court," *CT* 17 (16 February 1973): 32–33 and "Financing Murder" *CT* 15 (29 January 1971): 418.

64. Harold O. J. Brown, "The Passivity of American Christians," *CT* 20 (16 January 1976): 32–33.

65. "Birth Control: Which Methods Are Moral?" *CT* 12 (November 1967): 523–24. See also *CT* 11 (12 May 1967): 327, 829; John Warwick Montgomery, "News: Morality—Pope Faces Birth Control Crisis," *CT* 12 (16 August 1968): 1105–6; C. Stanley Lowell, "Protestant-Catholic Tensions," *CT* 7 (12 October 1962): 19–21; Robert Visscher, "Therapeutic Abortion: Blessing or Murder?": 1238–40.

66. "Editorial: Twisted Logic," *CT* 16 (22 December 1972): 308–9; David Kucharsky, "News: Rebirth of Opposition? The Abortion Issue," *CT* 15 (23 June 1971): 716–17; Harold Kuhn, "Now-Generation Churchmen and the Unborn," *CT* 15 (1971): 428; "Editorial: Baptist Bombast," *CT* 18 (12 April 1974): 829; "Tenth Anniversary of Vatican II," *CT* 17 (13 October 1973): 33.

67. "Editorial: Is Abortion a Catholic Issue?," *CT* 20 (16 January 1976): 219.

68. C. Everett Koop, *The Right to Live, the Right to Die* (Toronto, ON: Life Cycle Books, 1980).

69. For a more thorough discussion of anti-abortion clinics and crisis pregnancy centers, see Ginsburg, *Contested Lives,* 120, 123, 253.

70. Harold O. J. Brown, "The Passivity of American Christians," *CT* 20 (16 January 1976): 32–33.

71. *National Right to Life News* 1, no. 9 (September 1974): 8.

72. Harold O. J. Brown, "An Evangelical Looks at the Abortion Issue," *America* (25 September 1976): 161–64.

73. See Beth Bailey, *Sex in the Heartland* (Cambridge: Harvard University Press, 1999) for more detail on acceptance of the sexual revolution and emergence of sexual politics.

74. George Marsden, *Understanding Fundamentalism and Evangelicalism,* 95–96.

Flamm: The Politics of "Law and Order"

1. Wallace had entered the primary in an effort to prevent passage of the civil rights bill pending in Congress. See Dan T. Carter, *The Politics of Rage: George Wallace, the Origins of the New Conservatism, and the Transformation of American Politics* (New York: Simon and Schuster, 1995), 204–5. See also Stephan Lesher, *George Wallace: American Populist* (Reading, MA: Addison-Wesley Publishing Co.; 1994), 272–73.

2. For accounts of this incident and its aftermath, see "Shouts Back Wallace at Rally on South Side," *The Milwaukee Journal,* 2 April 1964, 1–2; Lesher, *George Wallace: American Populist,* 283–85; and Carter, *The Politics of Rage,* 206–7.

3. "Wallace Bid Brings Visit by Gronouski," *The Milwaukee Journal,* 3 April 1964, 1–2. Early polls showed him with less than 5% support, and Wallace privately expected to receive fewer than 50,000 votes. See Carter, *The Politics of Rage,* 206–7.

4. Certainly the option of crossover voting, the lack of a contest in the Republican primary, and the unpopularity of LBJ's stand-in, Governor John Reynolds (who had proposed the controversial open-housing bill), contributed significantly to Wallace's success. See Charles W. Windler, "The 1964 Wisconsin Presidential Primary," Ph.D. dissertation, Florida State University, 1983.

5. Goldwater's successful campaign for the nomination is described in detail in Rick Perlstein, *Before the Storm: Barry Goldwater and the Unmaking of the American Consensus* (New York: Hill & Wang Publishers, 2001); Theodore H. White, *The Making of the President 1964* (New York: Atheneum Publishers, 1965); Robert Alan Goldberg, *Barry Goldwater* (New Haven: Yale University Press, 1995); John A. Andrew III, *The Other Side of the Six-*

ties: Young Americans for Freedom and the Rise of Conservative Politics (New Brunswick, NJ: Rutgers University Press, 1997); Robert D. Novak, *The Agony of the GOP 1964* (New York: The Macmillan Company, 1965); Mary C. Brennan, *Turning Right in the Sixties: The Conservative Capture of the GOP* (Chapel Hill: University of North Carolina Press, 1995); and John H. Kessel, *The Goldwater Coalition: Republican Strategies in 1964* (New York: The Bobbs-Merrill Co. Inc., 1968). For participant accounts, see F. Clifton White, *Suite 3505: The Story of the Draft Goldwater Movement* (New Rochelle: Arlington House, 1967); Lee Edwards, *Goldwater: The Man Who Made a Revolution* (Washington: Regnery Publishing, Inc., 1995); Stephen Shadegg, *What Happened to Goldwater?* (New York: Holt, Rinehart & Winston, 1965); and Karl Hess, *In a Cause that Will Triumph: The Goldwater Campaign and the Future of Conservatism* (Garden City, NY: Doubleday, 1967).

6. For an anecdotal description of this process, see Samuel G. Freedman, *The Inheritance: How Three Families and America Moved from Roosevelt to Reagan* (New York: Simon and Schuster, 1996).

7. Thomas Byrne Edsall and Mary D. Edsall, *Chain Reaction: The Impact of Race, Rights, and Taxes on American Politics* (New York: Norton, 1991), 9. For a similar national perspective, see Allen J. Matusow, *The Unraveling of America: A History of Liberalism in the 1960s* (New York: Harper and Row, 1984). For a similar local perspective, see Jonathan Rieder, *Canarsie: The Jews and Italians of Brooklyn against Liberalism* (Cambridge: Harvard University Press, 1985).

8. He also argues that miscegenation was the main fear of whites in the 1950s. I would contend that by the 1960s street crime represented the main fear. Thomas J. Sugrue, "Crabgrass-Roots Politics: Race, Rights, and the Reaction against Liberalism in the Urban North, 1940–1964," *Journal of American History* 82 (September 1995): 578. See also Thomas J. Sugrue, *The Origins of the Urban Crisis: Race and Inequality in Postwar Detroit* (Princeton: Princeton University Press, 1996).

9. Thus a Charlestown, Massachusetts, housewife, Alice McGoff, could support the 1964 Civil Rights Act but later oppose forced busing. See J. Anthony Lukas, *Common Ground: A Turbulent Decade in the Lives of Three American Families* (New York: Alfred A. Knopf, 1985), 26.

10. Norman H. Vie, Sidney Verba, and John R. Petrocik, *The Changing American Voter* (Cambridge: Harvard University Press, 1979), 269.

11. They had "a reflexive, almost pathological, inability to get their hands around this issue." Ben Wattenberg, interview with author, 19 December 1997.

12. *Crime in the United States,* Uniform Crime Report (Washington, D.C.: The Federal Bureau of Investigation, 1970).

13. Special Message to the Congress on Crime and Law Enforcement, 7 February 1968, *Public Papers of the Presidents of the United States: Lyndon B. Johnson, 1968–69,* I (Washington, D.C.: U.S. Government Printing Office, 1969), 185.

14. Lyndon Baines Johnson, *The Vantage Point: Perspectives of the Presidency, 1963–1969* (New York: Holt, Rinehart and Winston, 1971), 549.

15. By ethnic I mean primarily those of Irish, Italian, Jewish, and East European ancestry.

16. Although police departments expanded at twice the rate of population growth during the 1960s, both clearance and conviction rates fell—the direct result of court rulings according to conservatives. Lucas A. Powe, Jr., *The Warren Court and American Politics* (Cambridge: Harvard University Press, 2000), 399–400, 408.

17. Even many liberals now concede that it was a mistake to extol untrammeled civil liberties at the expense of secure public spaces. See Harold Myerson, "Why Liberalism Fled

the City . . . And How It Might Come Back," *American Prospect* 37 (March–April 1998): 51–52.

18. James Sundquist, *Dynamics of the Party System: Alignment and Realignment of Political Parties in the United States* (Washington, D.C.: Brookings Institution, 1983), 383. "There was a conflation of all of these issues," recalls one administration official. "It wasn't genius—it was what the man on the street was doing." Ben Wattenberg, interview with author, 19 December 1997.

19. See Gerald Sorin, *The Nurturing Neighborhood: The Brownsville Boys Club and Jewish Community in Urban America, 1940–1990* (New York: New York University Press, 1990), 91, 159–63, 168.

20. "Rise in Murders Reported by City," *New York Times*, 18 July 1964, 23; "Gangs Beat and Rob 2 Riders on Upper Manhattan Subways," *New York Times*, 18 July 1964, 23; "Maccabees and the Mau Mau," *National Review*, 16 July 1964: 479–80.

21. James Lardner, *Crusader: The Hell-Raising Police Career of Detective David Durk* (New York: Random House, 1996), 75. Yorkville was a German neighborhood that supposedly had harbored pro-Nazi sentiments at one point. Two years later, during the Civilian Review Board controversy, Mayor John Lindsay charged that a neo-Nazi group regularly distributed literature there. See Ruth Cowan, "The New York City Civilian Review Board Referendum of November 1966," 346–47.

22. "Harlem: Hatred in the Streets," *Newsweek*, 3 August 1964, 19. Property losses ranged into the hundreds of thousands of dollars.

23. Letter, Mrs. Gertrude Schwebell of 549 Riverside Drive to Rockefeller, 19 July 1964, Reel 17, RG 15, Gubernatorial Office Records, Subject Files, NAR Collection, RAC; letter, Mr. Charles Shamoon of 70 La Salle St. to Rockefeller, 24 July 1964, Reel 17, RG 15, Gubernatorial Office Records, Subject Files, NAR Collection, Rockefeller Archives Center, Tarrytown, New York [hereafter RAC]. Rockefeller's correspondence is overwhelmingly in favor of "law and order" and opposed to the rioters. Very few mention, even obliquely, the social conditions in Harlem or cite them as exculpatory factors.

24. Michael R. Beschloss, *Taking Charge: The Johnson White House Tapes, 1963–1964* (New York: Simon and Schuster, 1997), 459 and 462.

25. Unsigned memo, Office of Jack Valenti to LBJ, 27 July 1964, Ex JL 3, WHCF, Box 25, Lyndon Baines Johnson Presidential Library, Austin, Texas [hereafter LBJ Library].

26. After the riots Johnson made an impassioned request to his FBI liaison: "Deke, you and the FBI have got to stop these riots. One of my political analysts tells me that every time one occurs, it costs me 90,000 votes." Cartha 'Deke' DeLoach, *Hoover's FBI: The Inside Story by Hoover's Trusted Lieutenant* (Washington, D.C.: Regnery Publishing Inc., 1995), 279.

27. Dayton, Ohio, 16 October 1964, box 16, PCF, Goldwater MSS. By September 1966—over a year before the riots in Newark and Detroit—a majority of whites felt that the anti-poverty program would not reduce racial unrest. Hazel Erskine, "The Polls: Demonstrations and Riots," *Public Opinion Quarterly* 31 (Winter 1967–68): 673.

28. Edwards, *Goldwater*, 309–311; White, *The Making of the President 1964*, 236 and 305.

29. Of the 507 southern counties that Goldwater won, 233 had never voted Republican before. Goldberg, *Barry Goldwater*, 232–35.

30. Confidential AFL-CIO Committee on Political Education (COPE) research memo, November 1964, box 3J9, BGC, Eugene C. Barker Center for American History, University of Texas at Austin [hereafter Barker Center].

31. In New York, murders rose over 23% in 1961. The overall crime rate set a record in 1962

and climbed steadily in 1963. See "Crimes Set Mark, Rising 3% in 1961," *New York Times,* 13 July 1962, 50, and "Crime Here Rises 9.1%; Murders Increase by 9.3%," *New York Times,* 15 October 1963, 78.

32. For a detailed account of the referendum battle and Lindsay's travails, see Vincent J. Cannato, *The Ungovernable City: John Lindsay and His Struggle to Save New York* (New York: Basic Books, 2001).

33. Ruth Cowan, "The New York City Civilian Review Board Referendum of November 1966: A Study in Mass Politics," unpublished. Ph.D. dissertation, NYU, 1970, 6, 393. See also James Priest Gifford, "The Political Relations of the PBA in the City of New York, 1946–1969," unpublished Ph.D. dissertation, Columbia, 1970, 386.

34. The final margin was 1,313,161 (63%) in favor of the referendum and 765,468 (32%) opposed. In Manhattan, the vote in favor of civilian review (and against the referendum) was 234,485 to 168,391. In the Bronx, the vote against civilian review was 235,310 to 128,084; in Brooklyn, 414,133 to 201,836; in Queens, 366,150–254,357 and in Richmond, 63,083 to 12,800. See Thomas R. Brooks, " 'No!' Says the PBA," *New York Times Magazine,* 16 October 1966; David W. Abbott, Louis H. Gold, and Edward T. Rogowsky, *Police, Politics, and Race: The New York City Referendum on Civilian Review* (Cambridge, MA: American Jewish Committee and the Joint Center for Urban Studies of MIT and Harvard, 1969), 7–8; and "Tally of Votes for Governor, Statewide Offices, Police Review Board, and Judgeships," *New York Times,* 10 November 1966, 10.

35. By October Lindsay was not confident of victory. "I am not at all sure that we're going to win. But one thing I am sure of—we're right. I have never been so sure of anything in my life." Woody Klein, *Lindsay's Promise: The Dream that Failed* (London: The Macmillan Co., 1970), 245, 250. "I thought it was a losing issue," recalled Aryeh Neier of the New York Civil Liberties Union (NYCLU) in March 1968. "It was not until the late days of the campaign that I deluded myself into thinking that we had a chance." Cowan, "The New York City Civilian Review Board Referendum of November 1966," 354.

36. The best account of this race is Matthew Dallek, *The Right Moment: Ronald Reagan's First Victory and the Decisive Turning Point in American Politics* (New York: The Free Press, 2000).

37. David Garth, campaign manager for FAIR, later termed the pursuit of Irish and Italian votes "a waste of time." Cowan, "The New York City Civilian Review Board Referendum of November 1966," 317, 331; Klein, *Lindsay's Promise,* 255; and Abbott, Gold, and Rogowsky, *Police, Politics, and Race,* 15.

38. More than 85% of whites said that blacks learned as well as whites and 75% said they would not object to minority neighbors if they had similar levels of income and education. Abbott, Gold, and Rogowsky, *Police, Politics, and Race,* 8, 17–18, 38, 42–44.

39. Lisa McGirr, "Suburban Warriors: Grass-Roots Conservatism in the 1960s," Ph.D. dissertation, Columbia University, 1995, 250. See also Lisa McGirr, *Suburban Warriors: The Origins of the New American Right* (Princeton, NJ: Princeton University Press, 2001).

40. Civil Rights and Backlash, "Dem. Party. General. Cong. Election Analysis, 1966–67," box 1057, Public Affairs Files, Vice Presidential Files, HHH Papers, Minnesota Historical Society [hereafter MHS]; "Illinois," n.d., 9/9, COPE Research Division Files, George Meany Memorial Archives [hereafter GMMA]; Alan Draper, *A Rope of Sand: The AFL-CIO Committee on Political Education, 1955–1967* (New York: Praeger, 1989), 123–24.

41. Draper, *A Rope of Sand,* 121–23; Minutes of AFL-CIO Executive Council Meeting, 15 November 1966, GMMA.

42. Memo, Wattenberg to LBJ, 21 November 1967, Ex PL/Kennedy, Robert F., WHCF, box 26, LBJ Library.

43. "Comment: Second Thoughts on Bobby," *Time,* 21 June 1968, 48.

44. "Between Remorse and Renewal," *Newsweek,* 24 June 1968, 25–26; "Once Again," *Newsweek,* 17 June 1968, 20–21; "Understanding Violence," *Newsweek,* 17 June 1968, 43; "Comment: Second Thoughts on Bobby," *Time,* 21 June 1968, 48.

45. Richard Harris, *The Fear of Crime* (New York: Praeger, 1968), 106–109.

46. George Kamenow to Celler, 23 May 1968, box 298, Celler MSS, Library of Congress, Washington, D.C. [hereafter Celler MSS]; interview with Celler, *WNBC's* "Man in Office," 7 December 1969, box 540, Celler MSS.

47. Roche to LBJ, 7 March 1968, box 3, WHOF of John Roche, LBJ Library; Finley to Clark, 6 June 1968, box 107, Ramsey Clark MSS, LBJ Library.

48. Statement Upon Signing the Omnibus Crime Control and Safe Streets Act of 1968, 19 June 1968, *Public Papers of the Presidents of the United States: Lyndon B. Johnson, 1968,* I: 725–29.

49. Califano to LBJ, 24 June 1968, box 22, WHOF of Joseph Califano, LBJ Library.

50. Minutes, 27 September 1968, "Pers Pol: Campaign Policy Committee Minutes," box 1, Personal Political Files, 1968 Campaign Files, HHH Papers, MHS; memo, Evron Kirkpatrick to Freeman, 4 October 1968, "Pers Pol: Freeman, Orville L," box 1, Personal Political Files, 1968 Campaign Files, HHH Papers, MHS.

51. Charles Roche to LBJ, 22 October 1968, box 3, WHOF of Charles Roche, LBJ Library; Voter Opinion on Campaign Issues, box 9, Research Files, 1968 Campaign Papers, Humphrey MSS; MHS; Panzer to LBJ, 28 October 1968, box 26, Ex PL/Nixon, Richard, WHSF, LBJ Library.

52. "Narrow Victory, Wide Problems," *Time,* 15 November 1968, 19; "Nixon's Hard-Won Chance to Lead," *Time,* 15 November 1968, 24–25. George Reedy to LBJ, 5 October 1968, box 26, Ex PL/Nixon, Richard, WHSF, LBJ Library; Theodore H. White, *The Making of the President 1968* (New York: Atheneum Publishers, 1969), 467; Gerald Hursh to Orville Freeman, 27 September 1968, box 16, Citizens for Humphrey Files, 1968 Campaign Papers, Humphrey MSS.

53. "Narrow Victory, Wide Problems," *Time,* 15 November 1968, 20; "The Way the Voting Went—And Why," *U.S. News & World Report,* 18 November 1968, 40, 42; "Nixon's Hard-Won Chance to Lead," *Time,* 15 November 1968, 22.

54. Curt Furr to Sam J. Ervin, Jr., June 18, 1968, Folder 669, box 204, Legislative Files, Samuel J. Ervin Papers, Southern History Collection, University of North Carolina at Chapel Hill.

LIST OF CONTRIBUTORS

David Farber is a professor of history at the University of New Mexico. His books include *The Age of Great Dreams: America in the 1960s* (1994), *The Columbia Guide to America in the 1960s* (2001), and *Sloan Rules: Alfred P. Sloan and the Triumph of General Motors* (2002).

Jeff Roche, an assistant professor of history at the College of Wooster, teaches courses on American political history. He is the author of *Restructured Resistance: The Sibley Commission and the Politics of Desegregation in Georgia* (1998), *Cowboy Conservatism: The Emergence of Western Political Culture, 1933–1984* (forthcoming) and several essays on the history and historiography of conservative politics.

Jonathan M. Schoenwald is Director of Studies at Rockefeller College, Princeton University. His study of modem American conservatism, *A Time for Choosing*, was published by Oxford University Press in 2001.

Evelyn A. Schlatter is an editor at the University of New Mexico Press. She completed her Ph.D. in history in 2000. Her research interests include white supremacist groups, gender, and social history.

Michelle Nickerson is a Ph.D. candidate in the American Studies program at Yale University. She is currently finishing her dissertation, "Domestic Threats: Women, Gender and Conservatism in Cold War Los Angeles, 1945–1966." Her articles on women and conservatism will be appearing in *The Journal of the West, The OAH Magazine of American History,* and the forthcoming anthology, *The Politics of Healing: Essays on the History of Alternative Medicine.*

Mary C. Brennan, born and educated in southwestern Ohio, currently resides in San Marcos, Texas. After receiving her doctorate at Miami University (Ohio), Mary taught briefly at Ohio State University before moving to Southwest Texas

State University. Mary is the author of *Turning Right in the Sixties* (1995). She is currently working on a book examining conservative, anticommunist women.

Kurt Schuparra is the author of *Triumph of the Right: The Rise of the California Conservative Movement, 1945–1966* (1998). He received a Ph.D. in history from the University of Arizona and is currently a policy adviser in the office of California governor Gray Davis.

Donald T. Critchlow is founding editor of the *Journal of Policy History* and the author/editor of twelve books including *Intended Consequences: Birth Control, Abortion, and the Federal Government* (2001). He is currently writing a study of Phyllis Schlafly and grassroots conservatism for Princeton University Press.

Scott Flipse is Associate Director of the University of Notre Dame's Washington Semester. He has a Ph.D. in history from Notre Dame and writes and teaches on the interplay of U.S. foreign policy, politics, and religion.

Michael W. Flamm is an assistant professor of history at Ohio Wesleyan University. He has written numerous articles and essays on the political culture of the 1960s. He is a co-author of "The Chicago Handbook of Teaching" (1999) and author of *Law and Order: Street Crime, Civil Disorder, and the Crisis of Liberalism* (forthcoming).

INDEX

Lightning Source UK Ltd.
Milton Keynes UK
UKHW051522140122
397146UK00015B/169